Data Modeling Essentials
Analysis, Design, and Innovation

Data Modeling Essentials
Analysis, Design, and Innovation

Graeme C. Simsion

VAN NOSTRAND REINHOLD
New York

I(T)P A division of International Thomson Publishing Inc.
       The ITP logo is a trademark under license.

Printed in the United States of America
For more information, contact:

Van Nostrand Reinhold
115 Fifth Avenue
New York, NY 10003

International Thomson Publishing GmbH
Konigswinterer Strasse 418
53227 Bonn
Germany

International Thomson Publishing
Berkshire House 168-173
High Holborn
London WCIV 7AA
England

International Thomson Publishing Asia
221 Henderson Road #05-10
Henderson Building
Singapore 0315

Thomas Nelson Australia
102 Dodds Street
South Melbourne, 3205
Victoria, Australia

International Thomson Publishing Japan
Hirakawacho Kyowa Building, 3F
2-2-1 Hirakawacho
Chiyoda-ku, 102 Tokyo
Japan

Nelson Canada
1120 Birchmount Road
Scarborough, Ontario
Canada M1K 5G4

International Thomson Editores Mexico
Campos Eliseos 385, Piso 7
Col. Polanco
11560 Mexico D.F. Mexico

ARCFF 16 15 14 13 12 11 10 9 8 7 6 5 4 3

Library of Congress Cataloging-in-Publication Data

Simsion, Graeme C.
    Data modeling essentials : analysis, design, and innovation /
Graeme C. Simsion.
        p.   cm.
Includes index.
ISBN 0-442-01654-9
1. Data base design. 2. Data structures (Computer science) I. Title.
QA76.9.D26S54   1993   93-21210
005.74—dc20   CIP

To my father, the memory of my mother, and my wife Anne.

Contents

Preface

Some years ago, I was interviewing a bank manager about the information he needed to assess customer profitability. I began to explain the information system changes that would be required. A look of exasperation crossed his face as he realized that this was going to be an expensive and time-consuming exercise. Finally, he interrupted. "I know that all the information I need is going into those blue boxes. How can it be so difficult to get it out?"

Last year I watched a large insurance company struggling to introduce a new product. The hold-up was the time required to develop a supporting information system. Meanwhile, one of the company's competitors was able to introduce a similar product, making use of an existing information system, and win a major share of the market.

Three banks of approximately the same size, using similar technology, spent several years developing information systems to address their core business. Their budgets varied by more than a factor of five. Yet an independent study found that only one had gained a competitive advantage – the bank that had spent the *smallest* amount.[1]

These are familiar themes for information systems developers and users: access to information, the ability to cope with change, and systems development productivity. What may not be so obvious is the central importance of data organization. The bank manager's requirements could not be met economically because the data held in the central databases was not organized to meet his needs. The insurance company's existing database was not adaptable enough to support the new product. The successful bank attributed the lower cost of its system to innovative data organization.

The task of specifying what data is to be stored, and how it is to be organized, is called *data modeling*. As both business requirements and database technology become more sophisticated, the need for good data modeling is increasingly apparent. Modern methodologies and computer-aided software engineering (CASE) tools now include data modeling as a key phase in the development life cycle, and the data model has taken its place alongside the functional specification as one of the major deliverables of systems analysis. Data modeling, once a specialist discipline, is now a required skill for virtually anyone involved in information systems design.

This book is intended both as an introduction to data modeling and a guide to handling the more common problems that arise in practice. It differs from other books on the subject in several important ways.

First, it is written *by* a practitioner *for* practitioners. I believe that academics and students will also find it useful, but my prime aim has been to convey the knowledge, techniques, and guidelines my colleagues and I use in designing data models for commercial information systems. The language and diagramming conventions reflect industry practice, as supported by the leading CASE products and database management systems.

Second, it recognizes the element of *choice* in data modeling. For a given problem there will usually be many possible models that satisfy the basic rules of sound design. To select the best model, we need to consider a variety of criteria, which will vary in importance from case to case. Throughout the book, the emphasis is on understanding the merits of different solutions, rather than prescribing a single "correct" answer.

Third, it examines the *process* by which data models are developed. Too often, authors assume that once we know the language and basic rules of data modeling, producing a data model will be straightforward. This is like suggesting that if we understand architectural drawing conventions, we can design buildings. In practice, data modelers draw on past experience, adapting models from other applications. They also use rules of thumb, standard patterns, and creative techniques to propose candidate models. These are the skills that distinguish the expert from the novice.

[1] Broadbent, M. and Weill, P., "Improving Business and Information Strategy Alignment: Learning from the Banking Industry," *IBM Systems Journal*, Vol. 32, No 1 (1993), pp 162 – 179.

Finally, I have been strictly honest in describing how I do data modeling in practice. In writing or teaching, there is always a temptation to tell the reader how it *should* be done – "do as I say, not as I do." But there are usually reasons for short cuts, simplifications, and deviations from the theoretical ideal. So the examples in the book include the awkward situations that crop up in real life, and the answers reflect solutions I would actually propose.

The book is in two parts. Part 1 covers the basics of data modeling. I suggest that you read these five chapters in sequence before tackling Part 2. Part 2 builds on the techniques covered in Part 1 to examine more advanced topics. The sequence is designed to minimize the need for "forward references." If you decide to read it out of sequence, you may need to refer to earlier chapters from time to time.

Acknowledgments

I had no idea when I started writing a book about a subject that I both practice and teach that it would take so long, raise so many questions, and generally be as demanding as it turned out to be. The fact that it was completed at all is due in a very large part to the support I received from others, particularly my colleagues at Simsion Bowles and my wife, Anne.

A number of people contributed directly to the content. Chief among these was my colleague Hu Schroor, who reviewed each chapter as it was produced, frequently covering the reverse side of every page with notes and suggestions. Graham Witt, Geoff Bowles, John Giles, Hugh Williams, Bill Haebich, Geoff Rasmussen, David Lawson, Chris Waddell, Mike Barrett, and Sue Huckstepp provided valuable input to individual chapters. Daryl Joyce of Ericssons and Steve Naughton of National Australia Bank reviewed the book as potential users, and made numerous suggestions to improve its clarity.

Graeme Shanks of Monash University and Edward Stow of Charles Sturt University provided an academic perspective – and the benefit of extensive teaching experience in the field. Their comments did much to improve the book's rigor, but they are most certainly not responsible for any failings in this area. In many instances, particularly in Part 1, I have deliberately deviated from a strict progressive development of concepts in order to give the reader a "flavor" of the topic. Undefined terms, informality, and any errors are entirely my responsibility.

Valuable and constructive as all this input was, I occasionally felt like offering the standard response to the critic: "Where were you when the paper was blank?" The person who *was* there at the beginning was Robin Wade, who worked from my dictation and briefings to produce an initial set of notes for the main chapters.

Others have contributed in an indirect but equally important way. Peter Fancke introduced me to formal data modeling in the late 1970s, when I was employed as a database administrator at Colonial Mutual Insurance, and provided an environment in which formal methods and innovation were valued. In 1984, I was fortunate enough to work in London with Richard Barker of Oracle Corporation. His extensive practical knowledge highlighted to me the missing element in most books on data modeling, and encouraged me to write my own. Richard beat me to it by writing *CASE Method Entity-Relationship Modelling* (Addison Wesley) in 1990, and it is this book I have recommended to practitioners since then. Hu Schroor, whose direct contribution I have already acknowledged, has been a constant source of ideas, insights, and encouragement. I have also learnt much from working with expert practitioners like Keith Finkelde, Brin Thiedeman, Hugh Drummond, and John Alexander, and from clients and students who ask the hard questions.

In putting the book together, I relied on Fiona Tomlinson, who produced the diagrams and camera-ready copy, and Sue Coburn who organized the text, changing innumerable "modelling"s to "modeling" and "normalisation"s to "normalization." Our other office staff provided valuable support. Ted Gannan and Rochelle Ratnayake of Thomas Nelson Australia, and Dianne Littwin, Chris Grisonich, and Risa Cohen of Van Nostrand Reinhold all provided encouragement and advice.

Finally, the most important contribution came from my wife Anne, who put up with weekends and evenings devoted to "the book," while managing two children, a career, an interstate move, and her own book.

Data Modeling Essentials
Analysis, Design, and Innovation

Part I

OVERVIEW OF DATA MODELING

1

What Is Data Modeling?

Ask not what you do, but what you do it to!
– Bertrand Meyer

1. INTRODUCTION

This book is about one of the most critical stages in the development of a computerized information system – the design of the *data model*. We begin by addressing some fundamental questions:

What is a data model?
Why is data modeling so important?
What makes a good data model?
Where does data modeling fit in systems development?
Who is involved in data modeling?

1.2.   A DATA-CENTERED PERSPECTIVE

We can usefully think of an information system as consisting of a database, containing stored data, together with programs that capture, store, manipulate, and retrieve the data (Figure 1-1). The programs are designed to meet a *functional specification*, describing the business functions which the system is to perform. In the same way, the database is specified by a *data model*, describing what sort of data will be held, and how it will be organized.

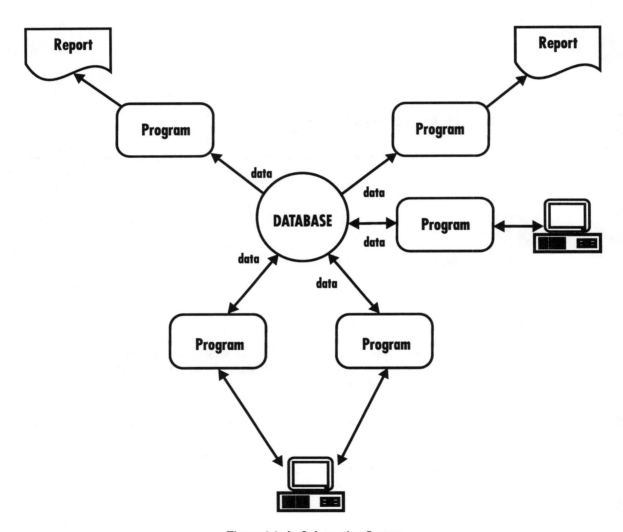

Figure 1-1. An Information System

1.3. A SIMPLE EXAMPLE

Before going any further, let's look at a simple data model. Figure 1-2 shows some of the data needed to support an insurance system.

POLICY TABLE

POLICY NO.	DATE ISSUED	TYPE	CUSTOMER NO.	COMMISSION	MATURITY DATE
V213748	02/29/2989	E20	SIDDM02	12%	02/29/2009
N065987	04/04/1984	E20	WALSH01	12%	04/04/2004
W345798	12/18/1987	WOL	FORET13	8%	06/12/2047
W678649	09/12/1967	WOL	RICHB76	8%	09/12/2006
V986377	11/07/1977	SUI	RICHB76	14%	09/12/2006

CUSTOMER TABLE

CUSTOMER NO.	NAME	ADDRESS	POST CODE	GENDER	AGE	DATE OF BIRTH
SIDDM02	M Siddke	48 South St	3070	F	38	04/12/1954
WALSH01	H Walsh	2 Allen Crt	3065	M	44	04/16/1947
FORET13	T Forest	69 Black St	3145	M	24	06/12/1967
RICHB76	B Rich	181 Kemp Rd	3507	M	50	09/12/1941

Figure 1-2. A Simple Data Model

We can see a few things straight away:

The data is organized into simple tables. This is exactly how a modern relational database stores data, and we could give the model to a technical database designer to build, just as an architect gives a house plan to a builder. Our job as data modelers is essentially to decide what tables and column headings are required. I've shown a few rows of data for illustration; in practice the database might contain thousands or millions of rows in the same format.

The data is divided into two tables – one for policy data and a separate one for customer data. Typical data models may specify anything from one to several hundred tables.

There is nothing technical about the model. You don't need to be a database expert or programmer to understand or contribute to the design.

A closer look at the data suggests some questions:

> *What exactly is a customer – the beneficiary or the person insured? Or perhaps the person who pays the premiums? Could a customer be more than one person – for example, a married couple? If so, how would we interpret Age, Gender, and Date of Birth?*

> *Do we really need to record customers' ages? Wouldn't it be easier to calculate them from Date of Birth whenever we needed them?*

> *Is the Commission Rate always the same for a given Policy Type? For example, do policies of type E20 always earn 12 percent commission? If so, we will end up recording the same rates many times. How do we record the commission rate for a new type of policy if we haven't yet sold any of that type?*

> *Customer Number consists of an abbreviated surname, initial, and a two-digit "tie-breaker" to distinguish customers who would otherwise have the same numbers. Is this a good choice?*

> *Would it be better to hold customer's initials in a separate column from their family names?*

Answering questions of this kind is what data modeling is about. In some cases, there is a single, correct approach. Far more often, there will be several options that represent different trade-offs amongst a set of objectives. Answering the questions and choosing the best options requires a detailed understanding of the relevant business area, as well as a knowledge of general data modeling principles. Professional data modelers therefore work closely with business specialists, usually the prospective users of the information system, in much the same way that architects work with the owners and prospective inhabitants of the buildings they are designing.

1.4.   DESIGN, CHOICE, AND CREATIVITY

The architect analogy is particularly appropriate, because architects are *designers*, and data modeling is also a design activity. In design, we do not expect to find a single correct answer, although we will certainly be able to identify many that are patently *incorrect*! Two data modelers (or architects) given the same set of requirements may produce quite different but nevertheless acceptable solutions.

We should not be too surprised that data modeling is not a deterministic process. At least three factors contribute to there being more than one workable answer in most practical situations:

First, our objective is to organize or classify data into tables and columns, and there is usually more than one way of doing this. In our insurance model, we might, for example, have specified separate tables for personal customers and corporate customers, or for accident insurance policies and life insurance policies.

Second, the requirements from which we work in practice are flexible enough to accommodate a variety of different solutions. Again, the architect analogy: rather than the client specifying the exact size of each room (which would give the architect little choice), he or she provides some broad objectives, and then evaluates the architect's suggestions in terms of how well they meet these, and what else they offer.

Third, in designing an information system, we have some choice as to which part of the system will handle each business requirement. For example, we might decide to write the rule that policies of type E20 had a commission rate of 12 percent into the relevant programs, rather than including it in the database. Working in the other direction, we might decide that the formulae for calculating benefits at maturity could be held in the database rather than in program logic. Either of these decisions would affect the data model simply by altering what was to be included.

Unfortunately, data modeling is not always recognized as being a design activity. The widespread use of the term "data analysis" as a synonym for data modeling has no doubt contributed to the confusion. The difference between analysis and design is sometimes characterized as one of *description versus prescription*.[1] We tend to think of analysts as being engaged in a search for truth rather than the generation and evaluation of alternatives. No matter how inventive or creative they may need to be in carrying out the search, the ultimate aim is to arrive at the single correct answer. A classic example is the chemical analyst using a variety of techniques to determine the make-up of a compound.

In simple textbook examples of data modeling, it may well seem that there is only one workable answer (although the experienced modeler will find it an interesting exercise to look for alternatives). In practice, data modelers have a wealth of options available to them and, like architects, cannot rely on simple recipes to produce the best design. Unfortunately, the terminology that is used in the information systems field tends to confuse the issue. The "analysis" phase within a systems development method often includes design activities, and data modeling is very likely to be the responsibility of a person with the job title of "systems analyst."

The distinction between analysis and design is nevertheless important, particularly when we discuss creativity. In analysis, creativity suggests interference with the facts. No honest accountant wants to be called "creative." On the other hand, creativity in design is valued highly. In this book, I try to emphasize the choices available at each stage of the data modeling process. I want you to learn not only to produce sound, workable models (buildings that won't fall down), but to be able to explore and compare a range of options, and occasionally experience the "aha!" feeling as a flash of insight produces an innovative solution to a problem. I use the term "creative modeling" when I want to emphasize the importance of actively searching for alternatives rather than merely selecting the most obvious option.

---

[1] See, for example, Olle, Hagelstein, MacDonald, Rolland, Sol, Van Assche, and Verrjin-Stuart, *Information Systems Methodologies – A Framework for Understanding*, Addison Wesley (1991)

We will look more closely at the creative process in Chapter 5, but let's clarify one thing right away. In recognizing the importance of choice and creativity in data modeling, we are not "throwing away the rule book" or suggesting that "anything goes," any more than we would allow architects or engineers to work without rules or to ignore their clients' requirements. On the contrary, creativity in data modeling requires familiarity with a full range of techniques, and rigorous evaluation of candidate models against a variety of criteria.

1.5.   WHY IS THE DATA MODEL SO IMPORTANT?

At this point, you may be wondering about the wisdom of devoting a lot of effort to developing the best possible data model, rather than just accepting the first adequate design. Should we not put similar effort into exploring alternative designs for programs and other system components?

The key reason for focusing on data organization is *leverage:* a small change to the data model may have a major impact on the system as a whole. For most commercial information systems, the programs are far more complex and take much longer to specify and construct than the database. But their content and structure are heavily influenced by the database design. Look at Figure 1-1 again. Most of the programs will be dealing with data in the database – storing, updating, deleting, manipulating, printing, and displaying it. Their structure will therefore be strongly influenced by the way the data is organized – in other words, by the data model.

The dependency of program design on data organization has important practical consequences.

A well-designed data model can make programming simpler and cheaper. Even a small change to the model may lead to significant savings in total programming cost.

Another consequence is that poor data organization is often expensive to fix. In the insurance example, imagine that we need to change the rule that each customer can have only one address. The change to the data model may well be reasonably straightforward – perhaps we will need to add a further two or three address columns to the Policy table. With modern database management software, the database can probably be reorganized to reflect the new model without much difficulty.

But the real impact is on the rest of the system. Report formats will need to be redesigned to allow for the extra addresses; screens will need to allow input and display of more than one address per customer; programs will need loops to handle a variable number of addresses, and so on. Changing the shape of the database may in itself be straightforward, but the costs come from altering all of the programs that use the affected part. In contrast, fixing a single incorrect program, even to the point of a complete rewrite, is a (relatively!) simple, contained exercise.

Problems with data organization arise not only from failing to meet the initial business requirements, but from changes to the business after the database has been built. A telephone billing database that allows only one customer to be recorded against each call may be correct initially, but be rendered unworkable by changes in billing policy, product range, or telecommunications technology. The cost of making changes of this kind has often resulted in an entire system being scrapped, or the business being unable to adopt a planned product or strategy.

A data model is also a very powerful tool for expressing and communicating business requirements. Its value lies partly in its *conciseness*. It implicitly defines a whole set of screens, reports, and functions needed to capture, update, retrieve, and delete the specified data. A thorough verification of a data model can therefore be far more valuable than a cursory evaluation of a functional specification amounting to many hundreds of pages. The data modeling process can similarly take us more directly to the heart of the business requirements. In their book "Object Oriented Analysis," [2] Coad and Yourdon describe the analysis phase of a typical project:

> Over time, the DFD [data flow diagramming or function modeling] team continued to struggle with basic problem domain understanding. In contrast, the Data Base Team gained a strong, in-depth understanding.

To summarize: the data model is a relatively small part of the total systems specification but has a high impact on the quality and useful life of the system. Time spent producing the best possible design is very likely to be repaid in the future.

1.6.   EVALUATION CRITERIA

What constitutes a "good" data model? If we are to evaluate alternative data models for the same business problem, we need some measures of quality. In the broadest sense, we are asking the question: "how well does the model support a sound overall system design that meets the users' requirements?" But we can be a bit more specific than this, and list some general criteria. We will come back to these again and again as we evaluate data models and data modeling techniques.

1.6.1.   Completeness

Does the model support all the necessary data? Our insurance model lacks, for example, a column to record a customer's occupation, and a table to record premium payments. If this data is required by the system, then these are serious omissions. More subtly, we have noted that we might be unable to register a commission rate if no policies had been sold at that rate. We also need to consider completeness in terms of reuseability, discussed below. Perhaps the model omits some data about persons or policies that is not required for the current application, but will be difficult to add later as new uses for the data are found.

---

[2] Coad, P., and Yourdon, E., *Object Oriented Analysis*, Second Edition, Englewood Cliff, NJ, Prentice Hall (1991).

1.6.2.   Nonredundancy

Does the model specify a database in which the same fact could be recorded more than once? In the example we saw that the same commission rate could be held in many rows of the Policy table. The Age column would seem to record essentially the same fact as Date of Birth, albeit in a different form. If we added another table to record insurance agents, we could end up holding data about people who happened to be both customers and agents in two places. Recording the same data more than once increases storage cost, requires extra processing to keep the various copies in step, and leads to consistency problems if the copies get out of step.

1.6.3.   Enforcement of Business Rules

How accurately does the model reflect the rules of the business? It may not be obvious at first glance, but our insurance model enforces the rule that each policy can be owned by only one customer, as there is provision for only one Customer Number in each row of the Policy table. No user or even programmer of the system will be able to break this rule: there is simply nowhere to record more than one customer against a policy (short of such extreme measures as holding a separate row in the *Policy* table for each customer associated with a policy). If this rule correctly reflects the business requirement, the resulting database will be a powerful tool in enforcing correct practice. On the other hand, any misrepresentation of business rules in the model may be very difficult to correct later.

1.6.4.   Data Reuseability

Will the data stored in the database be reuseable for purposes beyond those anticipated in the functional specification? Once an organization has captured data to serve a particular requirement, other potential uses and users almost invariably emerge. An insurance company might initially record data about policies to support the billing function. The sales department then wants to use the data to calculate commissions; the marketing department wants demographic information; regulators require statistical summaries. Seldom can all of these needs be predicted in advance.

If data has been organized with one particular application in mind, it is often difficult to use for other purposes. There are few greater frustrations for system users than to have paid for the capture and storage of data, only to be told that it cannot be made available to suit a new information requirement without extensive, and costly, reorganization.

In the last decade, there has been a growing realization that data is a valuable (and expensive) corporate resource, which should be properly managed for the benefit of *all* current and potential users. This has given rise to the discipline of *data management*, and many organizations now have data management teams responsible for ensuring that their computerized data is well organized, centrally documented, secure, and available to all those who require it. These teams place great emphasis on promoting sound data modeling practices as a means of improving data shareability. Data management is discussed in more detail in Chapter 12.

1.6.5. Stability and Flexibility

How well will the model cope with possible changes to the business requirements? Can any new data required to support them be accommodated in existing tables? Alternatively, will simple extensions to the model suffice? Or will we be forced to make major structural changes, with corresponding impact on the rest of the system?

The answers to these questions largely determine how quickly the system can respond to business change. In many cases, they determine how quickly the *business* can respond to change. The critical factor in getting a new product on the market or responding to a new regulation may well be how quickly the computer systems can be adapted. Frequently the reason for redeveloping a system is that the underlying database either no longer accurately represents the business rules or requires costly ongoing maintenance to keep pace with change.

A data model is *stable* in the face of a change to requirements if we do not need to modify it at all. We can sensibly talk of models being more or less stable, depending on the level of change required. A data model is *flexible* if it can be readily extended to accommodate likely new requirements with minimum impact on the existing structure.

Our insurance model is likely to be more stable in the event of changes to the product range if it uses a generic Policy table rather than separate tables (and associated processing, screens, reports, etc.) for each type of policy. New types of policies may be able to be accommodated in the existing Policy table, and to take advantage of existing programming logic common to all types of policies.

Flexibility depends on the type of change proposed. The insurance model would appear relatively easy to extend if we needed to include details of the agent who sold each policy. We could add an Agent Number column to the Policy table, and set up a new table containing details of all agents, including their Agent Numbers. However, if we wanted to change the database to cater for up to, say, three customers for each policy, the extension would be less straightforward. We could add columns Customer Number 2 and Customer Number 3 to the Policy table, but, as we shall see in Chapter 2, this is a less than satisfactory solution. Even intuitively, most information systems professionals would find it untidy, and likely to disrupt existing program logic. A proper solution would involve moving the original Customer Number from the Policy table, and setting up an entirely new table of

Policy Numbers and associated Customer Numbers. Doing this would significantly disrupt our existing programming logic, screens, and report formats for handling the customers associated with a policy. So, simplistically for the moment, our model is flexible in terms of adding agents, but less flexible in handling multiple customers for a policy.

1.6.6.   Simplicity and Elegance

Does the data model provide a reasonably natural and elegant classification of the data? If our Customer table were to include only insured persons, and not beneficiaries, we might need a separate Beneficiary table. To avoid recording the same fact more than once, we would need to exclude beneficiaries who were already recorded as Customers. Our Beneficiary table would then contain "beneficiaries who are not otherwise customers," an inelegant classification that would very likely lead to a clumsy system.

"Elegance" can be a difficult concept to pin down. But elegant models are typically simple, consistent, and easily described and summarized. ("This model recognizes that our basic business is purchasing raw materials and transforming them into beer through a number of brewing stages – the major tables hold data about the various raw, intermediate, and final products".) Functions and queries that are central to the business can be met in a simple, reasonably obvious way by accessing relatively few tables.

The difference in development cost between systems based on simple, elegant data models, and those based on highly complex ones can be considerable indeed. The latter models are often the result of incremental business changes over a long period without any re-thinking of processes and supporting data. Instead, each change is accompanied by requirements for new data and a corresponding increase in the complexity of the model. In our insurance model, we could imagine a proliferation of tables to cater to new products and associated persons as the business expanded. Some rethinking might suggest that all of our products fall into a few broad categories, each of which could be catered to by a single table, and that a simple "Person" table could accommodate all of the beneficiaries, policyholders, guarantors, assignees, etc.

The huge variation in the development costs for systems to support common applications, such as retail banking or asset management, can often be traced to the presence or absence of this sort of thinking during the data modeling phase of systems design.

1.6.7.   Communication Effectiveness

How effective is the model as a communication tool? Do the tables and columns represent business concepts the users and business specialists are familiar with, and can easily verify? The quality of the final model will depend very much on feedback from these people, who need to be comfortable with the model presented to them.

The most common communication problems arise from high levels of complexity, new concepts, and unfamiliar terminology. A model of even twenty or thirty tables will be overwhelmingly complex for most nonspecialists, unless presented in a summary form, ideally using graphics. Larger models need to be presented at different levels of complexity to allow the reader to take a "divide and conquer" approach to understanding.

Unfamiliar terminology is frequently the result of the data modeler striving to be rigorous and consistent in constructing column and table names, sometimes at the expense of familiar terms and concepts.

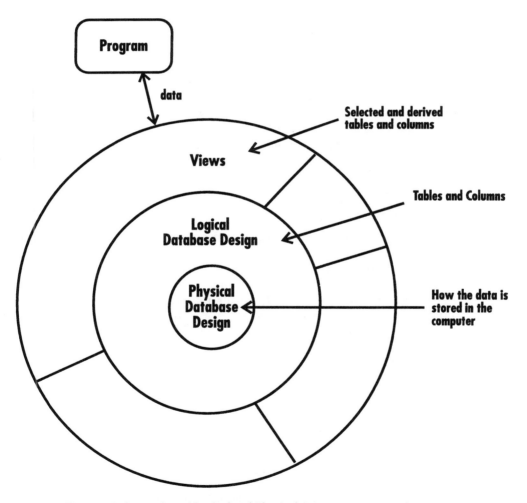

Figure 1-3. Separation of Logical and Physical Components of Database Design.

1.7.   CONFLICTING OBJECTIVES

In many cases, the above aims will conflict with one another. In striving for completeness, we may err towards redundancy. An elegant but radical solution may be difficult to communicate to conservative users. A model that accurately enforces a large number of business rules will be unstable if some of those rules change.

Our overall objective is to develop a model that provides at least a good (ideally, the best) trade-off amongst these comparative objectives. As in other design disciplines, this is a process of proposal and evaluation, rather than a step-by-step progression to the ideal solution. We may not realize that a better solution or trade-off is possible until we see it!

1.8.   PERFORMANCE AND IMPLEMENTATION ISSUES

You may have noticed an important omission from our list of criteria – performance. Certainly, the system user will not be satisfied if our complete, nonredundant, flexible and elegant database cannot meet throughput and response-time requirements. However, performance differs from our other criteria, in that it is *primarily* a problem for the physical (technical) database designer rather than the data modeler. This warrants some explanation, as the respective roles are frequently poorly defined or misunderstood.

1.8.1.   Logical and Physical Database Designs

Figure 1-3 shows an important feature of the organization of a modern database. The three-layer (or *three schema*) approach allows us to separate those aspects of the database of relevance to programmers and users from those related to the physical storage of data in the computer. In effect, we are able to keep the technical part of the design out of sight, and, more importantly, make changes to it without affecting programs. In more formal texts, the terms *internal schema, database schema*, and *external schema* are used for physical database design, logical database design, and views, respectively.[3]

The logical database design describes the organization of the data into tables and columns, as in our insurance example. Programs may work with these tables and columns either directly or via *views,* which restrict access to certain data or present data in a different way. A view can only select or rearrange data that is already specified in the logical database design.

---

[3] Even these terms are not used consistently. The usage here reflects Jardine, D.A., "Concepts and Terminology for the Conceptual Schema and the Information Base," *Computers and Standards 3* (1984) pp. 3-17. If using a relational database management system, it would be appropriate to use the term *relational schema* as an alternative to database schema. Some use the term *conceptual schema* in this role; others argue that the term should be used only for an implementation-independent design (i.e., our *data model*).

The physical database design is invisible to programmers and users. We can think of it as the inside of a black box, or the engine under the hood. (To pursue the architecture analogy, it represents the foundations, electrical wiring, and hidden plumbing: the owner will want only to know that the house will be sound and that the lights and faucets will work.)

The physical database design specifies how the data will be physically stored and accessed, using the facilities provided by a particular *database management system* (DBMS). For example, the data might be organized so that all the policies for a given customer were stored close together, allowing them all to be retrieved into the computer's memory in a single operation. An index might be provided to enable rapid location of customers by name. All this is the responsibility of the physical database designer, whose approach will be strongly influenced by the available DBMS.

Figure 1-4 is an overview of the inputs and outputs of the database design task. The job of the database designer is essentially to implement the data model so as to provide adequate performance for predicted transactions, using available hardware and DBMS software.

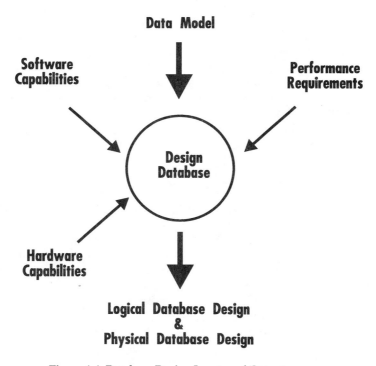

Figure 1-4. Database Design Inputs and Outputs.

So why differentiate between the data model and the logical database design? Ideally, they would be identical. There are three main reasons why they may not be.

Earlier I stated that in modern *relational* databases, data is organized into tables. The logical database design can therefore be an exact copy of the tables specified by the data model. But older database management systems, and some modern ones, are not based around simple tables, but support other data structures, such as hierarchies and networks. Data models based on tables will still serve perfectly well as specifications, but will need to be translated into logical database designs that suit the particular database software. This translation is largely mechanical, and is discussed in most texts on database design.[4] We will not pursue it further in this book.

The second reason is a variant of the first. There are advantages in extending our data model to include more than just tables. For example, we might want to show that customers could be subclassified into personal customers and corporate customers. At the end of the day, we will still have to specify tables, but the richer model can help us make better decisions as to what those tables should be. For example, we could choose between having separate tables for the different types of customers, or a single table for both. In effect, we can represent different options side by side in the same model.

The third reason is that sometimes the physical designer is unable to meet the performance requirements for all the specified functions with the available hardware and software. If this happens, one option is to implement a logical database design that is not a direct equivalent of the data model, but incorporates some compromises. Naturally, this needs to be done in consultation with the data modeler, and ultimately the person(s) paying for the system, just as a builder unable to implement an architect's design would need to consult with the architect and client. The client may well prefer to sacrifice some performance, or to buy more powerful hardware, rather than compromise flexibility or economy of programming.

1.8.2. Modifying the Data Model to Improve Performance

The alternative to implementing a logical database design that is not a direct translation of the data model is to modify the model itself. Perhaps the model can be changed to improve performance without prejudicing other objectives. More than once, an idea that has been prompted by the need to improve performance has led to improvements in other areas. The important thing is to keep in mind the fundamental premise of creative modeling: that there will be more than one workable solution. The aim should be to arrive at a model that still meets the original business objectives, as well as providing good performance. This is clearly a job for the data modeler, and is the reason I stated earlier that performance was *primarily* the responsibility of the physical database designer. Once the logical design is affected, the data modeler needs to be involved.

---

[4] For example, Hawryskziewycz, I.T., *Database Analysis and Design*, Second Edition, Maxwell MacMillan International Editions (1991).

1.8.3.   Roles of Data Modeler and Physical Database Designer

Unfortunately, the distinct roles and skills of the data modeler and physical database designer are not always recognized in practice. Data modelers frequently try to anticipate performance issues and compromise the data model even before the physical designer sees it. This is a mistake because the physical designer is generally far better placed to estimate performance, and to employ the full range of facilities available to optimize it. (Many data modelers have served apprenticeships as database designers, but are often not up to date with current database technology.) Even more importantly, the separation of stages in the process enables us to distinguish clearly "the design the business wants" from "what is possible using current technology."

Data modelers are not the only offenders in failing to separate the roles. Physical database designers (like some builders) do not always feel bound by the specification. Many a data model change has been introduced by a database designer under the guise of performance, often without adequate consultation with data modelers or the users whom they represent.

For data modelers, the best practical approach is to ignore performance issues in the initial modeling stage, and to present the database designer with an ideal logical database design. The data modelers also need to insist that any request for a change to the logical database design be fully justified with a *quantitative* assessment of impact (e.g., estimated transaction response times), and that data modelers and system owners are involved in proposing solutions and choosing the best trade-off. On no account should physical database designers make *any* change to the logical database design without such consultation. In my experience, organizations that have adopted this discipline find that the number of compromises actually required is relatively small.

In our favor is the fact that vendors of database management systems (the software component of the equation) are continually striving to improve what can be achieved at the physical level, without compromising the data model.

1.8.4.   When Performance Is Paramount

Occasionally, it is clear even before systems specification begins in earnest that achieving adequate performance will be a major challenge. The systems that fall into this category are usually core transaction processing systems which need to support high throughput and rapid response times. There is often a push to omit the data modeling phase and move directly to database design, on the basis that the ideal data model is likely to be unimplementable, and that the design will be largely determined by performance issues.

This is a *serious* mistake. Performance is of no value if the system does not provide the functionality required by the business. If anything, the need for good data modeling is even greater when we are going to be forced to consider difficult compromises among objectives. The data modeler's role in these circumstances, as always, is to help propose alternatives, and ensure that business needs and impact are properly taken into account.

1.9. WHERE DOES THE DATA MODEL FIT IN?

It should be fairly clear by now that we should not undertake database design without a complete and properly documented data model. Any sound methodology for systems development will therefore include a data modeling phase to be completed prior to database design. The main difference in methodologies is whether the data model is produced before, after, or in parallel with the functional specification.

Function-Driven Approaches

Traditional "function-driven" or "data flow-driven" approaches focus on the functional specification.[5] This is hardly surprising: we naturally tend to think of systems in terms of what they *do*. We first identify all of the functions and the data that each requires. The data modeler then designs a data model to support this fairly precise set of data requirements, typically using "mechanical" techniques such as normalization (the subject of Chapter 2). Some methodologies say no more about data modeling. If you are using a function-driven approach, I strongly suggest treating the initial data model as a "first cut" only, and reviewing it in the light of the evaluation criteria outlined earlier. This may result in alterations to the model, and subsequent amendments to the functional specification to bring it into line.

Data-Driven Approaches

"Data-driven" approaches[6] are more recent, but have been widely adopted, particularly by the vendors of CASE (Computer-Aided Software Engineering) tools, which provide automated support for systems developers.

The emphasis is on developing the data model *before* the detailed functional specification, in order to:

1. Promote reusability of data. We aim to organize the data independently of the functional specification, on the basis that the functions that it describes are merely the *initial* set that will access the data. The functional specification then becomes a test of the data model's ability to support a variety of unanticipated functions.

---

[5] See, for example, De Marco, T., Structured Analysis and Systems Specification, Yourdon Inc., 1978.

[6] Sometimes called "Information Engineering" approaches.

2. Establish a consistent set of names and definitions for data. If we develop the functional specification prior to the data model, we will end up *implicitly* defining the data concepts. A function called "Assign salesperson to customer" implies that we will hold data about salespersons and customers. But a second function "Record details of new client" raises the question (if we are alert): What is the difference between a client and a customer? Designing the data model prior to the detailed functional specification largely eliminates the need to sort out problems of this kind.

3. "Mechanically" generate a significant part of the functional specification. Just by looking at the insurance model, we can anticipate that we will need programs to:
    Store details of a new policy;
    Update policy details;
    Delete policy details;
    Report on selected policy details;
    List all policies belonging to a nominated customer;
    Store details of a new customer; etc.
    We don't need to know anything about insurance to propose these functions. In defining the data we intend to store, we have implicitly (and very concisely) identified a whole set of functions to capture, display, update, and delete that data. Some CASE tools make heavy use of the data model to generate programs, screens, and reports.

4. Provide a very concise overview of the system's scope. As discussed above, we can infer a substantial set of functions just by looking at the data. Not all of these will necessarily be implemented, but we can at least envision specifying them and having them built without too much fuss. Conversely, we can readily see that certain functions will *not* be supportable, simply because the necessary data has not been specified. More subtly, we can see what business rules are supported by the model, and assess whether these will unduly constrain the system. The data model is thus an excellent vehicle for setting the boundaries of the system – far more so than the often overwhelmingly large functional specification.

1.9.1.   Data-Driven Versus Function-Driven

Having grasped this theoretical distinction between function-driven and data-driven approaches, don't expect to encounter a pure version of either in practice. It is virtually impossible to do data modeling without some investigation of functions, or to develop a functional specification without considering data. At the very least, this means that function modelers and data modelers need to communicate regularly (they may well be the same person). An increasing number of methodologies now specify that the functional specification and data model be developed in parallel.[7]

1.9.2.   Prototyping Approaches

Finally, a few words on prototyping approaches. Rather than spend a long time developing a detailed paper specification, the prototyper adopts a "cut and try" approach – build something, show it to the client, modify it in the light of comments, show it to the client again and so forth. My experiences with prototyping have generally been positive, but they bear out what other experienced prototypers have observed: *you need to design a good data model early in the process*. It comes back to the very high impact of a change to the data model in comparison with the relatively low cost of changing a program. Once prototyping is underway, nobody wants to change the model. So prototypers need to adopt what is effectively a data-driven approach.

1.10.   WHO SHOULD BE INVOLVED IN DATA MODELING?

In Chapter 5, we look more closely at the *process* of developing a data model. At this stage, let's just note that at least the following people have a stake in the model, and should expect to be involved in its development or review.

The system users, owners and/or sponsors will need to verify that the model meets their requirements. Our ultimate aim is to produce a model that provides the most cost-effective solution for the business, and the users' *informed* agreement is an important part of ensuring that this is achieved.

Business specialists (sometimes called "subject matter experts") may be called upon to verify the accuracy and stability of business rules incorporated in the model, even though they themselves may not have any direct interest in the system. For example, we might involve strategic planners to assess the likelihood of various changes to product range.

The data modeler has overall responsibility for developing the model, and ensuring that other stakeholders are fully aware of its implications for them: "You realize that any change to your rule that each policy is associated with only one customer will be very expensive to implement later."

---

[7] For example SSADM – *Structured Systems Analysis & Design Methodologies*, NCC Blackwell.

Function modelers (systems analysts responsible for the functional specification) and program designers will need to specify programs to run against the database. They will want to verify that the data model supports all the required functions, and assess whether it will necessitate complex or sophisticated design and programming.

The database designer will need to assess whether the model can be implemented to provide adequate performance, or whether compromises will need to be negotiated.

The data administrator will be interested in how the new database will fit into the bigger picture: are there overlaps with other databases; does the coding of data follow organizational or external standards; have other users of the data been considered; are names and documentation in line with standards? In encouraging consistency, sharing, and reuse of data, the data administrator represents business needs beyond the immediate project.

Organizing the modeling task to ensure that all of these views are properly taken into account is one of the major challenges of data modeling.

1.11. COSTS AND BENEFITS OF DATA MODELING

Whatever approach to systems development you use, it must include a formal data modeling phase. I am frequently asked by project leaders and managers: "How much does data modeling add to the cost of a system?" or, conversely, "What are the benefits of data modeling?" The simple answer is that *data modeling is not optional*; no database was ever built without at least an implicit model, just as no house was ever built without a plan. In some cases the plan or model is not documented; but just as an architect can draw the plan of a building already constructed, a data modeler can examine an existing database and derive the underlying data model. The choice is not whether or not to model, but whether to do it *formally*, whom to involve, and how much effort to devote to producing a good design. If these issues are not explicitly addressed, the decisions are likely to be, respectively, "no," "a technical database specialist," and "not enough."

A formal data modeling phase, staffed with appropriate people, should reduce the costs of both database development (through the greater efficiency of properly qualified people), and the overall system (through the leverage effect of a good quality model). Unfortunately the question of cost is sometimes prompted by past problems with data modeling. In my experience, the two most common complaints are excessive, unproductive time spent in modeling, and clashes between data modelers and physical database designers. Overly long exercises are sometimes due to lack of familiarity with data modeling principles and standard approaches to problems. Surprisingly often, modeling is brought to a standstill by arguments as to which of two or more candidate models is correct – the "one-right-answer syndrome." Arguments between data modelers and physical database designers often reflect misunderstandings about roles and a lack of hard data to support opinions. Finally, some data modeling problems are just plain difficult, and may take some time to sort out. But we certainly won't solve them any more easily by leaving them to the physical database designers.

It is certainly possible for data modeling to cost too much, just as any activity that is performed incorrectly or not properly managed can cost too much. The solution, however, is to address the causes of the problem, rather than abdicating the job to people whose expertise is in other fields.

1.12. TERMINOLOGY – "DATA MODEL"

In data modeling, as in all too many other fields, academics and practitioners have developed their own terminologies, and do not always employ them consistently. We have already seen an example in the descriptions of different levels of database design: conceptual schema, database schema, internal schema, and external schema versus data model, logical database design, physical database design, and view. The professional data modeler will need to be familiar with both sets, if only to be able to read the literature. In this book, I stick as closely as possible with the terminology used by practitioners in industry, with passing references to the more formal academic terms.

The most important difference at this stage is the term "data model" itself. Practitioners use it as I have in this chapter, to refer to a representation of the data required to support a particular function or set of functions. Data models may be presented in different ways (e.g., with or without sample data; as tables or diagrammatically; in full or in summary form).

Academics use "data model" to describe a particular way of representing data: for example, in tables, hierarchically, or as a network. Hence they talk of the "relational model" (tables), the "entity relationship model," or the "network model." Be aware of this as you read texts aimed for the academic community or in discussing the subject with them. And encourage some awareness and tolerance of practitioner terminology in return!

1.13. ALTERNATIVE APPROACHES TO DATA MODELING

Practitioners differ from academics in another important way: their approach is heavily constrained by available tools. From a practical perspective, there is not much value in adopting a data modeling language that is not compatible with current database management systems or CASE products. In contrast, much of the academic literature on data modeling is devoted to exploring different languages, conventions, and database management system architectures.

As a practicing data modeler, I am often frustrated by the limitations of current tools. But in this book, I have stuck to the most widely used conventions, for documenting data models, and assumed that the models will be implemented using a traditional database management system.

1.14.   WHERE TO FROM HERE?

Let's now take a brief look at how the rest of this book is organized.

In the next four chapters, which complete Part 1 of the book, we look at the basic principles of data modeling.

In Chapter 2 we cover *normalization*, a formal technique for organizing data into tables. Normalization enables us to deal with certain common problems of redundancy and incompleteness according to straightforward and quite rigorous rules. In some texts, particularly those advocating a function-driven approach, this is all that is taught about data modeling. If you are new to the subject, Chapter 2 should give you a feeling for what a sound data model looks like.

In Chapter 3, we introduce a more convenient way of presenting complex models. In working with the insurance model, you may have found that some of the more important business rules (such as only one customer being allowed for each policy) were far from obvious. As we move to more complex models, it becomes increasingly difficult to see the key concepts and rules among all the detail. A typical model of 100 tables with five to ten columns each will appear overwhelmingly complicated. We need the equivalent of an architect's sketch plan to present the main points.

In Chapter 4, we look at subtyping and supertyping, and their use in exploring alternative designs and handling complex models. We have already touched on these when we discussed the possible breakdown of the Person table into separate tables for personal and corporate customers. Subtypes and supertypes are often treated as an advanced topic, and not all CASE tools provide support for them (though this is rapidly changing). On the contrary, I believe they are an important basic technique of modeling, and we will use them extensively in the remainder of the book.

Chapter 5 covers the process of modeling – how we go about actually designing a model in practice. It is possible to be very familiar with modeling conventions and principles of good design, but not be capable of applying them to model actual business requirements. I have confronted this often with graduate students who have studied modeling extensively, but actually developed few, if any, models for themselves.

Part 2 of the book expands on some of the topics covered in Part 1, and looks at problems and structures that the practicing data modeler will encounter regularly. While you may want to "dip in" to Part 2 as required, the sequence has been designed to introduce new concepts progressively. If you dip in, you may have to refer to earlier chapters from time to time.

In Chapter 12 we look at large scale (corporate) data modeling as a technique for information systems planning and coordination.

Appendix A is a checklist for data model review, summarizing material from throughout the book.

1.15.   SUMMARY

Data and databases are central to information systems. Every database is specified by a data model, even if only an implicit one. The data model is an important determinant of the design of the associated information systems. Changes in the structure of a database can have a radical and expensive impact on the programs that access it. It is therefore essential that the data model for an information system be an accurate, stable reflection of the business it supports.

Data modeling is a *design* process. The data model cannot be produced by a mechanical transformation from hard business facts to a unique solution. Rather, the modeler generates one or more candidate models, using analysis, abstraction, past experience, heuristics, and creativity. Quality is assessed according to a number of factors including completeness, nonredundancy, faithfulness to business rules, reuseability, stability, elegance, and communication effectiveness. There are often trade-offs involved in satisfying these criteria.

Performance of the resulting database is an important issue, but is primarily the responsibility of the physical database designer. The data modeler will need to be involved if changes to the data model or logical database design are contemplated.

In developing a system, data modeling and function modeling usually proceed in parallel. Prototyping approaches rely on a stable data model being developed at an early stage.

2

Basic Normalization

A place for everything and everything in its place.
– Homespun advice on kitchen organization.

In this chapter, we introduce *normalization,* a set of techniques for organizing data into tables, in such a way as to eliminate certain types of redundancy and incompleteness. Normalization is one of the most thoroughly researched areas of data modeling, and you will have little trouble finding other texts and papers on the subject. However, most take a fairly formal, mathematical approach. Here, I've tried to focus more on the steps in the process, what they achieve, and the practical problems you are likely to encounter. I have also highlighted areas of ambiguity and opportunities for choice and creativity.

The majority of the chapter is devoted to a rather long example. I encourage you to work through it. By the time you have finished, you will have covered virtually all of the issues involved in basic normalization.

2.1.   AN INFORMAL EXAMPLE OF NORMALIZATION

Normalization is essentially a two step task:

1. Put the data into tabular form (by removing repeating groups).
2. Remove duplicated data to separate tables.

A simple example will give you some feeling for what we are trying to achieve. Figure 2-1 shows a paper form (it could equally be a computer input screen) used for recording data about employees and their qualifications.

Employee Number: 01267	Employee Name: Clark		
Department Number: 05	Department Name: Auditing	Department Location:	HO
Qualification		Year	
Bachelor of Arts		1970	
Master of Arts		1973	
Doctor of Philosophy		1976	

Figure 2-1. Employee Qualifications Form

If we want to store this data in a database, our first task is to put it into tabular form. But we immediately strike a problem: because an employee can have more than one qualification, it's awkward to fit the qualification data into one row of a table (Figure 2-2). How many qualifications do we allow for? Murphy's law tells us that there will always be an employee who has one more qualification than the table will handle!

Employee Number	Employee Name	Department Number	Department Name	Department Location	Qualification 1	
					Description	Year
01267	Clark	05	Auditing	HO	Bachelor of Arts	1970
70964	Smith	12	Legal	MS	Bachelor of Arts	1969
22617	Walsh	05	Auditing	HO	Bachelor of Arts	1972
50607	Black	05	Auditing	HO		

Qualification 2		Qualification 3		Qualification 4	
Description	Year	Description	Year	Description	Year
Master of Arts	1973	Doctor of Philosophy	1976		
Master of Arts	1977				

Figure 2-2. Employee Qualifications Table

We can solve this by dividing the data between two tables: one for the basic employee data, and the other for qualification data – one row per qualification (Figure 2-3). In effect, we have removed the "repeating group" of qualification data to its own table. Note that we hold employee numbers in the second table to serve as a cross-reference back to the first, because we need to know to whom each qualification belongs. Now the only limit on the number of qualifications we can record for each employee is the maximum number of rows in the table – in practical terms, as many as we will ever need.

Employee Table

Employee Number	Employee Name	Department Number	Department Name	Department Location
01267	Clark	05	Auditing	HO
70964	Smith	12	Legal	MS
22617	Walsh	05	Auditing	HO
50607	Black	05	Auditing	HO

Qualification Table

Employee Number	Qualification Description	Qualification Year
01267	Bachelor of Arts	1970
01267	Master of Arts	1973
01267	Doctor of Philosophy	1976
70964	Bachelor of Arts	1969
22617	Bachelor of Arts	1972
22617	Master of Arts	1977

Figure 2-3. Separation of Qualification Data

Our second task is to remove duplicated data. For example, the fact that department number "05" is "Auditing" and is located at "HO" is repeated for every employee in that department. Not only do we waste space, but updating data is made more complicated. If we wanted to record that the Auditing department had moved to another location, we would need to update multiple rows in the employee table. This is a nice example of the "elegance" requirement being violated.

The basic problem is that department names and addresses are really data about *departments* rather than employees, and belong in a separate Department table. We therefore establish a third table for department data, resulting in the three-table model of Figure 2-4. Again we leave Department Number in the Employee table to serve as a cross-reference.

Employee Table

Employee Number	Employee Name	Department Number
01267	Clark	05
22617	Walsh	05
70964	Smith	12
50607	Black	05

Department Table

Department Number	Department Name	Department Location
05	Auditing	HO
12	Legal	MS

Qualification Table

Employee Number	Qualification Description	Qualification Year
01267	Bachelor of Arts	1970
01267	Master of Arts	1973
01267	Doctor of Philosophy	1976
70964	Bachelor of Arts	1969
22617	Bachelor of Arts	1972
22617	Master of Arts	1977

Figure 2-4. Separation of Department Data

This is a very informal example of what normalization is about. The rules of normalization have their foundation in mathematics, and have been very closely investigated by researchers. On the one hand, this means that we can have confidence in normalization as a technique; on the other, it is very easy to become lost in mathematical terminology and proofs, and miss the essential simplicity of the technique. The apparent rigor can also give us a false sense of security, by hiding some of the assumptions that have to be made before the rules are applied. Remember that data modeling is *design* – we should be wary of any process that seems to lead us to a single "right" answer.

You should also be aware that many data modelers profess not to use normalization, in a formal sense, at all. They would argue that they reach the same answer by other means, including common sense and intuition. Certainly, most practitioners would have had little difficulty solving the employee qualification example in this way.

However, common sense and intuition come from experience, and these experienced modelers have a good idea of what sound, normalized data models look like. Think of this chapter, therefore, as a way of gaining familiarity with some sound models, and, conversely, with some important and easily classified design faults. As you gain experience, you will find that you arrive at properly normalized structures as a matter of habit. Nevertheless, even the most experienced professionals make mistakes, or encounter difficulties with sophisticated models. At these times, it is helpful to get back onto firm ground by returning to first principles such as normalization. And when you encounter someone else's model which has not been properly normalized (a common experience for data modeling consultants!), it is useful to be able to demonstrate that some generally accepted rules have been violated.

2.2.   RELATIONAL NOTATION

Before tackling a more complex example, we need to introduce a more concise notation. The sample data in the tables takes up a lot of space, and is not strictly necessary to document the design (although it can be a great help in communicating it). If we eliminate the sample rows, we are left with the table names and columns.

EMPLOYEE (Employee Number, Employee Name, Department Number)

DEPARTMENT (Department Number, Department Name, Department Location)

QUALIFICATION (Employee Number, Qualification Description, Qualification Year)

Figure 2-5. Employee Model Using Relational Notation

EMPLOYEE

Employee Number	5 Numeric – Allocated by HR Dept
Employee Name	60 Characters – Surname plus initial
Department Number	Department which pays emp's salary

DEPARTMENT

Department Number	2 Numeric – To be re-allocated
Department Name	30 Characters
Department Location	30 Characters – city where located

QUALIFICATION

Employee Number	
Qualification Description	30 Characters
Qualification Year	Date – Optional

Figure 2-6. Employee Model Using List Notation

Figure 2-5 shows the normalized model of employees and qualifications using the *relational* notation of table name followed by column names in brackets. (The full notation requires that the key of the table be underlined – discussed in Section 2.4.4.) This convention is widely used in textbooks, and is convenient for presenting the minimum amount of information needed for most worked examples. In practice, however, we usually want to record more information about each column: format, optionality, and perhaps a brief note or description. Practitioners therefore usually use lists as in Figure 2-6.

2.3.   A MORE COMPLEX EXAMPLE

Armed with the more concise relational notation, let's now look at a slightly more complex example, and introduce the rules of normalization as we proceed. The rules themselves are not too daunting, but we'll spend some time looking at exactly what problems they solve.

The form in Figure 2-7 is based on one used in an actual survey of antibiotic drug usage in Australian hospitals. The survey team wanted to determine which drugs and dosages were being used for various operations, to ensure that patients were properly prescribed for, and that the public was not paying for unnecessary drugs.

Hospital Number:	H17	Hospital Name:		St Vincent's	Operation Number:	48		
Hospital Category:		P		Contact at Hospital:	Fred Fleming			
Operation Name:		Heart Transplant		Operation Code:	7A	Procedure Group:	Transplant	
Surgeon Number:	S15	Surgeon Speciality:		Cardiology		Total Drug Cost:	$75.50	
Drug Code		Full Name of Drug		Manufacturer		Method of Admin.	Cost of Dose ($)	Number of Doses
MAX 150mg		Maxicillin		ABC Pharmaceuticals		ORAL	$3.50	15
MIN 500mg		Minicillin		Silver Bullet Drug Co.		IV	$1.00	20
MIN 250mg		Minicillin		Silver Bullet Drug Co.		ORAL	$0.30	10

Figure 2-7. Drug Expenditure Survey

One form was completed for each operation. A little explanation is necessary to understand exactly how the form was used.

Each hospital in the survey was given a unique hospital number to distinguish it from other hospitals (in some cases two hospitals had the same name). All hospital numbers were prefixed "H" (for "Hospital").

Operation numbers were assigned sequentially by each hospital.

Hospitals fell into three categories: "T" for training, "P" for public, and "V" for private. All training hospitals were public ("T" implied "P").

The operation code was a standard international code for the named operation. Procedure group was a broader classification.

The surgeon number was allocated by individual hospitals to allow surgeons to retain a degree of anonymity – the prefix "S" stood for surgeon.

Total drug cost was the total cost of all drug doses for the operation. The bottom of the form recorded the individual antibiotic drugs used in the operation. The drug code consisted of a short name for the drug and the size of the dose.

As the study was extended to more hospitals, it was decided to replace the heaps of forms with a computerized database. Figure 2-8 shows the initial database design, using the relational notation. It consists of a single table, named Operation because each row represents a single operation. Don't be put off by the table's size: after the first 10 columns, there is a lot of repetition (which we are going to clean up once we start normalizing).

OPERATION (Hospital Number, Operation Number, Hospital Name, Hospital Category, Contact Person, Operation Name, Operation Code, Procedure Group, Surgeon Number, Surgeon Specialty, Total Drug Cost, Drug Code 1, Drug Name 1, Manufacturer 1, Method of Administration 1, Cost of Dose 1, Number of Doses 1, Drug Code 2, Drug Name 2, Manufacturer 2, Method of Administration 2, Cost of Dose 2, Number of Doses 2, Drug Code 3, Drug Name 3, Manufacturer 3, Method of Administration 3, Cost of Dose 3, Number of Doses 3, Drug Code 4, Drug Name 4, Manufacturer 4, Method of Administration 4, Cost of Dose 4, Number of Doses 4)

Figure 2-8. Initial Drug Expenditure Model

The data modeler (who was also the physical database designer and the programmer) took the simplest approach, exactly mirroring the form. Indeed, it is interesting to consider who really did the data modeling. Most of the critical decisions were taken by the designer of the form.

When I present this example in training workshops, I give participants a few minutes to see if they can improve on the design. I strongly suggest you do the same before proceeding. It's easy to argue *after* seeing a worked solution that the same result could be achieved intuitively – try it first!

2.4.   DETERMINING COLUMNS

Before we get started on normalization proper, we need to do a little preparation and tidying up. Normalization relies on certain assumptions about the way data is represented, and we need to make sure that these are valid. There are also some problems that normalization does not solve, and it is better to address these at the outset, rather than carrying excess baggage through the whole normalization process. The following steps are necessary to ensure that our initial model provides a sound starting point.

2.4.1.   One Fact per Column

First we make sure that *each column in the table represents one fact only*. The Drug Code column holds both a short name for the drug and a dosage size, two distinct facts. The dosage size in turn consist of a numeric size and a unit of measure. The three facts should be broken up into separate columns. We'll see that this decision makes an important difference to the structure of our final model.

A more subtle example of a multifact column is the Hospital Category. We are identifying whether the hospital is public or private (first fact) as well as whether the hospital provides training (second fact). We should establish two columns, Hospital Type and Training Status, to capture these distinct ideas.

The identification and handling of multifact columns is covered in more detail in Chapter 9.

2.4.2.   Hidden Data

The second piece of tidying up involves making sure that we have not lost any data in the translation to tabular form. The most common problem here is that *we cannot rely on the rows of the table being stored in any particular order*. Suppose the original survey forms had been filed in order of return. If we wanted to preserve this data, we would need to add a Return Date or Return Sequence column. If the hospitals used red forms for emergency operations and blue forms for elective surgery, we would need to add a column to record the category if it was of interest to the database users.

2.4.3.   Derivable Data

We need to remove any data that can be derived from other data in the table, and amend the columns accordingly. Remember our basic objective of nonredundancy. The Total Drug Cost is derivable by adding together the Drug Costs multiplied by the Numbers of Doses. We therefore remove it, noting in our supporting documentation how it can be derived (someone is bound to notice it missing, and we need to be able to prove to them that it can be reconstructed).

We might well ask why the total was held in the first place. In some cases, derived data is included unknowingly; more often it is added with the intention of improving performance. Even from that perspective, we should realize that there will be a trade-off between data retrieval (faster if we don't have to assemble the base data and calculate the total each time) and data update (the total will need to be recalculated if we change the base data). Far more importantly, though, performance is none of our business at this stage. If the physical designers cannot achieve the required performance, then carrying redundant data is *one* option we might consider and properly evaluate.

We can also drop the practice of prefixing Hospital Numbers with "H" and Surgeon Numbers with "S." The prefixes add no information, as we will always look at the hospital numbers and surgeon numbers in the context of their column headings.

2.4.4. Determining the Key

Finally, we determine a *key* for the table. The subject of keys warrants a full chapter (Chapter 8); for the moment we'll simply note that the key is *a minimal set of columns that hold a different combination of values for each row of the table.* Another way of looking at it is that each value of the key *uniquely identifies* one row of the table. In this case, a combination of Hospital Number and Operation Number will do the job. To clarify: if we nominate a particular hospital number and operation number, there will be at most *one* row with that particular combination of values. The purpose of the key is exactly this: to enable us to refer unambiguously to a specific row of a table ("Give me the row for hospital number 33, operation 109"). We can check this with the user by asking: "Could there ever be more than one form with the same combination of Hospital Number and Operation Number?" Incidentally, any combination that *includes* these two columns (e.g., Hospital Number, Operation Number, and Surgeon Number) will also identify only one row, but will violate our requirement that the key be minimal (i.e., just big enough to do the job).

Figure 2-9 shows the result of tidying up the initial model of Figure 2-8. Note that Hospital Number and Operation Number are underlined. *This is the standard convention for identifying the columns that form the key.*

OPERATION Hospital Number, Operation Number, Hospital Name, Hospital Type, Training Status, Contact Person, Operation Name, Operation Code, Procedure Group, Surgeon Number, Surgeon Specialty, Drug Short Name 1, Drug Name 1, Manufacturer 1, Size of Dose 1, Unit of Measure 1, Method of Administration 1, Cost of Dose 1, Number of Doses 1, Drug Short Name 2, Drug Name 2, Manufacturer 2, Size of Dose 2, Unit of Measure 2, Method of Administration 2, Cost of Dose 2, Number of Doses 2, Drug Short Name 3, Drug Name 3, Manufacturer 3, Size of Dose 3, Unit of Measure 3, Method of Administration 3, Cost of Dose 3, Number of Doses 3, Drug Short Name 4, Drug Name 4, Manufacturer 4, Size of Dose 4, Unit of Measure 4, Method of Administration 4, Cost of Dose 4, Number of Doses 4)

Figure 2-9. Drug Expenditure Model After Tidying Up

2.5.   REPEATING GROUPS AND FIRST NORMAL FORM

Let's start cleaning up this mess! Earlier we saw that our first task in normalization was to put the data in tabular form. It might seem that we've done this already, but in fact we've only managed to hide a problem with the data about the drugs administered.

2.5.1.   Limit on Maximum Number of Occurrences

The drug administration data is the major cause of the table's complexity and inelegance, with its Drug Short Name 2, Drug Name 4, Number of Doses 3, and so forth. The columns needed to accommodate up to four drugs account for most of the complexity. And why only four – why not five or six or more? Four drugs represented a maximum arrived at by asking one of the survey team, "What would be the maximum number of different drugs ever used in an operation?" In fact, this number was frequently exceeded, with some operations using up to ten different drugs. Part of the problem was that the question was poorly put: a line on the form was required for each *drug-dosage combination*, rather than just for each different drug. And even if this had been allowed for, drugs and procedures could later have changed in such a way as to increase the maximum likely number of drugs. The model rates poorly against the stability criterion.

With the original clerical system, this didn't present much of a problem. Many of the forms were returned with a piece of paper taped to the bottom, or with additional forms attached with only the bottom section completed to record the additional drug administrations. In a computer system, the change to the database to add the extra columns could be easily made, but the associated changes to programs would be much more painful. Indeed, the system developer decided that the easiest solution was to leave the database structure unchanged, and to hold multiple rows for these operations, suffixing the Operation Number with "a," "b," or "c" to indicate a continuation. This also involved changes to program logic and compromised the original simplicity of the system.

So one problem with our "repeating group" of drug administration data is that we have to set an arbitrary maximum number of repetitions. Ten repetitions is at least untidy and possibly inefficient, considering that 75 percent of operations used no antibiotic drugs at all. But this is not the major problem.

2.5.2.   Data Reuseability and Program Complexity

The main difficulties are with data reuseability and management of program complexity. It is relatively easy to write a program to answer questions like "How many operations were performed by neurosurgeons?" or "Which hospital is spending the most money on drugs?" A simple scan through the relevant columns will do the job. But it gets more complicated when we ask a question like "How much money was spent on the drug Ampicillin?" Similarly, "Sort into Operation Code sequence" is simple to handle, but "Sort into Drug Name sequence" can't be done at all without reshaping the table.

You might argue that some enquiries are always going to be intrinsically more complicated than others. But consider what would have happened if we had designed the table on the basis of "one row per drug." This might have been prompted by a different data collection method – perhaps the hospital drug dispensary filling out one survey form per drug. We would have needed to allow a repeating group (probably with many repeats!) to cater for all the operations that used each drug, but we would find that the queries that were previously difficult to program had become straightforward, and vice versa. Here is a case of data being organized to suit a specific set of processes, rather than as a resource available to all potential users.

Consider too the problem of updating data within the repeating group. Suppose we wanted to delete the second drug administration for a particular operation (perhaps it was a nonantibiotic drug, entered in error). Would we shuffle the third and fourth drugs back into slots two and three, or would our programming now have to cater to intermediate gaps? Either way, the programming is messy because our data model is inelegant.

2.5.3.   Recognizing Repeating Groups

To summarize: we have a set of columns repeated a number of times – a "repeating group" – resulting in inflexibility, complexity, and poor data reusability. The table design hides the problem by using numerical suffixes to give each column a different name.

We are better off to face the problem squarely, and document our initial structure as in Figure 2-10. The curly brackets indicate a repeating group with an indefinite number of occurrences: it's a useful convention, but it describes something we can't implement with a simple table. In technical terms, our data is *unnormalized*.

> **OPERATION (Hospital Number, Operation Number, Hospital Name, Hospital Category, Training Status, Contact Person, Operation Name, Operation Code, Procedure Group, Surgeon Number, Surgeon Specialty, {Drug Short Name, Drug Name, Manufacturer, Size of Dose, Unit of Measure, Method of Administration, Cost of Dose, Number of Doses})**

Figure 2-10. Drug Expenditure Model Showing Repeating Group

A general and flexible solution should not set any limits on the maximum number of occurrences, and should also neatly handle the situation of few or no occurrences (the drug-free operation).

2.5.4.   Removing Repeating Groups

This brings us to the first step in normalization:

> **STEP 1:**   Put the data in tabular form by identifying and eliminating repeating groups.

The procedure is to split the file into two tables: one for the basic operation data and one for the (repeating) drug administration data, as follows:

1. Remove all repeating group columns to a new table, so that each occurrence of the group becomes a row in the new table.
2. Include the key of the original table in the new table, to serve as a cross reference (we call this a *foreign key*).
3. If the sequence of the original repeating group had business significance, introduce a "Sequence" column to the new table.
4. Name the new table.
5. Identify and underline the key of the new table, as described in the next subsection.

Figure 2-11 shows the two tables that result from applying these rules to the Operation table.

OPERATION (<u>Hospital Number</u>, <u>Operation Number</u>, Hospital Name, Hospital Type, Training Status, Contact Person, Operation Name, Operation Code, Procedure Group, Surgeon Number, Surgeon Specialty).

DRUG ADMINISTRATION (<u>Hospital Number</u>, <u>Operation Number</u>, <u>Drug Short Name</u>, <u>Size of Dose</u>, <u>Unit of Measure</u>, <u>Method of Administration</u>, Cost of Dose, Number of Doses, Drug Name, Manufacturer).

Figure 2-11. Repeating Group Removed to Separate Table

We have named the new table Drug Administration, since each row in the table records the administration of a particular drug dose, just as each row in the original table records an operation.

2.5.5.   Determining the Key of the New Table

Finding the key of the new table wasn't easy (in fact this is usually the trickiest step in the whole normalization process). We had to ask, "What is the minimum combination of columns needed to uniquely identify one row (i.e., one specific administration of a drug)?" Certainly we needed Hospital Number and Operation Number to pin it down to one operation, but to reliably identify the individual administration we had to specify not only the Drug Short Name, but also the Size of Dose, Unit of Measure, and Method of Administration – a six-column key.

In verifying the need for this long key, we would need to ask: "Can the same drug be administered in different dosages for the one operation?" (yes), and: "Can the same drug and dose be administered using different methods for the one operation?" (yes again).

The reason for including the key of the Operation table in the Drug Administration table should be fairly obvious – we need to know which operation each drug administration applies to. It does, however, highlight the importance of keys in providing the links between tables. It's worth considering the problems that would arise if we could have two or more operations with the same combination of Hospital Number and Operation Number. There would be no way of knowing which of the operations a given drug administration applied to.

To recap: keys are an essential part of normalization.

In determining the key for the new table, you will *usually* need to include the key of the original table, as in this case (Hospital Number and Operation Number form part of the key). This is not always so, despite what some widely read texts, including Codd's[1] original paper, suggest (see the example of insurance agents and policies in Section 7.6.3).

The sequence issue is often overlooked. In this case, the sequence of the drugs was not, in fact, significant, but the original data structure did allow us to distinguish between first, second, third, and fourth administrations. A sequence column in the Drug Administration table would have enabled us to retain that data if needed.

2.5.6.   First Normal Form

Our tables are now technically in *First Normal Form* (often abbreviated to 1NF). What have we achieved?

1. All data of the same kind is now held in the same place: for example, all drug names are now in a common column. This translates into elegance and simplicity in both data structure and programming (we could now sort the data by Drug Name, for example).

2. The number of different drug dosages that can be recorded for an operation is limited only by the maximum possible number of rows in the Drug Administration table – effectively unlimited. Conversely, an operation that does not use any drugs will not require any rows in the Drug Administration table.

---

[1] Codd, E. F., "A Relational Model of Data for Large Shared Data Banks," *Communications of the ACM*, (1970). This was the first paper to advocate normalization as a data modeling technique.

2.6.   SECOND AND THIRD NORMAL FORMS

2.6.1.   Problems With Tables in First Normal Form

Look at the Operation table in Figure 2-11.

Every row that represents an operation at, say, hospital number 17 will contain the facts that its name is St. Vincent's, that Fred Fleming is the contact person, that its training status is T, and its type is P. At the very least, our criterion of non-redundancy is not being met. But there are other associated problems. Changing any fact about a hospital (e.g., the contact person) will involve updating every operation for that hospital. And if we were to delete the last operation for a hospital, we would also be deleting the details of that hospital. Think about this for a moment. If we have a transaction "Delete Operation," its usual effect will be to delete the record of an operation only. But if the operation is the last for a particular hospital, the transaction has the additional effect of deleting data about the hospital as well. If we want to prevent this, we will need to explicitly handle "last operations" differently, a clear violation of our elegance criterion.

2.6.2.   Eliminating Redundancy

We can solve all of these problems by removing the hospital information to a separate table, in which each hospital number appears once only (and therefore is the obvious choice for the table's key). Figure 2-12 shows the result. We keep Hospital Number in the original Operation table to tell us which row to refer to in the Hospital table if we want relevant hospital details. Once again, it's vital that Hospital Number identifies one row only, to prevent any ambiguity.

OPERATION (<u>Hospital Number</u>, <u>Operation Number</u>, Operation Name, Operation Code, Procedure Group, Surgeon Number, Surgeon Specialty).

HOSPITAL (<u>Hospital Number</u>, Hospital Name, Hospital Type, Training Status, Contact Person).

DRUG ADMINISTRATION (<u>Hospital Number</u>, <u>Operation Number</u>, <u>Drug Short Name</u>, <u>Size of Dose</u>, <u>Unit of Measure</u>, <u>Method of Administration</u>, Cost of Dose, Number of Doses, Drug Name, Manufacturer).

Figure 2-12. Hospital Data Removed to Separate Table

We've gained quite a lot here. Not only do we now hold hospital information once only; we are also able to record details of a hospital even if we don't yet have an operation recorded for that hospital.

2.6.3. Determinants

It's important to understand that this whole procedure of separating hospital data relied on the fact that for a given hospital number there could be only one hospital name, contact person, hospital type, and training status. In fact we could look at the dependency of hospital data on hospital number as the cause of the problem: every time a particular hospital number appeared in the operation table, the hospital name, contact person, hospital type, and training status were the same. Why hold them more than once?

Formally, we say that Hospital Number is a *determinant* of the other four columns. We can show this as:

> Hospital Number => Hospital Name, Contact Person, Hospital Type, Training Status.
>
> where we read "=>" as "determines" or "is a determinant of."

Determinants need not consist of only one column; they can be a combination of two or more columns. For example: Hospital Number + Operation Number = Surgeon Number.

This leads us to a more formal description of the procedure:

1. Identify any determinants, other than the key, and the columns they determine. (We qualify this rule slightly in the section on candidate keys).
2. Establish a separate table for each determinant and the columns it determines. The determinant becomes the key of the new table.
3. Name the new tables.
4. Remove the determined columns from the original table. Leave the determinants to provide links between tables.

Our "other than the key" exception in (1) is interesting. The problems with determinants arise when the same value appears in more than one row of the table. Because hospital number 17 could appear in more than one row of the Operation table, the corresponding values of Contact Person and other columns that it determined were also held in more than one row – hence the redundancy. But each value of the *key* can appear only once, by definition.

We've already dealt with "Hospital Number => Hospital Name, Contact Person, Hospital Type, Training Status."

Let's check the tables for other determinants. We find:

Operation Table

> Hospital Number + Surgeon Number => Surgeon Specialty
> Operation Code => Operation Name, Procedure Group

Drug Administration Table

> Drug Short Name => Drug Name, Manufacturer
> Drug Short Name + Method of Administration + Size of Dosage + Unit of
> Measure = Cost of Dose

How did we know that, for example, each combination of Drug Short Name, Method of Administration, and Size of Dose would always have the same cost? Without knowledge of every row that might ever be stored in the table, we had to look for a general rule. In practice, this means *asking the business specialist*. Our conversation might have gone along the following lines:

Modeler:	What determines Drug Cost?
User:	It depends on the drug itself and the size of the dose.
Modeler:	So any two doses of the same drug and same size would always cost the same?
User:	Assuming, of course, they were administered by the same method – injections cost more than pills.
Modeler:	Ah, and wouldn't cost vary from hospital to hospital (and operation to operation)?
User:	Strictly speaking, that's true, but it's not what we're interested in. We want to be able to compare prescribing practices, not how good each hospital is at negotiating discounts. So we use a standardized cost.
Modeler:	So maybe we could call this column "Standard Cost" rather than "Cost." By the way, where does the Standard Cost come from?

And so on. Finding determinants may look like a technical task, but in practice most of the work is in understanding the business requirements.

The determinant of Surgeon Specialty is interesting. Surgeon Number alone will not do the job, because the same surgeon number could be allocated by more than one hospital. We need to add Hospital Number to form a true determinant. But think about the implications of this means of identifying surgeons. The same surgeon could work at more than one hospital, and would be allocated different surgeon numbers. Because we have no way of keeping track of a surgeon across hospitals, our system will not fully support queries of the type "List all the operations performed by a particular surgeon." As data modelers, we need to ensure the user understands this limitation of the data, a result of the strategy used to ensure surgeon anonymity.

By the way, are we sure that a surgeon can have only one specialty? If not, we would need to show Surgeon Specialty as a repeating group. For the moment, we'll assume that the model correctly represents reality, but the close examination of the data that we do at this stage of normalization often brings to light issues that may take us back to the earlier stages of preparation for normalization and removal of repeating groups.

2.6.4. Third Normal Form

Figure 2-13 shows the final model. Every time we removed data to a separate table, we eliminated some redundancy, and allowed the data in the table to be stored independently of other data (for example, we can now hold data about a drug, even if we haven't used it yet).

OPERATION (<u>Hospital Number, Operation Number,</u> Operation Code, Surgeon Number)

SURGEON (<u>Hospital Number, Surgeon Number,</u> Surgeon Specialty)

OPERATION TYPE (<u>Operation Code,</u> Operation Name, Procedure Group)

DRUG DOSAGE (<u>Drug Short Name, Method of Administration, Size of Dose, Unit of Measure,</u> Standard Cost)

DRUG (<u>Drug Short Name,</u> Drug Name, Manufacturer)

HOSPITAL (<u>Hospital Number,</u> Hospital Name, Hospital Category, Contact Person)

DRUG ADMINISTRATION (<u>Drug Short Name, Size of Dose, Unit of Measure, Method of Administration, Hospital Number, Operation Number,</u> Number of Doses)

Figure 2-13. Fully Normalized Drug Expenditure Model

Intuitive designers call this "creating look-up tables." Using normalization terminology we say that the model is now in *third normal form* (3NF). I'll anticipate a few questions right away.

What happened to Second Normal Form?

Our approach took us directly from first normal form (data in tabular form) to third normal form. Most texts treat this as a two-stage process, dealing first with determinants that are part of the table's key, and later with nonkey determinants. For example, Hospital Code is part of the key of Operation, so we would establish the Hospital table in the first stage. Similarly, we would establish the Drug and Dose tables. At this point we would be in Second Normal Form (2NF), with the Operation Type and Surgeon information still to be separated out. The next stage would handle these, taking us to 3NF.

But be warned: most explanations that take this line suggest that you handle determinants which are part of the key first, then determinants which are made up from nonkey columns. What about the determinant of Surgeon Specialty? This is made up of one key column (Hospital Number) plus one nonkey column (Surgeon Number), and is in danger of being overlooked. *Use the two stage process to break up the task if you like, but run a final check on determinants at the end.*

Most importantly, we only see 2NF as a stage in the process of getting our data fully normalized, never as an end in itself.

Is "Third Normal Form" the same as "Fully Normalized?"

Unfortunately, no. There are three further important normal forms: Boyce-Codd Normal Form (BCNF), Fourth Normal Form (4NF), and Fifth Normal Form (5NF). We'll discuss these in Chapter 7. The good news is that in most cases, including this one, data in 3NF is already in these other normal forms. In particular, 4NF and 5NF are relevant only when dealing with tables in which every column is part of the key. By the way, "all key" tables are legitimate and occur quite frequently, usually without causing any 4NF and 5NF problems.

What about performance? Surely all those tables will slow things down?

There are certainly a lot of tables for what might seem to be relatively little data. This is partly because I deliberately left out quite a few columns, such as Hospital Address, which did not do much to illustrate the normalization process. This is done in virtually all illustrative examples, so they have a "stripped down" appearance compared with those you'll encounter in practice.

But the important point, made in Chapter 1, is that *performance is not an issue at this stage*. We don't know anything about performance requirements, data and transaction volumes, or the hardware and software to be used. Time after time modelers given this problem will do (or not do) things "for the sake of efficiency." For the record, the actual system was implemented completely without compromise, and performed as required.

Finally, recall that in preparing for normalization, we split the original Drug Code into Drug Short Name, Size of Dose, and Unit of Measure. At the time, I mentioned that this would affect the final result. We can see now that had we kept them together, the key of the Drug table would have been Drug Code. A look at some sample data from such a table will illustrate the problem this would have caused (Figure 2-14).

Drug Code	Drug Name
Max 50 mg	Maxicillin
Max 100 mg	Maxicillin
Max 200 mg	Maxicillin

Figure 2-14. Drug Table Resulting From Complex Drug Code

We are carrying the fact that "Max" is the short name for Maxicillin redundantly, and would be unable to neatly record a short name and its meaning unless we had established the available doses – typical symptoms of unnormalized data.

2.7.   DEFINITIONS AND A FEW REFINEMENTS

We've taken a rather long walk through what was, on the surface, a fairly simple example. In the process, though, we've encountered most of the problems that arise in getting data models into 3NF. Because we'll be discussing normalization issues throughout the book, and because you'll encounter them in the literature, it's worth clarifying the terminology, and picking up a few additional important concepts.

2.7.1.   Determinants and Functional Dependency

We've already covered determinants in some detail. Remember that a determinant can consist of one or more columns, and must fit the following formula:

> "For each value of the determinant, there can only be one value of some other nominated column(s) in the table at any point in time." Equivalently we can say that the other nominated columns are *functionally dependent* on the determinant.

The determinant concept is what 3NF (and BCNF) is all about – we are simply grouping data items around their determinants.

2.7.2.   Primary Keys

We've introduced the underline convention to document the key of each table, and emphasized the importance of keys in normalization. More precisely we are talking about the *primary* keys. A primary key is a nominated column or combination of columns that has a different value for every row in the table. Each table has only one primary key. When checking this with a business person, I say, "If I nominated, say, a particular Account Number, would you be able to *guarantee* that there was *never* more than one Account with that number?" We look at primary keys in more detail in Chapter 8.

2.7.3.   Candidate Keys

Sometimes more than one column or combination of columns could serve as a primary key. For example, we could have chosen Drug Name rather than Drug Short Name as the primary key of the Drug table (assuming, of course, that no two drugs could have the same name). We refer to such possible primary keys, whether chosen or not, as *candidate keys*. From the point of view of normalization, the important thing is that candidate keys that have not been chosen as the primary key, such as Drug Name, will be determinants of every column in the table, just as the primary key is. Under our normalization rules, as they stand, we would need to create a separate table for the candidate key and every other column, a step which would add complexity to the model without any reduction in redundancy (since, by definition, each candidate key value will appear once only).

To cater to this situation, we need to be more specific in our rule for which determinants to use as the basis for new tables. We previously excluded the primary key; we need to extend this to all candidate keys. Our first step then should strictly begin:

> "Identify any determinants, *other than candidate keys* ..."

2.7.4.   A Formal Definition of Third Normal Form

The concepts of determinants and candidate keys provide a nice lead-in to a more formal definition of 3NF:

> A table is in 3NF if the only determinants of nonkey columns are candidate keys.

This makes sense: our procedure took all determinants other than candidate keys, and removed the columns they determined. The only determinants left should therefore be candidate keys. Once you've come to grips with the concepts of determinants and candidate keys, this definition of 3NF is a succinct and practical test to apply to data structures. The oft-quoted maxim "Each non key column must be determined by the key, the whole key, and nothing but the key" is a good way of remembering first, second, and third normal forms, but not quite as tidy and rigorous.

Incidentally, the definition of BCNF is even simpler: a table is in BCNF if the only determinants of *any* columns (including key columns) are candidate keys. The reason that we defer discussion of BCNF to Chapter 7 is that identifying a BCNF problem is one thing – fixing it may be another!

2.7.5.   Foreign Keys

Recall that when we removed repeating groups to a new table, we carried the primary key of the original table with us, to cross-reference or "point back" to the source. Similarly, in moving from first to third normal form, we left determinants behind as cross-references to the relevant rows in the new tables.

These cross-referencing columns are called "foreign keys," and are our means of linking data from different tables. For example, Hospital Number (the primary key of Hospital) appears as a foreign key in the Surgeon and Operation tables, in each case pointing back to the relevant hospital information. Another way of looking at it is that we are using the foreign keys as surrogates or abbreviations for hospital data – we can always get the full data about a hospital by looking up the relevant row in the Hospital table.

Note that "elsewhere in the data model" may include "elsewhere in the same table." For example, an Employee table might have a primary key of Employee Number. We might also hold the employee number of each employee's manager (Figure 2-15). The Manager's Employee Number would be a foreign key. This structure appears quite often in models as a means of representing hierarchies. The traditional convention for highlighting the foreign keys in a model is an asterisk, as shown.

EMPLOYEE (<u>Employee Number</u>, Name, Manager's Employee Number*,....)

Figure 2-15. Foreign Key Convention

For the sake of brevity, I use the asterisk convention in this book. But when dealing with more complex models, and recording the columns in a list as in Figure 2-6, I suggest you distinguish each foreign key by labeling the columns FK-Hospital, FK-Drug, etc., identifying the tables to which they point. Some columns will be part of more than one primary key, and hence potentially of more than one foreign key: for example, Hospital Number is the primary key of Hospital, but part of the primary key of Operation, Surgeon, and Drug Administration.

It is a good check on normalization to mark all the foreign keys, and then to check whether any column names appear more than once in the overall model. If they are marked as foreign keys, they are serving the required purpose of cross-referencing the various tables. If not, there are three likely possibilities:

1. We have made an error in normalization – perhaps we have moved a column to a new table, but forgotten to remove it from the original table.
2. We have used the same name to describe two different things – perhaps we have used the word "Unit" to mean both "unit of measure" and "(organizational) unit in which the surgeon works" (as in fact actually happened in the early stages of designing this model).
3. We have failed to correctly mark the foreign keys.

In Chapter 3, foreign keys will play an important role in translating our models into diagrammatic form.

2.7.6. Referential Integrity

Imagine we are looking at the values in a foreign key column – perhaps Hospital Number in the Operation Table, which is a foreign key pointing to Hospital (where Hospital Number is the primary key). We would expect every hospital number in the Operation table to have a matching hospital number in the Hospital table. If not, our database would be internally inconsistent; critical information about the hospital at which an operation was performed would be missing.

Modern database management systems provide *referential integrity* features that ensure automatically that each foreign key value has a matching primary key value.

2.7.7. Denormalization and Unnormalization

As we know, from time to time it is necessary to compromise one data modeling objective in favor of another. Occasionally, we will be obliged to implement logical database designs that are not fully normalized in order to achieve some other objective – almost invariably performance. When doing this, it is important to look beyond "normalization" as a goal in itself, to the underlying benefits it provides: completeness, nonredundancy, flexibility of extending repeating groups, ease of data reuse, and programming simplicity. These are what we are sacrificing when we implement unnormalized or only partly normalized structures.

In many cases, these sacrifices will be prohibitively costly, but in others they may be acceptable. Figure 2-16 shows two options for representing data about a fleet of aircraft. The first model consists of a single, unnormalized table; the second is a normalized version of the first, comprising four tables.

(a) Unnormalized Model

AIRCRAFT (Aircraft Tail Number, Date Purchased, Model Name, Variant Code,

Variant Name, Manufacturer Name, Manufacturer Supplier Code)

(b) Normalized Model

AIRCRAFT (Aircraft Tail Number, Date Purchased, Variant Code*)

VARIANT (Variant Code, Variant Name, Model Name*)

MODEL (Model Name, Manufacturer Name*)

MANUFACTURER (Manufacturer Name, Manufacturer Supplier Code)

Figure 2-16. Normalization of Aircraft Data

If we were to find that the performance cost of accessing the four tables to build up a picture of a given aircraft was unacceptable, we might consider a less-than-fully-normalized structure, although not necessarily the single table model of Figure 2-16(a). In this case, it may be that the Variant, Model, and Manufacturer tables are very stable, and that we are not interested in holding the data unless we have an aircraft of that type. Nevertheless, we would expect that there would be some update of this data, and would still have to provide the less-elegant update programs no matter how rarely they were used.

Considered decisions of this kind are a far cry from the database design folklore which regards denormalization as the first tactic in achieving acceptable performance, and sometimes even as a standard implementation practice regardless of performance considerations! Indeed, the words "denormalization" and "unnormalization" are frequently used to justify all sorts of design modifications that have nothing to do with normalization at all. I once saw a data model *grow* from 25 to 80 tables under the guise of "denormalization for performance."

To summarize:

1. Normalization is aimed at achieving many of the basic objectives of data modeling, and any compromise should be evaluated in the light of the impact on those objectives.
2. There are other techniques for achieving better database performance, many of them affecting only the physical design. These should always be thoroughly explored before compromising the logical database design.
3. No change should ever be made to a logical database design without consultation with the data modeler.

2.8.   CHOICE, CREATIVITY, AND NORMALIZATION

Choice and creativity have not featured much in our discussion of normalization. Indeed, normalization itself is a deterministic process, which makes it particularly attractive to teachers – it's always nice to be able to set a problem with a single right answer. The rigor of normalization, and the emphasis placed on it in teaching and research, has sometimes encouraged a view that normalization is the only technique required in modeling.

On the contrary, normalization is only one part of the modeling process. Let's look at our example again with this in mind.

We started the problem with a set of columns. Where did they come from? Some represented well-established classifications – Operation Code was defined according to an international standard. Some classified other data sought by the study – Hospital Name, Contact Person, Surgeon Specialty. And some were "invented" by the form designer (the *defacto* modeler) – the study group had not asked for Hospital Number, Drug Short Name, or Surgeon Number.

We'll look at column definition in some detail in Chapter 9; for the moment, let's note that there are real choices possible here. For example, we could have allocated nonoverlapping ranges of surgeon numbers to each Hospital so that Surgeon Number alone was the determinant of Specialty. And what if we hadn't invented a Hospital Number at all? Hospital Name and Contact Person would have remained in the Operation table, with all the apparent redundancy that implies. We couldn't remove them, because we would not have a reliable foreign key to leave behind.

All of these decisions, quite outside the normalization process, and almost certainly "sellable" to the business users (after all, they accepted the *unnormalized* design embodied in the original form), would have affected our final solution. The last point is particularly pertinent. We invented a Hospital Number and, at the end of the normalization process, we had a Hospital table. Had we not recognized the concept of "hospital" (and hence the need for a hospital number to identify it) before we started normalization, we wouldn't have produced a model with a Hospital table. There's a danger of circular reasoning here: we implicitly recognize the need for a hospital table, so we specify a Hospital Number to serve as a key, which in turn leads us to specify a hospital table.

A particularly good example of concepts being embodied in keys is the old account-based style of banking system. Figure 2-16 shows part of a typical savings account file (a savings account *table*, in modern terms). Similar files would have recorded personal loan accounts, cheque accounts, etc. This file may not be normalized (for example, Account Class might determine Interest Rate), but no amount of normalizing will provide two of the key features of many modern banking data models: recognition of the concept of "customer," and integration of different types of accounts. Yet we can achieve this very simply by adding a Customer Number (uniquely identifying each customer) and replacing the various specific account numbers with a generic Account Number.

SAVINGS ACCOUNT (<u>Savings Account Number</u>, Name, Address, Account Class, Interest Rate, ...)

Figure 2-16. Traditional Savings Account Model

Let's be very clear about what's happening here. At some stage in the past, an organization may have designed computer files or manual records and invented various "numbers" and "identifiers" to identify individual records, forms, or whatever. If these identifiers are still around when we get to normalization, our new data model will contain tables that mirror these old classifications of data, which may or may not suit today's requirements.

In short, uncritical normalization perpetuates the data organization of the past.

In our prenormalization tidying-up phase, we divided complex facts into more primitive facts. There is a degree of subjectivity in this. By eliminating a multifact column, we add apparent complexity to the model (the extra columns); on the other hand, if we use a single column, we may hide important relationships amongst data, and will need to define a code for each allowable combination.

We will need to consider:

1. The value of the primitive data to the business.
    A retailer might keep stock in a number of colors, but would be unlikely to need to break the color codes into separate primary color columns (Percentage Red, Percentage Yellow, Percentage Blue); but a paint manufacturer who was interested in the composition of colors might find this a workable approach.

2. Customary and external usage.
    If a way of representing data is well established, particularly outside the business, we may choose to live with it rather than become involved in "reinventing the wheel" and translating between internal and external coding schemes. Codes that have been standardized for electronic data interchange are frequently overloaded, or suffer from other deficiencies, which we'll discuss in Chapters 8 and 9. Nevertheless, the best trade-off often means accepting these codes with their limitations.

Finally, identification of repeating groups requires a decision about *generalization*: in the example we decide that (for example) Drug Name 1, Drug Name 2, Drug Name 3, and Drug Name 4 are in some sense the "same sort of thing," and represent them with a generic "Drug Name." It's hard to dispute this case, but what about the example in Figure 2-18?

CURRENCY (<u>Currency ID</u>, <u>Date</u>, Spot Rate, Exchange Rate 3 Days, Exchange Rate 4 Days, Exchange Rate 5 Days, ...)

Figure 2-18. Currency Exchange Rates

Here we have different currency exchange rates, depending on the number of days until the transaction will be settled (i.e., money actually changing hands). There seems to be a good argument for generalizing most of the rates to a generic Rate, giving us a repeating group, but should we include Spot Rate, which covers settlement in two days? On the one hand, renaming it "Exchange Rate 2 Days" would probably push us towards including it; on the other, the business has traditionally adopted a different naming convention, perhaps because they see it as somehow different from the others. In fact, spot deals are often handled differently, and I've seen experienced data modelers in similar banks choose different options, without violating any rules of normalization.

In this section, we've focused on the choices that are not usually explicitly recognized in the teaching and application of normalization theory, in particular the degree to which key selection pre-empts the outcome. It is tempting to argue that we might as well just define a table for each concept, and allocate columns to tables according to common sense. This approach would also help to overcome another problem with the normalization process: the need to start with all data organized into a single table. In a complex "real world" model, such a table would be close to unmanageably large.

Indeed, this is the flavor of Chapter 3. In practice, however, normalization provides a complementary technique to ensure that columns are indeed where they belong, and that we haven't missed any of the less obvious tables. We will see how normalization can be complemented with a top-down approach, which gives us a first-cut set of tables, and then uses normalization as a final test to ensure that these tables are free of the avoidable problems we have discussed in this chapter.

2.9.   TERMINOLOGY

In this chapter we've used terminology based around *tables*: more specifically *tables, columns,* and *rows.* These correspond fairly closely with the familiar (to older computer professionals!) concepts of *files, data items,* and *records,* respectively.

Most theoretical work uses the relational terminology: *relations, attributes,* and *tuples,* respectively. This is because much of the theory of tabular data organization, including normalization, comes from the mathematical areas of relational calculus and relational algebra.

All that this means to most practitioners is a proliferation of different words for essentially the same concepts. We'll stick with tables, columns, and rows, but will call models in this form relational models. If you are working with a relational database management system, you'll almost certainly find the same convention used, but be prepared to encounter the full relational terminology in books and papers, and to hear practitioners talking about files, records, and items. Old habits die hard!

2.10.   SUMMARY

Normalization is a set of techniques for organizing data into tables in such a way as to eliminate certain types of redundancy and incompleteness. The modeler starts with a single file and divides it into tables based on dependencies among the data items. The process is mechanical, but the initial data will always contain assumptions about the business that will affect the outcome.

Normalization relies on correct identification of determinants and keys. In this chapter, we covered normalization to third normal form (3NF). A table is in 3NF if every determinant of a nonkey item is a candidate key. A table can be in 3NF but still not fully normalized. Higher normal forms are covered in Chapter 7.

In practice, normalization is used primarily as a check on the correctness of a model developed using a top-down approach.

3

The Entity Relationship Approach

3.1. INTRODUCTION

This chapter presents a top-down approach to data modeling, supported by a widely used diagramming convention. In Chapter 2, the emphasis was on confirming that the data organization was technically sound. The focus of this chapter is on ensuring that the data reflects business requirements.

We start by defining a procedure for representing existing models in diagram form. We then look at developing the diagrams directly from business requirements, and introduce a more business-oriented terminology, based around entities (things of interest to the business) and the relationships between them. Much of the chapter is devoted to the correct use of the terminology and diagramming conventions, which provide a common language for all participants in the data modeling process.

3.2.   A DIAGRAMMATIC REPRESENTATION

Figure 3-1 is the model we produced in Chapter 2 for the drug expenditure example. Imagine for a moment that you are encountering it for the first time. Whatever its merits as a rigorous specification for a database designer, its format does not encourage a quick appreciation of the main concepts and rules. For example, the fact that each operation can be performed by only one surgeon (because each row of the Operation table allows only one surgeon number) is an important constraint imposed by the data model, but it may not be immediately apparent. This is as simple a model as we're likely to encounter in practice. As we progress to models with more tables and more columns per table, the problem of presentation becomes more serious.

OPERATION (<u>Hospital Number*</u>, <u>Operation Number</u>, Operation Code*, Surgeon Number*)

SURGEON (<u>Hospital Number*</u>, <u>Surgeon Number</u>, Surgeon Specialty)

OPERATION TYPE (<u>Operation Code</u>, Operation Name, Procedure Group)

STANDARD DRUG DOSAGE (<u>Drug Short Name*</u>, <u>Method of Administration</u>, <u>Size of Dose</u>, <u>Unit of Measure</u>, Standard Cost of Dose)

DRUG (<u>Drug Short Name</u>, Drug Name, Manufacturer)

HOSPITAL (<u>Hospital Number</u>, Hospital Name, Hospital Category, Contact Person)

DRUG ADMINISTRATION (<u>Drug Short Name*</u>, <u>Method of Administration*</u>, <u>Size of Dose*</u>, <u>Unit of Measure*</u>, <u>Hospital Number*</u>, <u>Operation Number*</u>, Number of Doses)

Figure 3-1. Drug Expenditure Model in Relational Format

Function modelers solve this sort of problem by using diagrams showing the most important features of their models. Data flow diagrams, as used in structured analysis, are typical. Complex function models can be handled by levelled diagrams, with diagrams at each level showing different amounts of detail.

We can approach data models the same way. This chapter introduces a widely used convention for diagrammatic representation of data models, and Chapter 4 covers an approach to levelling complex models.

3.2.1.   The Basic Symbols

Our data model diagrams (sometimes called *data structure diagrams*) are based on two symbols:

1. A "box" (strictly speaking, a rectangle with rounded corners) represents a table.
2. A line drawn between two boxes represents a foreign key pointing back to the table where it appears as a primary key.

The first part is easy. Simply draw a box for every table in the model (Figure 3-2), with the name of the table inside it.

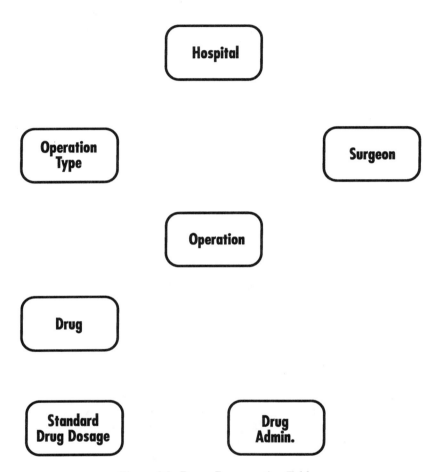

Figure 3-2. Boxes Representing Tables

3.2.2. Diagrammatic Representation of Foreign Keys

To understand how to draw the lines, look at the operation and Surgeon tables. The primary key of Surgeon (Hospital Number + Surgeon Number) appears in the operation table as a foreign key. Therefore draw a line between the two boxes, and indicate the direction of the link by putting a "crow's foot" at the foreign key end (Figure 3-3). If you like, you can think of the crow's foot as an arrow pointing back to the relevant surgeon for each operation.

Figure 3-3. Foreign Key Represented by Line and Crow's Foot.

3.2.3.   Interpreting the Diagram

If presented only with this diagram, we could deduce at least four important things:

1. The model specifies a Surgeon table (hence we want to keep data about Surgeons).
2. The model specifies an Operation table (hence we want to keep data about Operations).
3. Each Operation can be associated with only one Surgeon (because there is only provision for the key of Surgeon to appear once in each row of the Operation table).
4. Each Surgeon could be associated with many Operations (because there is nothing to stop many rows of the Operation table pointing to the same Surgeon).

The first two rules would have been obvious from the relational representation, the other two much less so. With the diagram, we have succeeded in summarizing the relationships between tables implied by our primary and foreign keys, without having to actually list any column names at all.

We could now ask a business specialist, referring to the diagram: "Is it true that each operation is performed by one surgeon only?" It is possible that this is not so, or cannot be relied upon to be so in future. Fortunately, we will have identified the problem while the cost of change is still only a little time reworking the model (we would need to represent the Surgeon information as a repeating group in the Operation table, then remove it using the normalization rules).

Another possible answer to our question could be that while more than one surgeon could participate in an operation, the client is only interested in recording details of one – perhaps the surgeon who *managed* the operation. Having made this decision, it is worth recording it on the diagram (Figure 3-4), first to avoid the question being revisited, and second to specify more precisely what data will be held. It is now clear that the database will not be able to answer the question: "In how many operations did surgeon number 12 at hospital number 18 *participate*?" It *will* support "How many operations did surgeon number 12 at hospital number 18 *manage*?"

As well as annotating the diagram, we should change the name of the Surgeon Number column in the Operation table to Managing Surgeon Number.

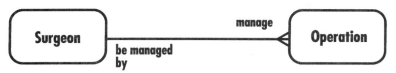

Figure 3-4. Annotated Relationship.

3.2.4.   Optionality

The diagram may also raise the possibility of operations that don't involve any surgeons at all: "We don't involve a surgeon when we are attending to a patient who presents with a small cut, but we still need to record whether any drugs were used." In this case, some rows in the Operation table may have a null value for Surgeon Number. We can show whether the involvement of a surgeon in an operation is *optional* or *mandatory* by using the conventions of Figure 3-5. You can think of the circle as a zero and the perpendicular bar as a "1," indicating the minimum number of surgeons per operation or (at the other end of the line) operations per surgeon.

Our diagram now contains just about as much information about the Surgeon and Operation tables and their inter relationships as can be recorded without actually listing columns and text descriptions of their meanings.[1] The result of applying the rules to the entire drug expenditure model is shown in the diagram in Figure 3-6.

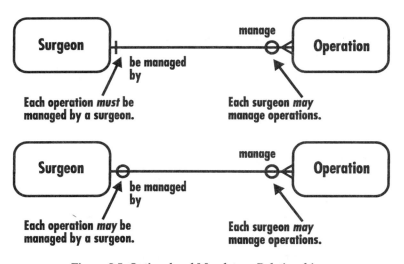

Figure 3-5. Optional and Mandatory Relationships.

---

[1] This is not quite all we can usefully record, but few CASE tools support more than this. See Section 6.3 for a diagramming convention for nontransferability. Some tools support the *weak entity* concept discussed in Section 8.6.3.

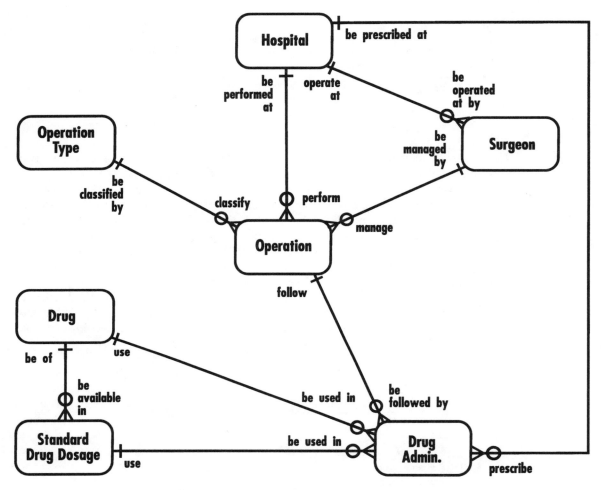

Figure 3-6. Diagram of Drug Expenditure Model.

3.2.5. Verifying the Model

The diagram provides an excellent starting point for verifying the model with users and business specialists. Intelligent, thorough checking of each line on the diagram will often reveal unsound assumptions and misunderstandings or, equally useful, increase confidence in the model on the part of both user and modeler.

We have already looked at the relationship between Operation and Surgeon. Now, consider the relationship between Operation and Operation Type. It prompts the question : "Are we sure that each operation can be of only one type?" This is the rule held in the model, but how would we represent a combined gall bladder removal and appendectomy? There are at least two possibilities:

1. Allow only "simple" operation types such as "Gall Bladder Removal" and "Appendectomy." If this course was selected, the model would need to be redesigned, based on the operation type information being a repeating group within the operation; or
2. Allow complex operation types such as "Combined Gall Bladder Removal and Appendectomy."

Both will work and the decision may be made for us by the existence of an external standard. If the system already exists, option (two) will be much easier to implement. But option (one) is more elegant, in that, for example, a single code will be used for all appendectomies. Queries of the form "list all operations that involved appendectomies" will therefore be simpler to specify and program.

Note that examining the relationship between the two tables led to thinking about the meaning of the tables themselves. Whatever decision we made about the relationship, we would need to document a clear definition of what was and wasn't a legitimate entry in the Operation Type table.

3.2.6. Redundant Lines

Look at the lines linking the Hospital, Operation, and Surgeon tables. There are lines from Hospital to Surgeon and from Surgeon to Operation. Also there is a line from Operation direct to Hospital. Does this third line add anything to our knowledge of the business rules supported by the model? It tells us that each operation must be performed at one hospital. But we can deduce this from the other two lines that specify each operation must be managed by a surgeon and each surgeon operates at a hospital. The line also shows a program could "navigate" directly from a row in the Operation table to the corresponding row in the Hospital table. But our concern is with business rules rather than navigation. Accordingly, we can remove the "short-cut" line from the diagram, without losing any information about the business rules that the model enforces.

Figure 3-7 summarizes the rule for removing redundant lines, but the rule has some important caveats:

> If it were possible for an operation to be recorded without a surgeon (i.e., if the link to the Surgeon table were *optional*), we could not remove the short-cut line, which shows that *every* Operation is performed at a hospital, something we could no longer deduce from the other lines.

> If the line from Surgeon to Hospital was named (for example) "be trained at," then the direct link from Operation to Hospital would represent different information than the combined link. The former would tell at which hospital the operation was performed, the latter which hospital trained the surgeon who performed the operation.

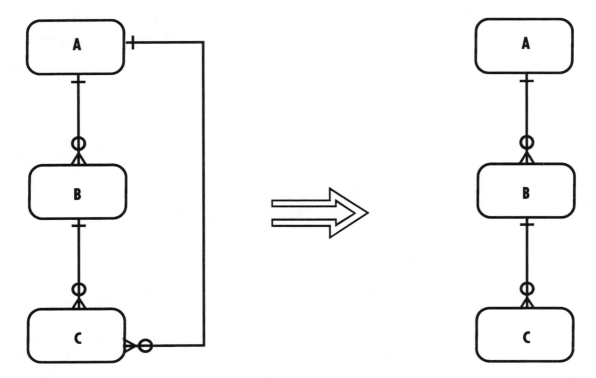

See Caveats in Text!

Figure 3-7. Removing Redundant Lines.

The value of recording names and optionality on the lines should now be a little clearer – for one thing, they allow the correct decision to be made about which lines on the diagram are redundant and can be removed. Figure 3-8 shows the result of applying the redundant line rule to the whole model.

3.3.   THE TOP-DOWN APPROACH: ENTITY-RELATIONSHIP MODELING

In the preceding section, a reasonably straightforward technique was used to represent a data model in diagram form. Although the diagram contains little new information, it communicates the principal rules so much more clearly that you should never review or present a model without drawing one. In the past, databases were often designed without the use of diagrams. It is interesting to prepare a diagram for such a database and show it to programmers and analysts who have been working with the database for some time. Frequently they have never explicitly considered many of the rules and limitations that the diagram highlights.

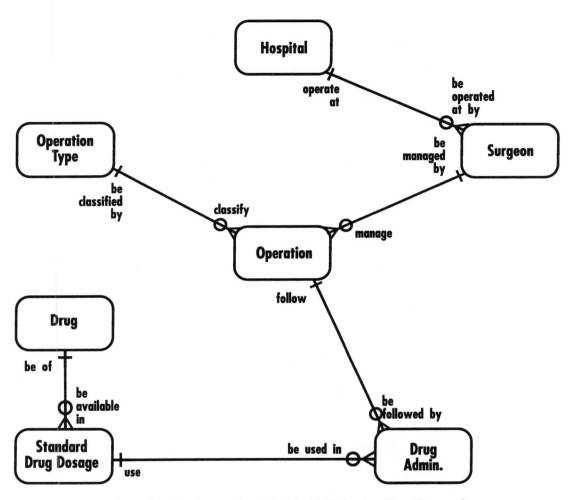

Figure 3-8. Drug Expenditure Model with Redundant Lines Removed

3.3.1. Developing the Diagram Top Down

The most interesting thing about the diagram is that it prompts a suspicion that normalization and subsequent translation into boxes and lines was not necessary at all. If instead we had asked the client "What things do you need to keep data about?" wouldn't we have received answers such as "hospitals, operations, and surgeons?" If we'd asked how they were related, might we not have been able to establish that each operation was managed by one surgeon only, and so forth? With these questions answered, couldn't we draw the diagram immediately, without bothering about normalization?

In fact, this is the approach most often taken in practice. The modeler develops a diagram that effectively describes which tables will be required, and how they will need to be related, and *then* allocates columns to the tables. Normalization becomes a final check to ensure that the "grammar" of the model is correct. For experienced modelers, the check becomes a formality, as they will have already anticipated the results of normalization and incorporated them into the diagram.

The reason we looked at normalization first is that in order to produce a normalized model, you need to know what one looks like, just as an architect needs to have examined some completed buildings before attempting to design one. At the end of the day, we want a design made up of sound, fully normalized tables that meets our criteria of completeness, nonredundancy, stability, reuseability, and elegance – not a mish-mash of business concepts. The frequently given advice to "ask what things the business needs to keep information about, and draw a box for each of these" is overly simplistic, although it indicates the general direction of the approach.

The need to produce a normalized model should be in the back of our minds, and we will therefore split out repeating groups and "look-up tables" as we discover them. For example, we might identify a table called "Aircraft." We recognize that some data will be the same for all aircraft of a particular type, and that normalization would produce an "Aircraft Type" look-up table for this data. Accordingly a box named Aircraft Type is drawn. We are actually doing a little more than normalization here, as we don't actually know that there is an existing determinant of Aircraft Type in the data (e.g., Aircraft Model Number). No matter – we reserve the right to define one if we need it!

In dealing with a Customer table, we may recognize that a customer may have more than one occupation, and that data about occupations therefore forms a repeating group that normalization would remove. We can anticipate this and define a separate Occupation table, again without knowledge of actual columns and determinants.

The top-down approach also overcomes most of the limitations of normalization used by itself. We do not need to start with a formidably complex single table, nor do we need to accept the tables implicitly defined by our historical choice of determinants. However, as we shift focus from the technical structure of the tables to the broader business requirements, it helps to introduce a more business-oriented terminology.

3.3.2. Terminology

The relational models were built on three basic concepts: tables, columns, and keys. Our new terminology is more business-oriented. Again, there are three concepts,:

1. Entities – things of interest to the business. Represented by boxes on the diagram, and implemented as tables.
2. Attributes – what we want to know about entities. Not usually shown on the diagram. They will be implemented as columns in tables.
3. Relationships – relationships between entities are represented by lines on the diagram and implemented through foreign keys.

The process of designing an appropriate set of entities and relationships to meet a business problem (i.e., getting as far as the diagram) is called, reasonably enough, entity relationship modeling or E-R modeling for short. A data model in this format is often called an E-R model, and the diagram an E-R diagram.

Don't be daunted by the new terms. Broadly speaking, we have just introduced a less technical language, to enable us to talk about (say) "the relationship between a hospital and a surgeon," rather than "the existence of the primary key of Hospital as a foreign key in the Surgeon table."

In the following sections, these new terms and their representation are examined in more detail.

3.4. ENTITIES

An entity is the "real world" class of things that a table represents, such as "Hospital." Strictly, we should distinguish between *entities*, such as "St. Vincent's Hospital" and *entity types* such as "Hospital." In practice, we tend to use the word entity loosely to mean entity type; and *entity instance* on those fairly rare occasions when we want to refer to a single instance (which would translate into a *row* in a table).

All entities will meet the criterion of being "a class of things we need to keep information about," as long as we are happy for "thing" to include more abstract concepts such as events (e.g., Operation) and classifications (e.g., Operation Type). However, the converse is not true – many classes that a user might nominate in response to the question "what do you need to keep information about?" would not end up as entities. Some concepts suggested by the user will be complex, and will need to be represented by more than one entity. For example, invoices would not usually be represented by a single Invoice entity, but by two entities – Invoice Header and Invoice Item (the result of removing the repeating group of invoice items to form a separate entity). Other user requirements will be derivable from more primitive data – for example "Quarterly Profit" might be derivable from sales and expense figures represented by other entities.

Still other "real world" classes will overlap, and would therefore violate our non-redundancy requirement. If our model already had "Personal Customer" and "Corporate Customer" entities, we would not add a "Preferred Customer" entity if such customers were already catered to by the original entities.

Finally, some concepts will be represented by attributes or relationships. There is a degree of subjectivity in deciding whether some concepts are best represented as entities or relationships: is a marriage better described as a relationship between two people, or as "something we need to keep information about?"

There is almost always an element of choice in how data is classified into entities. Should a single entity represent all employees or should we define separate entities for part-time and full-time employees? Should we use separate entities for insurance policies and cover notes or is it better to combine them into a single Policy entity? We'll discuss ways of generating and choosing alternatives in Chapters 4 and 5; for the moment, just note that such a choice does exist, even though it may not be obvious in these early examples.

Now, a few rules for representing entities. Recommending a particular set of conventions is one of the best ways of starting an argument among data modelers, and there was a time when there seemed to be as many diagramming conventions as modelers. In the last few years there has been greater standardization, thanks mainly to the increasing use of CASE tools, which enforce reasonably similar conventions. The rules for drawing entities and relationships presented in this chapter are typical of current practice.

3.4.1.   Entity Diagramming Convention

Entities are represented by boxes with rounded corners. We use the rounded corners to distinguish E-R diagrams from final logical database designs (square corners). The latter may include compromises required to achieve adequate performance or to suit the constraints of the implementation software. By using two conventions, we can quickly identify whether we are looking at what was specified (the model) or what was built (the final database design).

There are no restrictions, other than those imposed by your CASE tool, on the size or color of the boxes. If drawing a box larger or in another color aids communication, by all means do it. For example, you might have a Customer entity, and several associated entities resulting from removing repeating groups: Address, Occupation, Dependant, and so on. Just drawing a larger box for the Customer entity might help readers approach the diagram in a logical fashion.

3.4.2.   Entity Naming

The name of an entity must be in the singular. The entity name refers to a single instance (in relational terms, a row) – not to the whole table.

For example, we use:

> *Account* rather than *Accounts*
>
> *Customer* rather than *Customer File* or *Customer Table ,* or even *Customer Record*
>
> *Product* rather than *Product Catalogue*
>
> *Historical Transaction* rather than *Transaction History*
>
> *Scheduled Visit* rather than *Visiting Schedule*

We do this for three reasons:

1. *Consistency* – it is the beginning of a naming standard for entities.
2. *Communication* – an entity is "something we want to keep information about," such as a customer rather than a customer file.
3. *Compatibility with Relationship Names* – which we'll look at in the following section.

A common mistake is to name the entity after the most "important" attribute – for example, Drug Cost rather than Standard Drug Dosage, or Specialty rather than Surgeon. This is particularly tempting when we have only one nonkey attribute. It looks much less reasonable later when we add further attributes, or if the original attribute is normalized out to another entity. You should also avoid giving an entity a name that reflects only a subset of the roles it plays in the business. For example, consider using Material Item rather than Component, Person rather than Witness, and Stock Item rather than Returned Item.

3.4.3.   Entity Definitions

Entity names must be supported by definitions.

In the early stages of data modeling, we work mainly with the diagram. But that is asking a lot of the entity names – they need to communicate without ambiguity exactly what real world data they represent. Does the Operation Type entity cover hybrid operations? Does Surgeon include a general practitioner who performs an operation, or only formally qualified specialists? What exactly qualifies as an "Operation?" The answers to these questions will affect the overall shape of the model, as we discovered when we discussed the definition of Operation Type earlier in this chapter.

Frequently in data modeling you need to decide on the best terminology to use. It may be that you need to discard familiar terms in favor of less widely used terms that do not carry the same diversity of meaning. This is particularly so for the most commonly used terms, which may have acquired all sorts of context-dependent meanings over a period of time. To a railroad company, the word "train" may mean a particular service (the 8.15 P.M. train from Sydney to Melbourne), a physical object (Old Number 10), or perhaps a marketed product (the Orient Express).

But at some point in the development process (preferably sooner rather than later) we need to supplement the names in the boxes with more detailed and precise definitions. A good definition will clearly answer two questions:

1.   What distinguishes instances of this entity from instances of other entities?
2.   What distinguishes one instance from another?

Good examples of each, focusing on the marginal cases, are the best method of pinning this down. The primary key and a few other sample attributes can also do much to clarify the definition prior to the full set of attributes being defined.

For example, we might define Drug as follows:

> An antibiotic drug as marketed by a particular manufacturer. Variants which are registered as separate entries in *Smith's Index of Therapeutic Drugs* are treated as separate instances. Excluded are generic drugs such as penicillin. Examples are: Maxicillin, Minicillin, Extracycline.

Note that there is no rule against using the entity name in the definition – we are not trying to write an English dictionary.

I can't over-emphasize the importance of good entity definitions. From time to time, data modelers get stuck in long arguments without much apparent progress. Almost invariably, they have not put adequate effort into pinning down some working definitions, and are continually making subtle adjustments, which are never recorded. Modelers frequently (and, I believe, unwittingly) shift definitions in order to support their own position in discussion – "Yes, we could accommodate a patient who transfers hospitals while undergoing treatment by defining Hospital to mean the hospital where the treatment commenced," and later, "Of course we can work out how much each hospital spent on drugs – all the relevant hospitals are represented by the Hospital entity."

As well as helping to clarify the modelers' thinking, definitions provide guidance on the correct use of the resulting database. Many a user interrogating a database with a query language has been misled because of incorrect assumptions about what its tables contained. And many a programmer has effectively changed the data model by using tables to hold data other than that intended by the modeler. The latter constitutes a particularly insidious compromise to a model. If someone (perhaps the physical database designer) makes explicit changes to the logical database design, we can at least see the changes and raise the alarm. But bypassing a definition is far more subtle, as the violation is buried in program specifications and logic.

The result can be inconsistent use of data by programmers, and consequent system problems ("I assumed that surgeons included anyone who performed an operation" or even "I used the Surgeon table for pharmacists – they're all prefixed with a 'P'"). The database may even be rendered unworkable because a business rule specified by the model does not apply under the (implicit) new definition. For example, the rule that each drug has only one manufacturer will be violated if the programmer uses the table to record generic drugs, in violation of a definition that allows only for branded drugs. Changes of this kind are often made after a database has been implemented, and fails to support a new requirement. A failure on the stability criterion leads to compromises in elegance and communication.

Thus, it is vital that definitions are not only written but used. Sometimes we have a choice of either "tightening up" the definition of an existing term, or introducing a new term. The first approach produces a diagram that is more accessible to people familiar with the business, and apparently more meaningful; on the other hand, readers are less likely to look up the definition. Keep this in mind: "communication" must include an understanding of the meaning of entities as well as a superficial comfort with the diagram.

3.5.   RELATIONSHIPS

In our drug expenditure model, the lines between boxes can be interpreted in "real world" terms as relationships between entities. There are relationships between, for example, hospitals and surgeons, and between operations and drug administrations.

3.5.1.   Relationship Diagramming Conventions

We have already used a convention for annotating the lines to describe their *meaning* (relationship names), *cardinality* (the crow's foot can be interpreted as meaning "many," its absence as meaning "one"), and *optionality* (the circles and bars representing "optional" and "mandatory," respectively).

The convention is shown in Figure 3-9 and is typical of several in common use and supported by CASE tools. Figure 3-10 shows some variants.

Note that we have named the relationship in both directions: "issue" and "be issued by." This enables us to interpret the relationship in a very structured, formal way:

"Each company may issue one or more shares"

and

"Each share must be issued by one company."

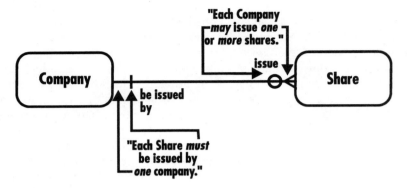

Figure 3-9. Relationship Notation

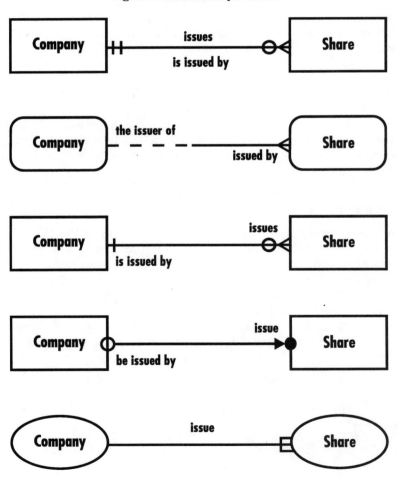

Figure 3-10. Alternative Relationship Notations

The value of this sentence form is in improving communication. While diagrams are great for conveying the big picture, they don't encourage systematic and detailed examination, particularly by business specialists. Generating the sentence is an *almost* entirely mechanical process (forming the plurals of the entity names can't be totally automated). Many CASE tools support this, using a more or less similar formula.

I like to use "one or more" rather than "many," which may have a connotation of "lots" ("Oh no, nobody would have *many* occupations, two or three would be the most"). I also like the "may" and "must" approach to describing optionality, rather than the "zero or more" and "one or more" wording used by some. "Zero or more" is an expression only a programmer could love, and our aim is to communicate with business specialists in a natural way without sacrificing precision.

An alternative to using "must" and "may" is to use "always" and "sometimes:" "Each company sometimes issues one or more shares" and "Each share is always issued by one company."

In order to be able to mechanically translate relationships into business sentences, a few rules need to be established.

We have to select relationship names that fit the sentence structure. It's worth trying to use the same verb in both directions ("hold" and "be held by," "be responsible for" and "be the responsibility of") to ensure that the relationship is not interpreted as carrying two separate meanings.

We have to name the relationships in both directions, even though this adds little to the meaning. I make a practice not only of placing each relationship name close to the entity that is the object of the sentence, but also of arranging the names above and below the line so they are read in a clockwise direction when generating the sentence (as, for example, in Figure 3-9).

We need to be strict about using singular names for entities. As mentioned earlier, this discipline is worth following regardless of relationship naming conventions.

Finally, we need to show the optional/mandatory symbol at the crow's foot end of the relationship, even though this will not usually be enforceable by the database management system (at the non-crows-foot end, "optional" is implemented by allowing the foreign key to take a null value).

Figures 3-11 and 3-12 show some relationships typical of those we encounter in practice.

Note that:

1. A crow's foot may appear at neither, one, or both ends of a relationship. The three alternatives are referred to as one-to-one, one-to-many, and many-to-many relationships, respectively.
2. There may be more than one relationship between the same two entities.
3. It is possible for the same entity to appear at both ends of a relationship – this is called a "self-referencing" or "recursive" relationship.

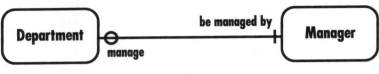

one-to-one

Each Department must be managed by one Manager.
Each Manager may manage one Department.

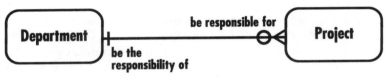

one-to-many

Each Department may be responsible for one or more Projects.
Each Project must be the responsibility of one Department.

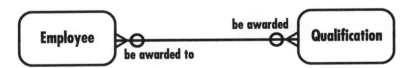

many-to-many

Each Employee may be awarded one or more Qualifications.
Each Qualification may be awarded to one or more Employees.

Figure 3-11. Examples of Relationships

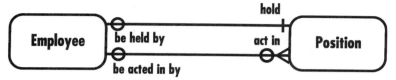

two relationships

Each Employee must hold one Position.
Each Position may be held by one Employee.

and

Each Employee may act in one or more Positions.
Each Position may be acted in by one Employee.

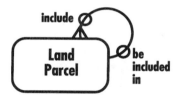

self-referencing one-to-many

Each Land Parcel may include one or more Land Parcels.
Each Land Parcel may be included in one Land Parcel.

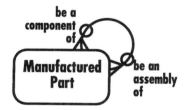

self-referencing many-to-many

Each Manufactured Part may be an assembly of one or more
Manufactured Parts.

Each Manufactured Part may be a component of one or more
Manufactured Parts.

Figure 3-12. Examples of Relationships

When drawing one-to-many relationships, I suggest you orient the entities so that the crow's foot is nearer the bottom of the page. This means that hierarchies appear in the expected way, and diagrams are easier to compare. For horizontal relationship lines, the convention (by no means followed by all modelers) is to orient the crow's foot to the right). You won't always be able to follow these conventions, especially when you use subtypes, which we introduce in Chapter 4. Once again, don't sacrifice effectiveness of communication for blind adherence to a layout convention.

Similarly, in laying out diagrams, it usually helps to eliminate crossing lines wherever possible. But carrying this rule too far can result in large numbers of close parallel lines not dissimilar in appearance (and comprehensibility) to the tracks on a printed circuit board.

Another useful technique is to duplicate entities on the diagram to avoid long and difficult-to-follow relationship lines. You need to have a symbol (provided by some CASE tools) to identify a duplicated entity; a dotted box is a good option.

3.5.2.   Many-to-Many Relationships

Many-to-many relationships crop up regularly in E-R diagrams in practice. But if you look again at the drug expenditure diagram in Figure 3-8 you will notice that it contains only one-to-many relationships. This is no accident, but a consequence of the procedure we used to draw the diagram from normalized tables. Remember that each value of a foreign key pointed to *one* entity instance, and that each value could appear *many* times; hence we only ever end up with one-to-many relationships when working from a relational model.

Look at the many-to-many relationship between Employee and Qualification in Figure 3-13.

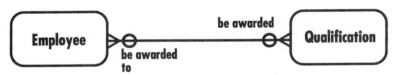

Figure 3-13. Many-to-Many Relationship

How would we implement the relationship using foreign keys? The answer is that we can't. We can't hold the key to Qualification in the Employee table, because an employee could have several qualifications. The same applies to the Qualification table, which would need to support multiple Employee keys. A normalized model cannot represent many-to-many relationships with foreign keys, yet such relationships certainly exist in the real world.

A quick preview of the answer: although we can't represent the many-to-many relationship with a foreign key, we *can* represent it with a table. But let's tackle the problem systematically.

3.5.2.1. *Applying Normalization to Many-to-Many Relationships*

Although we can't capture the relationship in a fully normalized model using only Employee and Qualification tables, we can handle it with an *unnormalized* representation, using a repeating group (Figure 3-14).

EMPLOYEE (Employee Number, Employee Name, {Qualification ID, Qualification Name, Date Qualification Received})

Figure 3-14. Employee and Qualification Unnormalized

I've had to make up a few plausible columns to give us something to normalize!

Proceeding with normalization (Figure 3-15), we remove the repeating group, and identify the key of the new table as Employee Number + Qualification ID (if an employee could receive the same qualification more than once, perhaps from different universities, we would need to include Date Qualification Received in the key to distinguish them).

Looking at our 1NF tables, we note the following dependency:

Qualification ID = > Qualification Name

Hence we provide a look-up table for qualification details. The tables are now in 3NF. You may like to confirm that we would have reached the same result if we had represented the relationship initially with a repeating group of employee details in the Qualification table.

Unnormalized:

EMPLOYEE (Employee Number, Employee Name, {Qualification ID, Qualification Name, Date Qualification Received})

First Normal Form:

EMPLOYEE (Employee Number, Employee Name)

EMPLOYEE QUALIFICATION (Employee Number*, Qualification ID, Qualification Name, Date Qualification Received)

Second and Third Normal Forms:

EMPLOYEE (Employee Number, Employee Name)

EMPLOYEE QUALIFICATION RELATIONSHIP (Employee Number*, Qualification ID*, Date Qualification Received)

QUALIFICATION (Qualification ID, Qualification Name)

Figure 3-15. Normalization of Employee and Qualification

Naming the tables presents a bit of a challenge. Employee and Qualification are fairly obvious, but what about the other table? "Employee-Qualification Relationship" is one option, and makes some sense because this less obvious table represents the many-to-many relationship between the other two. The result is shown diagrammatically in Figure 3-16.

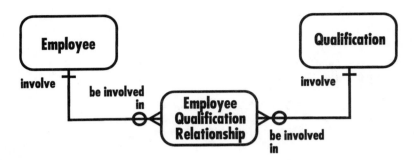

Figure 3-16. Many-to-Many Relationship Resolved

This example illustrates an important general rule. Whenever we encounter a many-to-many relationship between two entities, we can represent it with a new entity, linked to the two original entities. We call this process "resolving a many-to-many relationship" and the new entity a "resolution entity" (or "intersection entity"). There is no need to go through the normalization process each time – we simply recognize the pattern and handle it in a standard way.

3.5.2.2. Choice of Representation

We are now faced with an interesting choice. We can represent the same real world situation either with a many-to-many relationship, or with an entity and two new relationships.

The many-to-many notation preserves consistency: we use a line to represent each real world relationship, whether it is one-to-many or many-to-many (or one-to-one, for that matter). But we now have to perform some conversion to get to a relational representation. Worse, the conversion is not totally mechanical, in that we have to determine the key of the resolution table (which, in our example, might or might not have included Date Qualification Received). And how do we represent any nonkey attributes that might apply to the resolution entity – do we need to allow entities *and* relationships to have attributes?

On the other hand, if we restrict ourselves to one-to-many relationships, we seem to be stuck with the clumsy idea of an entity whose name implies that it is a relationship! And if this box actually represents a real world relationship rather than an entity, what about the two one-to-many "relationships" with the original entities? Can we really interpret them as real world relationships, or are they just "links" between relationships and entities?

The solution to this apparent mess lies in the fact that there is usually some choice as to whether to classify a particular concept as an entity or a relationship. For example, we could model the data relating prospective employees and job positions with either a relationship ("apply for/be applied for by") or an entity ("Application"). Here are some more examples:

Relationship	**Resolution Entity**
Students *enroll in* Subjects	Enrollment
Companies *employ* Persons	Employment
Employees *are responsible for* Assets	Responsibility

The name of the many-to-many relationship is usually a good source of an appropriate entity name. Perhaps we could use "Award" as an alternative to "Employee-Qualification Relationship."

Experienced data modelers take advantage of this choice, and are adept at selecting names that allow boxes to represent entities and lines to represent relationships. As a last resort, they would name the box representing a many-to-many relationship as "entity-1 entity-2 Relationship" (e.g., Employee-Asset Relationship), and thereafter treat it as an *entity*. This practice is so universal that most data modelers refer to all boxes as entities and all lines as relationships. Many would be unaware that this is only possible because of choices they have made during the modeling process.

This may all sound a little like cheating! Having decided that a particular concept is going to be implemented by a foreign key (because of the way our database management system works), we then decide that concept is a relationship. Likewise, if a particular concept is to be implemented as a table, we decide to call that concept a real world entity! And we may change our view along the way, if we discover, for example, that a relationship we originally thought to be one-to-many is in fact many-to-many.

We come back to the questions of design, choice, and creativity. If we think of the real world as being naturally preclassified into entities and relationships, and our job as one of analysis and documentation, then we are in trouble. On the other hand, if we see ourselves as designers who can choose the most useful representation, then this classification into entities and relationships is a legitimate part of our task.

3.5.2.3. The Chen Convention for Relationships

Some in the academic world choose the first option: that there are entities and relationships "out there" that we need to document consistently. When reading the literature, watch out for this assumption – it isn't always explicitly stated. This leads to the argument that we need to use a consistent symbol for relationships, regardless of cardinality or the number of participating entities. The most common symbol is the diamond, introduced by Chen in his very important paper "The Entity Relationship Model – Toward a Unified View of Data."[2]

---

[2] *ACM Transactions on Database Systems,* (March 1976).

Figure 3-17 shows the Employee-Asset example using the Chen convention. If we had started out thinking that the relationship was one-to-many, but on checking with the user found that it was many-to-many, we would only need to make a minor change to the diagram (changing the "l" to "m"). This seems more appropriate than introducing a Responsibility entity (" Fine," says the user, "but why didn't we need this entity before?").

Figure 3-17. Chen Convention for Relationships

Despite this, I don't recommend the convention, for three practical reasons.

First, it simply puts too many objects on the page. With our boxes and lines convention, we tend to look at the boxes first, then the lines, allowing us to come to grips with the model in two logical stages. In my experience, diamonds make this much harder, and practical Chen models can be quite overwhelming. Some academics even extend the convention to include attributes, shown as circles connected to the entities and relationships – excellent for illustrating simple examples, but even more unwieldy for practical problems.

Second, most CASE tools don't support the diamond convention. A few provide a special symbol for intersection entities, but still require one-to-many relationships to be documented using lines.

Third, many of the people who contribute to and verify the model will also need to see the final database design. End users may access it through query languages, and analysts will need to specify processes against it. If the final database design uses the same concepts as the verified model, these people don't have the problem of coming to grips with two different views of their data.

None of these problems need bother researchers, who typically work with fairly simple examples. A number of texts explain the Chen convention in detail;[3] they are worth reading if you want to pursue modeling theory further or to better understand some of the assumptions underlying the methods we use in practice.

In this book, we will steer a middle course, which will keep us in line with most CASE products. In the earlier stages of analysis, we will allow many-to-many relationships as a convenient and easily checked shorthand. But we will attach attributes only to entities (not to relationships), and the final model presented to the database designer will not contain any many-to-many relationships.

---

[3] For example, Batini, Ceri, Navathe, *Conceptual Database Design*, Redwood City, CA, Benjamin Cummings (1992).

3.5.3.   One-to-One Relationships

We'll leave a detailed discussion of one-to-one relationships until Chapter 6, as they are relatively uncommon (but nevertheless a legitimate and important structure in modeling). For the moment, note that you should not *automatically* combine the entities linked by a one-to-one relationship into a single entity, as is sometimes suggested.

3.5.4.   Self-Referencing Relationships

Look at Figure 3-18. This type of relationship is sometimes called a "head scratcher," not only because of its appearance, but because of the difficulty many people have in coming to grips with the recursive structure it represents.

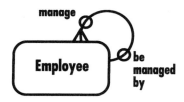

Figure 3-18. Self-Referencing One-to-Many Relationship

We interpret this in the same way as any other relationship, except that both participants in the relationship are the same entity:

"Each Employee may manage one or more Employees"
and
"Each Employee may be managed by one Employee."

The model represents a simple hierarchy of employees as might be shown on an organization chart. To implement the relationship using a foreign key, we would need to carry the key of Employee (say, Employee ID) as a foreign key *in the Employee table*. We would probably call it "Manager ID" or similar. We encountered the same situation in Section 2.7.5 when we discussed foreign keys which pointed to the primary key of the same table.

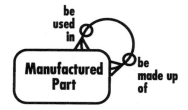

Figure 3-19. Self-Referencing Many-to-Many Relationship

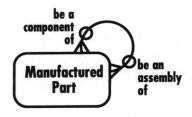

(a) Starting Point

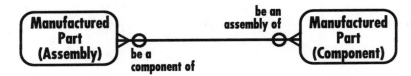

(b) Temporarily Showing Manufactured Part as Two Entities

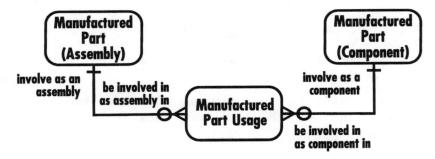

(c) Resolving Many-to-Many Relationship

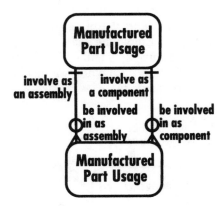

(d) Re-combining the Two Manufactured Part Entities

Figure 3-20. Resolving a Self-Referencing Many-to-Many Relationship

Note that the relationship is optional in both directions. This reflects the fact that the organizational hierarchy has a top and bottom (some employees have no subordinates, one employee has no manager). A mandatory symbol on a self-referencing relationship should always raise your suspicions.

Self-referencing relationships can also be many-to-many. Figure 3-19 shows such a relationship on a Manufactured Part entity. In business terms, we are saying that a part can be made up of parts, which themselves can be made up of parts and so on. Furthermore, we allow a given part to be used in the construction of more than one part – hence, the many-to-many relationship.

This relationship, being many-to-many, cannot be represented by a single table with suitable foreign key(s). We can, however, resolve it in much the same way as a many-to-many relationship between two different entities.

Figure 3-20 shows an intuitive way of tackling the problem directly from the diagram. We temporarily split the Manufactured Part entity in two, giving us a familiar two-entity many-to-many relationship, which we resolve as described earlier. We then recombine the two parts of the split entity, taking care not to lose any relationships.

Figure 3-21 shows the same result achieved by representing the structure with a repeating group and normalizing.

MANUFACTURED PART (<u>Manufactured Part Number,</u> Description, {Component Manufactured Part Number, Quantity Used})

Removing repeating group....

MANUFACTURED PART (<u>Manufactured Part Number,</u> Description)

MANUFACTURED PART USAGE (<u>Assembly Manufactured Part Number*</u>, <u>Component Manufactured Part Number*,</u> Quantity Used)

Figure 3-21. Using Normalization to Resolve a Self-Referencing Many-to-Many Relationship

The structure shown in Figure 3-20(d) can be used to represent any self-referencing many-to-many relationship. It is often referred to as the "Bill of Materials" structure, because in manufacturing, a bill of materials lists all the lowest level components required to build a particular product by progressively breaking down assemblies, sub-assemblies, and so forth. Note that the Manufactured Part Usage entity holds two foreign keys pointing to Manufactured Part (Assembly Manufactured Part Number and Component Manufactured Part Number) to support the two relationships.

3.5.5.   Relationships of Higher Degree

All our relationships so far have involved only two entities. How would we handle a real world relationship involving three or more entities?

A welfare authority might need to record which services were provided by which organizations in which areas. From a relational modeling viewpoint, our three basic tables might be Service, Organization, and Area. The objective is to record each allowable combination of the three. For example, the Service "Child Care" might be provided by "Family Support Inc." in "Greentown." We can easily do this by defining a table in which each row holds an allowable combination of the three primary keys. The result is shown diagrammatically in Figure 3-22, and it can be viewed as an extension of the technique used to resolve two-entity many-to-many relationships. The same principle applies to relationships involving four or more entities.

Once more, in modeling the real world using an E-R model, we find ourselves representing a relationship with a box rather than a line. Modelers using the Chen convention would use a diamond in this case. However, once again we can change our perspective and view the relationship as an entity – in this case we might name it Service Availability (" Allowed Combination" or similar is often a good choice). We discuss relationships involving three or more entities in Chapters 6 and 7.

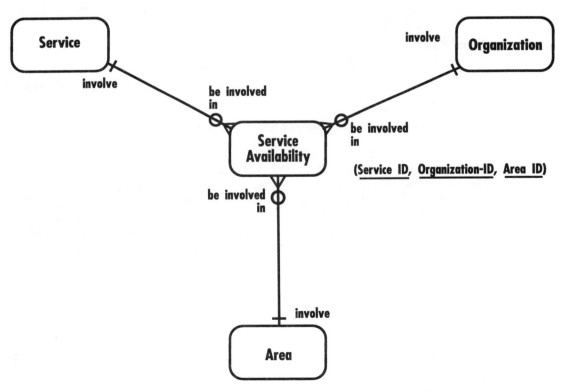

Figure 3-22. Resolution Entity Representing a Ternary (3-entity) Relationship

3.5.6. Relationship Names

Finally, a few words on one of the areas most often neglected in modeling – the naming of relationships. It is usual in the early stages of modeling to leave relationships unnamed. This is fine while the basic entities are still being debated, but the final model should always be properly annotated with meaningful relationship names – *not* "associated with" or "related to." The exception to this rule is the two relationships that arise from resolving a many-to-many relationship, because the name of the relationship has usually been used to name the new entity. I suggest "involve" and "be involved in" as workable names, as in Figure 3-16.

A good example of the need for meaningful names is the relationship between Country and Currency, as might be required in a database to support foreign currency dealing. Figure 3-23 shows the two entities.

Figure 3-23. Unnamed Relationship

What is the relationship between these two entities? One to many? Many to many? We can't answer these questions until the meaning of the relationship has been clarified. Are we talking about the fact that currency is *issued* by a country? Or *legal tender* in the country? Or *able to be traded* in that country? The result of our investigation may well be that we identify more than one relationship between the same pair of entities.

There is another problem here which may affect cardinalities. What do we mean by "country?" Exactly what is a currency? Again these words can have many meanings. Does San Marino qualify as a country? It issues lire with the same value as Italian lire. Should they be considered the same currency?

Is the European Currency Unit (ECU) a currency? If so, the "be issued by" relationship to Country may be optional. And so on.

The point is that definition of the relationship is closely linked to definitions of the participating entities. We focus on the entity definitions first, but our analysis of the relationships may lead us to revise these definitions.

3.6.   ATTRIBUTES

I've left the easiest concept until last. Attributes in an E-R model correspond to columns in a relational model.

We sometimes show a few attributes, particularly keys, on the diagram for clarification of entity meaning, or to illustrate a particular point. But we don't generally show *all* of the attributes on the diagram, primarily because we would end up swamping our "big picture" with detail. They are normally recorded in simple lists for each entity, either on paper or in an automated CASE tool or data dictionary.

Attributes represent an answer to the question "what data do we want to keep about this entity?" The rules we applied to the definition of columns in Chapter 2 apply equally here: each attribute should represent a primitive fact, and no attribute value should be derivable from others.

In the process of defining the attributes we may find a repeating group, common information requiring a look-up table, or some other deviation from a fully normalized model. If so, we normalize, then modify the E-R model accordingly.

Recall that in a relational model, every table must have a key. In E-R modeling, we can identify entities prior to defining their keys. Ultimately (and better sooner than later), we will need to nominate a key for each entity, either drawn from existing attributes, or invented for the purpose. For example, we may already have a company-defined Employee ID. On the other hand, we would need to define a new one if the existing Employee ID didn't cover, for instance, casual employees.

We discuss attributes in more detail in Chapter 9, and the selection of keys in Chapter 8.

3.7.   CREATIVITY AND E-R MODELING

The element of choice is far more apparent in E-R modeling than in normalization, as we would expect. In E-R modeling we are defining our categories of data; in normalization these have been determined (often by someone else) before we start. The process of categorization is so subjective that even our broadest division of data, into entities and relationships, offers some choice, as we have seen.

It is helpful to think of E-R modeling as "putting a grid on the world": we are trying to come up with a set of non-overlapping categories so that each fact in our world fits into one category only. Different modelers will choose differently shaped grids to achieve the same purpose. Current business terminology is invariably a powerful influence, but we still have room to select, clarify, and depart from this.

Consider just one area of our drug expenditure model – the classification of operations into operation types. As discussed earlier, we could define Operation Type to either include or exclude hybrid operations. If we chose the latter course, we would need to modify the model as in Figure 3-24(a) to allow an operation to be of more than one operation type.

Alternatively, we could define two levels of operation type: Hybrid Operation Type and Basic Operation Type, giving us the model in Figure 3-24(b). Or we could allow operation types to be either basic or hybrid as in the original model, but record the component operations of hybrid operations, resulting in Figure 3-24(c).

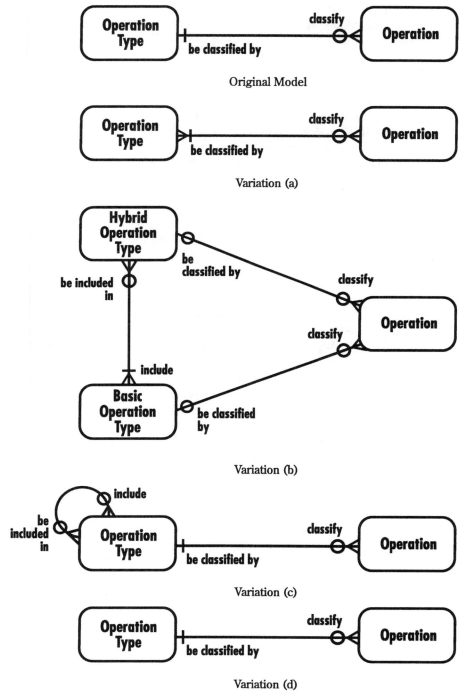

Figure 3-24. Alternative Models for Operations and Operation Types

Another option is to represent a hybrid operation as two separate operations, possibly an inelegant solution, but one we might end up adopting if we hadn't considered hybrid operations in our initial modeling (Figure 3-24(d)). This diagram looks the same as the original, but the definitions of Operation and Operation Type will be different. This gives us five solutions altogether (including the original one), each with different implications. For example, Figure 3-24(b), Figure 3-24(c), and the original model allow us to record standard hybrids, while the other options only allow their definition on an operation-by-operation basis. How many of these possibilities did you consider as you worked with the model?

Creativity in modeling is a progressively acquired skill. Once you make a habit of looking for alternative models, finding them becomes easier. You also begin to recognize common structures. The Operation Type example provides patterns that are equally relevant to dealing with customers and customer types or payments and payment types.

But we can also support the search for alternative models with some formal techniques. In the next chapter we'll look at one of the most important of these.

3.8.   SUMMARY

Data models can be presented diagrammatically by using a box to represent each table and a line for each foreign key relationship. Further diagramming conventions allow the name, cardinality, optionality, and transferability of the relationships to be shown.

We can view the boxes as representing entities – things about which the business needs to keep information, and the lines as representing business relationships between entities. This provides a language and diagramming formalism for developing data models "top down" prior to identifying attributes. The resulting model is called an Entity-Relationship (E-R) model.

Many-to-many real world relationships cannot be directly implemented using foreign keys, but require the introduction of a "resolution" entity.

Entity identification is essentially a process of classifying data, and there is considerable room for choice and creativity in selecting the most useful classification.

4

Subtypes and Supertypes

"A very useful technique ... is to break the parts down into still smaller parts and then recombine these smaller units to form larger novel units."
– Edward de Bono, *The Use of Lateral Thinking*

4.1. INTRODUCTION

In this chapter, we look at a particular, and very important, type of choice in data modeling. In fact, it is so important that we introduce a special convention – subtyping – to allow our diagrams to show several different options at the same time. We will also find subtyping useful for concisely representing rules and constraints, and for managing complexity.

4.2.   DIFFERENT LEVELS OF GENERALIZATION

Suppose we are designing a database to record family trees. We need to hold data about fathers, mothers, their marriages, and children. I've presented this apparently simple problem many times to students and practitioners, and have been surprised by the sheer variety of workable, if sometimes inelegant, ways of modeling it. Figure 4-1 shows two of the possible designs.

Incidentally, the Marriage entity is the resolution of a many-to-many relationship "be married to" between Person and Person in (a) and Man and Woman in (b). The many-to-many relationships arise from persons possibly marrying more than one other person, usually over time rather than concurrently.

Note the optionality of the relationships "mother of" and "father of," particularly in the first model, where they are self-referencing. (Recall my advice in Section 3.5.4 to beware of mandatory self-referencing relationships). While the rule "every person must have a mother" may seem reasonable enough at first glance, it is not true of that subset of persons of interest to us, i.e., family members whom we can identify from historical records. Long before we need to face the real world problem of "who was the first woman?," we simply run out of data: we reach an ancestor whose mother we do not know.

The important issue, however, is our choice of entities. We can't use the nouns ("mother," "father," "child") given in the problem description, because these will overlap – a given person can be both a mother and a child, for example. Implementing Mother and Child entities would therefore compromise our objective of nonredundancy, by holding details of some persons in two places. We need to come up with another set of concepts, and in Figure 4-1 we see two different approaches to the problem: the first uses the person concept, the second the two nonoverlapping concepts of man and woman.

Aside from this difference, the models are essentially the same (although they need not be!) They appear to address our criterion of completeness equally well. Any person who can be represented by the first model can also be handled by the second, and vice versa. Neither model involves any redundant data. Although no attributes are shown, simple attributes such as Name, Date of Birth, and Place of Marriage could be allocated to either model without causing any normalization problems.

The difference lies in the level of generalization we have selected for the entities. Person is a *generalization* of Man and Woman, and, conversely, Man and Woman are *specializations* of Person. This helps us to understand how the two models relate, and raises the possibility that we might be able to propose other levels of generalization, and hence other models – perhaps specializing Man into Married Man and Unmarried Man, or generalizing Marriage to Personal Relationship.

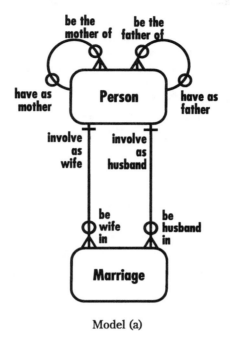

Model (a)

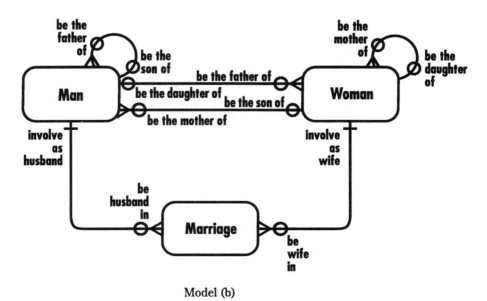

Model (b)

Figure 4-1. Alternative Family Tree Models

It's important to recognize that our choice of level of generalization will have a profound effect not only on the database but on the design of the total system. The most obvious effect of generalization is to reduce the number of entities, and, on the face of it, simplify the model. Sometimes this will translate into a significant reduction in system complexity, through consolidating common program logic. In other cases, the increase in program complexity from combining the logic needed to handle quite different subtypes outweighs the gains. Estimates of system size based on function point counts tend to favor more generalized models, particularly if the estimates are based on the data model alone.

4.3.   RULES VERSUS STABILITY

To select the most appropriate level of generalization, we start by looking at an important difference between the models: the number and type of *rules* (*constraints*) that each supports. The man-woman model has three entities and six relationships, whereas the person model has only two entities and four relationships. The man-woman model seems to be representing more rules about the data.

For example, the man-woman model insists that a marriage consists of one man and one woman, while the person model allows a marriage between two men or two women (one of whom would participate in the "wife of" relationship and the other in the "husband of" relationship, irrespective of gender!). The person model would allow a person to have two parents of the same gender; the man-woman model insists that the mother must be a woman, and the father a man.

The man-woman model is looking pretty good! But remember that we can enforce rules elsewhere in the system as well. If we adopt the person model, we only need to write a few lines of program code to check the gender of marriage partners and parents when data is entered, and return an error message if any rules are violated. We could even set up a table of allowed combinations, which was checked whenever data was entered. The choice, therefore, is not whether to build the rules into the system, but whether the database structure, as specified by the data model, is the best place for them.

Recall that one of the reasons we give so much attention to designing a sound data model is the impact of changing the database structure after it is implemented. On the other hand, changing a few lines of program code, or data in a table, is likely to be much less painful. Accordingly, we included stability as one of the criteria for data model quality. Stability is the counter balance to enforcement of constraints.

Put simply, the more constraints a data model enforces, the more likely one or more of them will change during the life of the system. In our example, we need to trade off the power of representing the rules about marriage in the model against the risk that the rules may change during the life of the system. In some countries, the man-woman model would already be unworkable. Once again there is a need for some forward thinking and judgment on the part of those involved in the modeling process.

Let's just look at how strongly the man-woman model enforces the constraint on marriages. The Marriage entity contains, as foreign keys, a Man ID and a Woman ID. Programs will be written to interpret these as pointers to the Man and Woman tables, respectively. If we want to record a marriage between, say, two men without redesigning the database and programs, the most obvious "work around" is to record one as a man and one as a woman. What if both have previously been married to women? How will we need to modify reports such as "list all men?" Some complicated logic is going to be required, and our criterion of elegance is going to be severely tested.

We can express the flexibility requirement as a guideline:

> *Don't build a rule into the data structure of a system unless you are reasonably confident that the rule will remain in force for the life of the system.*

As a corollary, we can add:

> *Use generalization to remove unwanted rules from the data model.*

It's sometimes difficult enough to determine the *current* rules that apply to business data, let alone those that may change during the life of a system. Sometimes our systems are expected to outlast the strategic planning time-frame of the business: "We're planning five years ahead, but we're expecting the system to last for ten."

The models developed by inexperienced modelers often incorporate too many rules, primarily because familiar concepts and common business terms may themselves not be sufficiently general. Conversely, once the power of generalization is discovered, there is a tendency to overdo it. Very general models can seem virtually immune to criticism, on the basis that they can accommodate almost anything! This is not brilliant modeling, but an abdication of design in favor of the function modeler, or the user, who will now have to pick up all the business rules missed by the data modeler.

4.4.   REPRESENTATION OF SUBTYPES AND SUPERTYPES

It is not surprising that many of the arguments that arise in data modeling are about the appropriate level of generalization, although they are not always recognized as such. We can not easily resolve such disputes by turning to the rule book, nor do we want to throw away interesting options too early in the modeling process. While our final decision might be to implement the "person" model, it would be nice not to lose the (perhaps unstable) rules we have gathered. Even if we don't implement them in our final database design, we can pass them on to the function modeler.

So we defer the decision on generalization, and treat the problem of finding the correct level as an opportunity to explore different options. To do this, we allow two or more models to exist on top of one another on the same diagram. Figure 4-2 shows how this is achieved.

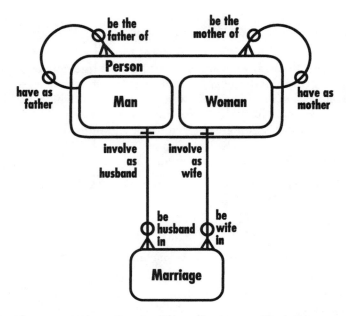

Figure 4-2. Different Levels of Generalization on a Single Diagram

The ability to represent different levels of generalization has cost us a new diagramming convention, the box-in-box. You should be very wary about over-complicating diagrams with too many different symbols, but this one literally adds another dimension (generalization/specialization) to our models.

We call the use of generalization and specialization in a model "subtyping."

Man and Woman are *subtypes* of Person.

Person is a *supertype* of Man and of Woman.

We'll now look at the main rules for using subtypes and supertypes.

4.5.   SUBTYPES AND SUPERTYPES AS ENTITIES

Much of the confusion that surrounds the proper use of subtypes and supertypes can be cleared with a simple rule: subtypes and supertypes are *entities*.

Accordingly:

1. We use the same diagramming convention (the box with rounded corners) to represent all entities, whether or not they are subtypes or supertypes of some other entity(ies).
2. Subtypes and supertypes must be supported by definitions.
3. Subtypes and supertypes can have attributes. Attributes particular to individual subtypes are allocated to those subtypes; common attributes are allocated to the supertype.
4. Every subtype or supertype must have a primary key.

5. Subtypes and supertypes can participate in relationships. Notice in our family tree model how neatly we have been able to capture our "mother of" and "father of" relationships by tying them to entities at the most appropriate level. In fact, this diagram shows most of the sorts of relationships that seem to worry modelers – in particular the relationship between an entity and its own supertype.

6. Subtypes can themselves have subtypes. We need not restrict ourselves to two levels of subtyping. In practice, we tend to represent most concepts at one, two, or three levels of generality, although four or five levels are useful from time to time.

4.6.   DIAGRAMMING CONVENTION

In this book, I use the "box-in-box" convention for representing subtypes. It's not the only option, but is compact, widely used, and supported by several popular CASE tools, including Oracle CASE Designer from Oracle Corporation and Information Engineering Facility from Texas Instruments. Virtually all of the alternative conventions are based around lines between supertypes and subtypes. These are easily confused with relationships, and can give the impression that the model allows redundant data. (In our example, Person, Man, and Woman would appear to overlap, until we recognized that the lines joining them represented subtype-supertype associations, rather than relationships.)

Some CASE tools do not provide a separate convention for subtypes at all, and the usual suggestion is that they be shown as one-to-one relationships. This is a pretty poor option, but better than ignoring subtypes altogether. If forced to use it, I suggest you adopt a relationship name, such as "be," which is reserved exclusively for subtypes ("is a" is more common, but does not fit with the formula for constructing business rules presented in Section 3.5.1). Above all, do not confuse relationships with subtype-supertype associations just because a similar diagramming convention is used. This is a common mistake, and the source of a great deal of confusion in modeling.

4.7.   DEFINITIONS

Every entity in a data model must be supported by a definition, as discussed in Section 3.4.3. To avoid unnecessary repetition, a simple rule applies to the definition of a subtype:

An entity inherits the definition of its supertype.

If the entity Job Position is subtyped into Permanent Position and Temporary Position, the definition of Permanent Position will be "a Job Position that ..." In effect we build a vocabulary from the supertypes, allowing us to define subtypes more concisely.

4.8.   ATTRIBUTES AND PRIMARY KEYS OF SUPERTYPES AND SUBTYPES

Where do we record the attributes of an entity that has been divided into supertypes and subtypes? In our example, it makes sense to document attributes that can apply to all persons against Person, and those that can apply only to men or only to women against the respective entities. So we would hold Date of Birth as an attribute of Person, and Maiden Name as an attribute of Woman. By adopting this discipline, we are actually modeling constraints: "Only a Woman can have a Maiden Name."

Sometimes we can add meaning to the model by representing attributes at two or more levels of generalization. For example, we might have an entity Contract, subtyped into Renewable Contract and Fixed-Term Contract. These subtypes could include attributes Renewal Date and Expiry Date, respectively. We could then generalize these attributes to End Date, which we would hold as an attribute of Contract. You can think of this as subtyping at the attribute level. It's vital that documentation of the model makes it clear that such attributes are associated, rather than distinct.

In order for each level of subtyping to represent a valid implementation option, we need to be able to specify a primary key for every entity, regardless of whether it is a supertype or subtype. In fact, as long as all the entities have a primary key nominated at one level of subtyping, we can generate primary keys for the other levels. For example, if Person had a primary key of Person ID, we could use that attribute as the primary key for both Man and Woman. Similarly, if Man had a primary key of Man ID and Woman a primary key of Woman ID, we could use these, plus an attribute to distinguish men from women, as the primary key of Person. This provides a solution, but not always the most elegant one. The final choice of primary keys is discussed further in Chapter 8.

4.9.   CONVERSION TO A RELATIONAL MODEL

When we started with a set of tables, and used them to draw an E-R diagram, we didn't come up with any subtypes or supertypes. This is because relational data organization doesn't provide direct support for subtypes or supertypes. Therefore, at the end of the modeling process, we will need to produce a subtype-free model as a specification for the logical database design. I call this "leveling the model." It is interesting to note that one of the advantages claimed for object-oriented database management systems over relational database management systems is support for *inheritance*, which enables a model with subtypes to be implemented directly.[1]

---

[1] Atkinson, M., Bancilhon, F., DeWitt, D., Dittrich, K., Maier, D., Zdonik, S., *The Object Oriented Database System Manifesto*, Rapport Technique Altair (August 1989).

4.9.1.   Implementation at a Single Level of Generalization

One way of leveling the model is to select a single level of generalization from each hierarchy of subtypes. In our example, we can do this by discarding Person, in which case we specify only its subtypes, Man and Woman, or by discarding Man and Woman and specifying only their supertype, Person.

Actually, "discard" is far too strong a word. A model with subtypes describes rules and data that the system will need to implement somehow. Some will be retained in the final model. Others will be represented as data *values*, such as "Male" or "Female." We pass on what is left to the function modelers, to be included in their specification.

We certainly won't discard any attributes. We need to *inherit* the attributes of any supertypes, and *roll up* the attributes of any subtypes. So if we implement Man and Woman, each entity will inherit all the attributes of Person. Conversely, if we implement Person, we need to roll up any attributes specific to Man or Woman. These attributes would become *optional* attributes of Person, i.e., null values would be permissible. In some cases, we might choose to combine attributes from different subtypes to form a single attribute. For example, in rolling up Purchase and Sale into Financial Transaction we might combine Price and Sale Value into Amount. This is generalization at the attribute level, and is discussed in more detail in Section 9.4.

If we implement at the supertype level, we also need to add "type" attributes to allow us to preserve any distinctions that the discarded subtypes represented and that cannot be derived from existing attributes of the supertype. In this example we would introduce a Gender attribute to allow us to distinguish those persons who are men from those who are women.

If we are rolling up two or more levels of subtypes, we have some choice as to how many "Type" attributes to introduce. For a generally workable solution, I suggest you simply introduce a single "Type" attribute based on the lowest level of subtyping. Look at Figure 4-3. If you decide to implement at the Customer level, add a single Customer-Type attribute, which will hold values of "Company," "Partnership," "Government Body," "High Net Worth Person," and "Ordinary Consumer." If you want to distinguish which of these are Persons and which are Organizations, you will need to introduce an additional look-up table with five rows as in Figure 4-4.

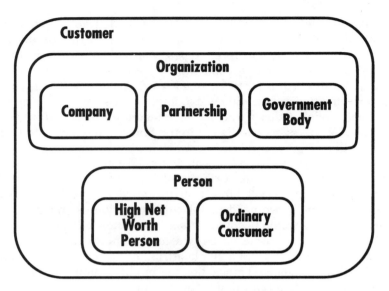

Figure 4-3. Customer Model with Three Levels of Generalization

Customer Type	Person/Organization Indicator
Company	Organization
Partnership	Organization
Government Body	Organization
High Net Worth Person	Person
Ordinary Consumer	Person

Figure 4-4. Look-Up Table of Customer Types

4.9.2.   Implementation at Multiple Levels of Generalization

Returning to our family tree example, a third option is to implement all three entities in the Person hierarchy as tables (Figure 4-5). We link the tables by carrying the foreign key of Person in the Man and Women tables. The appeal of this option is that we don't need to discard any of our concepts. On the other hand, we can easily end up with a proliferation of tables, violating our aim of simplicity. And these tables will usually not correspond on a one-to-one basis with familiar concepts – the Woman table in this model does not hold all the attributes of women, but only those that are not common to all persons. The concept of woman is represented by the Person *and* Woman tables in combination.

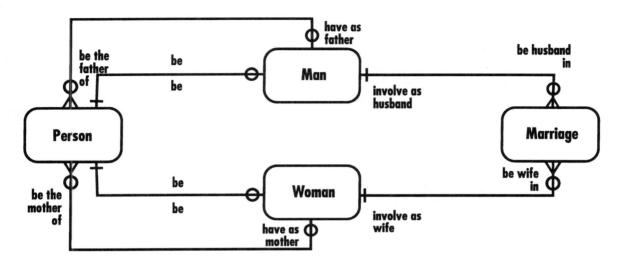

Figure 4-5. Direct Implementation of Person, Man, and Woman Entities

4.9.3. Construction of Views

As mentioned briefly in Chapter 1, we do not always access the tables of a relational database directly. Usually, we access them through *views,* which can consist of simple tables, or of tables combined or selected in various ways. We can use the standard facilities available for constructing views to present data at the subtype or supertype level, regardless of whether we have chosen to implement subtypes, supertype, or both. However, there are some limitations. Not all views allow the data presented to be updated. This is sometimes due to restrictions imposed by the particular database management system, but there are also some logical constraints on what types of views can be updated. These arise where data has been combined from more than one table, and it is not possible to unambiguously interpret a command in terms of which underlying tables are to be updated. It is beyond the scope of this book to discuss view construction and its limitations in any detail. Broadly, the implications for the three implementation options described above are:

1. Implementation at the supertype level. If we implement a Person table, a simple selection operation will allow us to construct Man and Woman views. These views will be logically updateable.

2. Implementation at the subtype level. If we implement separate Man and Woman tables, a Person view can be constructed using the "union" operator. Views constructed using this operator are not updateable.

3. Implementation of both supertype and subtype tables. If we implement Man, Woman, and Person tables, full views of Man and Woman can be constructed using the "join" operator. These will not be updateable. They can be combined using the "union" operator to produce a Person view, which again will not be updateable.

Nonrelational database management systems offer different facilities, and may make one or other of the options more attractive. The ability to construct useful, updateable views becomes another factor in selecting the most appropriate implementation option.

The important thing, however, is to recognize that views are not a substitute for careful modeling of subtypes and supertypes, and consideration of the appropriate level for implementation. Identification of useful data classifications is part of the data modeling process – not something that should be left to some later task of view definition. If subtypes and supertypes are not recognized in the modeling stage, we cannot expect the functional specification to take advantage of them. There is little point in constructing views unless we have planned to use them in our programs.

4.9.4.   What Happens to Relationships?

When we select a level for implementation, we need to do something about relationships involving discarded subtypes and supertypes. The approach is the same as for attributes (after all, one-to-many relationships are implemented using attributes). We inherit relationships from discarded supertypes and roll up relationships from discarded subtypes. In rolling up, we will make some relationships "optional," and may generalize or aggregate two or more to a single relationship, as we did with attributes. Figures 4-6 (a), (b) and (c) show some examples. We discuss the handling of relationships in more detail in Section 6.7.

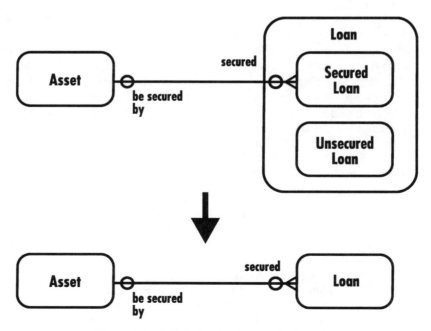

Figure 4-6 (a). Relationship Generalization

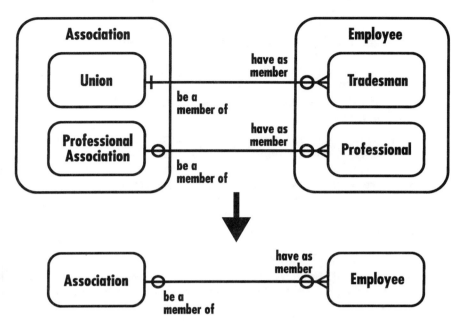

Figure 4-6 (b). Relationship Generalization

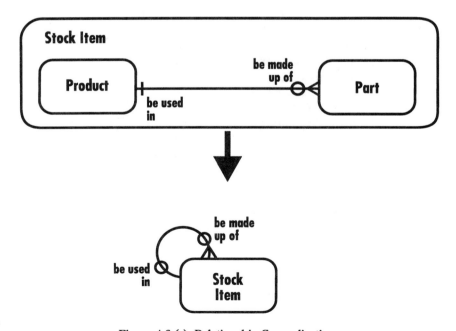

Figure 4-6 (c). Relationship Generalization

4.10.   NONOVERLAPPING AND EXHAUSTIVE

The subtypes in our family tree model obeyed two important rules:

> They were *nonoverlapping* – a given person cannot be both a man and a woman.

> They were *exhaustive* – a given person must be either a man or a woman, nothing else.

In fact, these two rules are necessary in order for each level of generalization to be a valid implementation option in itself. Consider a model in which Trading Partner is subtyped into Buyer and Seller. If a buyer can also be a seller, then the subtypes overlap. If we were to discard the supertype and implement the two subtypes, our database would hold redundant data: those trading partners who were both buyers and sellers would appear in both tables.

Now look again at the family tree model. In the real world, it may be true that all people are either men or women, but sometimes our *data* about the real world is incomplete, and we may not have enough information to classify all persons whom we want to record. Implementing Man and Woman tables only would result in a database that was not able to hold an important category of persons – those whose gender was unknown.

To summarize: in order to allow each level to represent a sound option for implementation, subtypes must be nonoverlapping and exhaustive. This makes the final leveling of the model considerably easier, but restricts our choice in selecting subtypes, and consequently our ability to represent rules applying to specific subtypes. Whether the sacrifice is worth it is a contentious issue.

The most common argument against restrictions on subtyping is that we should not allow the facilities available for implementation (i.e., simple tables) to limit the power of our data modeling language. This is a nice idea in theory, but there are many facts about data that cannot be represented even by overlapping, non-exhaustive subtypes. Genuine observance of this principle would seriously complicate our data modeling language and conventions with constructs that could not be translated into practical database designs using available technology. This has not stopped researchers from developing richer languages, for example, Nijssen and Halpin's fact-based approach,[2] but practitioners have been reluctant to extend their modeling much beyond that needed to specify a database design. Indeed, many practitioners do not even use subtypes.

---

[2] Nijssen, G.M. and Halpin, T.A., *Conceptual Schema and Relational Database Design – A Fact Based Approach*, Prentice Hall (1989).

Another, more convincing, argument is that the value of our models is reduced (particularly in the areas of communication and representation of constraints) if we cannot represent common but overlapping business concepts. This happens most often when modeling data about people and organizations. Typical businesses deal with people and organizations in many roles: supplier, customer, investor, account holder, guarantor, and so forth. Almost invariably the same person or organization can fill more than one of these roles; hence we cannot subtype the entities Person and Organization into these roles without breaking the "no overlaps" rule. But leaving them out of the model may make them difficult to understand ("where is Customer?") and will limit our ability to capture important constraints ("only a customer can have a credit rating"). This is certainly awkward, but in practice is seldom a problem outside the domain of persons and organizations. I once supervised a graduate student who was investigating the issues of modeling roles, and he encountered great difficulty finding further real world examples. Some tactics for dealing with situations that seem to demand overlapping subtypes are discussed in the next section.

It's worth comparing the situation with function modeling. The rules for functional decomposition and data flow diagrams do not normally allow functions at any level to overlap. Most of us don't even stop to consider this, but happily model nonoverlapping functions without thinking about it. Much the same applies in data modeling: we are used to modeling nonoverlapping entities in a level (subtype-free) model, and we tend to carry this over into the modeling of subtypes.

Some of the major CASE tool manufacturers have chosen the restrictive route, in part, no doubt, because translation to relational tables is simpler. If you're using these tools, the choice will be made for you. The academic community has tended to allow the full range of options, in some cases recommending diagramming conventions to distinguish the different possible combinations of overlap and completeness.

On balance, my recommendation is that you discipline yourself to use only non overlapping, exhaustive subtypes, as I do in practice and in the remainder of this book.

4.11.   OVERLAPPING SUBTYPES AND ROLES

Having established a rule that subtypes must not overlap, we are left with the problem of handling certain real world concepts and constraints that seem to require overlapping subtypes to model. As mentioned earlier, the most common examples are the various roles played by persons and organizations. Many of the most important terms used in business (Client, Employee, Stockholder, Manager, etc.) describe such roles, and we are likely to encounter at least some of them in almost every data modeling project.

There are several tactics we can use to model these roles without breaking the "no overlaps" rule.

4.11.1.   Ignoring Real World Overlaps

Sometimes it is possible to model as if certain overlaps did not exist. We have previously distinguished real world rules ("every person must have a mother") from rules about the data that we need to hold or are able to hold about the real world ("we only know some peoples' mothers"). Similarly, while a customer and a supplier may in fact be the same person, the business may be happy to treat them as if they were separate individuals. Indeed, this may be legally required. In such cases, we can legitimately model the roles as nonoverlapping subtypes.

You obviously need to be careful in using this approach. Its inappropriate application is one of the most common faults in older database designs, and it is most unlikely that it will provide a complete solution to the role problem. Its value is in excluding a few key entities from the problem. Often these are entities that are handled quite differently by the business, so useful gains in simplicity and elegance can be achieved. A banking model is unlikely to treat borrowers, guarantors, and depositors as separate entities, but may well separate stockholders and suppliers.

Data modelers are inclined to reject this approach on the grounds of infidelity to the real world, rather than any negative impact on the resulting database or system. This is a simplistic argument, and not likely to convince other stakeholders in the database design.

4.11.2.   Modeling Only the Supertype

One of the most common approaches to modeling the roles of persons and organizations is to use only a single supertype entity to represent all possible roles. If subtyping is done at all, it is on the basis of some other criterion, such as "legal entity type" – partnership, company, individual, etc. Naming the supertype entity presents a challenge, but Party, Involved Party, and Legal Entity are regularly used.

The problem of communicating this high-level concept to business people has been turned into an opportunity to influence thinking and terminology in some organizations. In particular, it can encourage a move from managing "customer" relationships to managing the total relationship with persons and organizations. A database that includes a table of parties rather than merely those who fulfill a narrower definition of "customer" provides the data needed to support this approach.

The major limitation of the approach is the inability to model rules specific to particular roles. The simplest solution is to accept that these will not be represented in the database structure, and to include them in the functional specification.

4.11.3. Modeling the Roles as Participation in Relationships

In the supertype-only model described above, roles can often be described in terms of participation in relationships. For example, we can describe a customer as a party who owns an account, and a supplier as a party who participates in a contract for supply. Chen[3] actually describes a convention to support this (Figure 4-7).

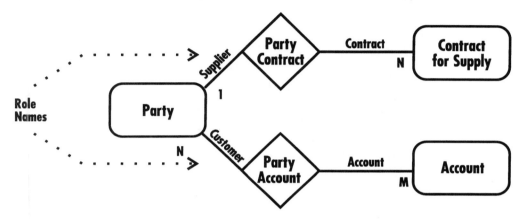

Figure 4-7. Chen Convention for Roles

Rather than further complicate relationship notation for the sake of one section of a model, I suggest you document such rules within the definition of the main entity. For example, "A guarantor is a party who participates in the (guarantee) relationship with Loan."

4.12.   USING ROLE ENTITIES AND ONE-TO-ONE RELATIONSHIPS

An approach that allows us to record the business terminology as well as the specific attributes and relationships applicable to each role is shown in Figure 4-8. The role entities can be supertyped into Party Role to facilitate communication, although we would be most unlikely to implement at this level – we would then lose the distinction among roles that the role entities were designed to provide. However, intermediate supertyping is often useful. For example, we might decide that a single Customer Role would cover all roles involving participation in insurance policies, regardless of the type of policy or participation.

---

[3] Chen, "The Entity-Relationhship Model – Toward a Unified View of Data," *ACM Transactions on Database Systems,* Volume 1, No. 1 (1976), pp 9-36.

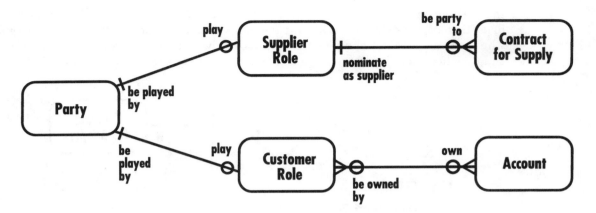

Figure 4-8. Role Entities and One-to-One Relationships

Note the entity names. The word "role" is included to indicate that these entities do not hold the primary data about customers, suppliers, etc. There is a danger here of blurring the distinction between subtypes and one-to-one relationships. You should think of the model as documenting the implementation option shown in Figure 4-5, in which we represented entities at more than one level of generalization, and the lines on the diagram as representing subtype associations rather than one-to-one relationships.

Despite this inelegance in distinguishing relationships from subtypes, the role entity approach is usually the neatest solution to the problem when there are significant differences in the attributes and relationships applicable to different roles.

4.12.1. Multiple Partitions

At least one popular CASE tool (Information Engineering Facility from Texas Instruments) supports a partial solution to overlapping subtypes by allowing multiple breakdowns (*partitions*) into complete, nonoverlapping subtypes (Figure 4-9). In the example, the two different subtypings of Company enable us to model the constraints that, for example:

Only a public company can be listed on a stock exchange.

Only an overseas company can be represented by a local company.

If a given company could be both public and local, for example, it would be difficult to model both of these constraints if we were restricted to a single partition.

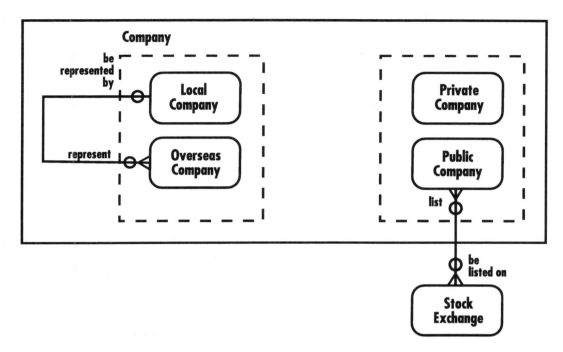

Figure 4-9. Multiple Partitions

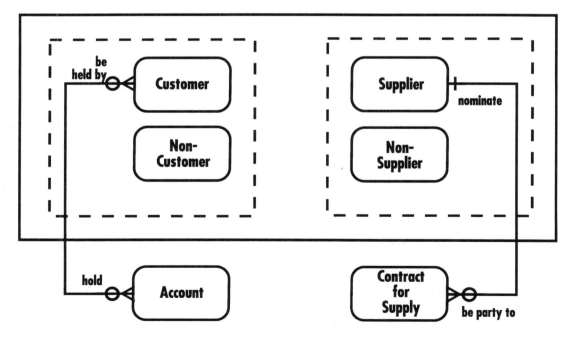

Figure 4-10. Representing Roles Using Multiple Partitions

The multiple partition facility is useful when we have two or three alternative ways of subtyping according to our rules. It is less helpful in handling the roles problem, as we end up with the less-than-elegant partitioning shown in Figure 4-10. Translation to relational database design is also more difficult. We can either implement the highest level supertype (straightforward, but not always the best choice) implement multiple levels (as we did for the Marriage model in Figure 4.5) or select one of the partitions. If we choose the last alternative, we need to ensure that relationships and attributes from the other partitions are reallocated to the chosen subtypes.

4.13. HIERARCHY OF SUBTYPES

I have already used the term "subtype hierarchy." Each subtype can have only one immediate supertype (in a hierarchy, everybody has one immediate boss only – except the person at the top who has none). This follows from the "no overlap" requirement, as two supertypes that contained a common subtype would overlap. Again, adherence to this rule produces a model that is more readily translated into an implementable form with each fact represented in one place only.

Few conventions or tools support multiple supertypes for an entity, possibly because they introduce the sophistication of "multiple inheritance," whereby a subtype inherits attributes and relationships directly from two or more supertypes. Multiple inheritance is a major issue in object-oriented design. The object-oriented designers' problem is almost the opposite of ours: their programming languages provide the facilities, but the questions of how and where they should be used, if at all, are still contentious.

4.14. BENEFITS OF USING SUBTYPES AND SUPERTYPES

We've introduced subtypes and supertypes as a means of comparing many possible options on the one diagram. Each level in each subtype hierarchy represents a particular option for implementing the business concepts embraced by the highest level supertype. But subtypes and supertypes offer benefits not only in presenting options, but in supporting creativity and handling complexity.

4.14.1. Creativity

Our use of subtypes in the creative process has been a bit passive so far. We have assumed that two or more alternative models have already been designed, and used subtypes to compare them on the same diagram. This is a very useful technique when different modelers have been working on the same problem and (as almost always happens) produced different models. Generally, though, we use these conventions to enhance creativity in a far more active way. Rather than design several models and attempt to bring them together, we work with one multilevel model. As we propose entities we ask:

"Can this entity be subtyped into more specific entities that represent distinct business concepts?" and

"Are any of the entities candidates for generalization into a common supertype?"

The first question is usually reasonably straightforward to answer, although it may require some research and perhaps some thinking as to the best breakdown. However, the second frequently prompts us to propose new supertype entities that represent novel but useful classifications of data. Let's assume we already have a model that is complete and nonredundant. Experimenting with different supertypes will preserve these properties, and we can focus on other objectives, such as simplicity and elegance. "Taking the model down another level" by further subtyping existing entities will give us more raw material to work with. We'll look at this technique more closely in Chapter 5. For the moment, take note that the use of subtyping and supertyping is one of the most important aids to creativity in modeling.

4.14.2. Presentation – Level of Detail

Subtypes and supertypes provide a mechanism for presenting data models at different levels of detail. This can make a huge difference to our ability to communicate and verify a complex model. If you are familiar with function modeling techniques, you will know the value of leveled data flow diagrams in communicating first the "big picture," then the detail as required. The concept is applied in many, many disciplines, from the hierarchy of maps in an atlas, to the presentation of a company's accounts. Subtypes and supertypes form the basis of a similar *structured* approach to data modeling.[4]

We can summarize a data model simply by removing subtypes, choosing the level of summarization by how many levels of subtyping we leave. We can even vary this across the model, to show the full detail in an area of interest, while showing only supertypes outside that area. For example, our model might contain (among other things) details of contracts and the employees who authorized them. The human resources manager might be shown a model in which all the subtypes of Employee were included, with a relationship to the simple supertype entity Contract. Conversely, the contract manager might be shown a full subtyping of contracts, with a relationship to the supertype entity Employee (Figure 4-11).

Each sees only what is of interest to them, without losing the context of external data.

---

[4] Described in Simsion, G.C., "A Structured Approach to Data Modelling," *Australian Computer Journal* (August 1989).

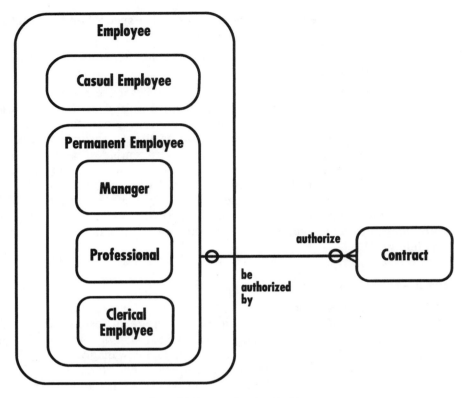

View (a) Human Resources Focus

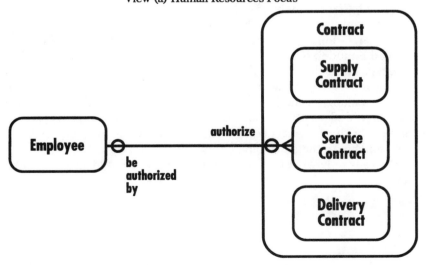

View (b) Contract Management Focus

Figure 4-11. Different Views of a Model

In practice, when presenting a very high-level model, I often selectively delete those entities that do not fit into any of the major generalizations, and that are not critical to conveying the overall "shape" of the model. In doing this, I lose the completeness of coverage that a strict supertype model provides. While the model no longer specifies a viable design, it serves as a starting point for understanding. Anyone who has tried to explain a data model for even a medium-sized application to a non-technical person will appreciate the value of such a high-level starting point.

4.14.3. Communication

Communication is not only a matter of dealing with complexity. Terminology is also frequently a problem. A vehicles manager may be interested in trucks, but the accountant's interest is in assets. Our subtyping convention allows Truck to be represented as a subtype of Asset, so both terms appear on the model, and their relationship is clear.

This is particularly useful to the creative modeler, who may want to introduce or use a less-familiar concept. By showing a new entity in terms of old, familiar entities, the model can be verified without business people becoming stuck on the unfamiliar term. Perhaps our organization trades in bonds and bills, and we are considering representing both by a single entity type Financial Instrument. To the organization, they are separate and have always been treated as such. By showing Financial Instrument subtyped into Bond and Bill, we provide a starting point for understanding. If they prefer, the business specialists need never use the new word, but can continue to talk about "bonds or bills."

In one organization, senior management wanted to develop a consolidated asset management system, but divisional management wanted local systems, arguing that their own requirements were unique. Rather than try to develop a consolidated model straight away (with little cooperation), I developed two separate models, using local terminology, but with one eye on consistency. I then combined the models, preserving all the local entities, but introducing supertypes to show the commonality. With the understanding that their specific needs had been accommodated (and the differences – and there were some – recognized), the managers agreed to proceed with the consolidated system.

When using subtypes and supertypes to help communicate a model, remember that we need have no intention of implementing them as tables: communication is a sound enough reason in itself for including them.

4.14.4. Classifying Common Patterns

We can also use supertypes to help us classify and recognize common patterns. In the later chapters of this book, we look at a number of structures that appear again and again in models. In most cases, we first look at an example of the structure (such as the different ways of modeling Operation Type and Operation in Section 3.7), then apply what we have learned to the general case (Thing and Thing Type, if you like). *Without generalization, we cannot apply what we learn in designing one model to the design of another.* Supertypes and subtypes provide a formal means of doing this.

I once had to review several models covering different stages in the brewing of beer. The models had been produced independently, but some common patterns began to emerge, so that I developed a mental generic model roughly applicable to any stage. I could then concentrate on how the models differed. Reviewing one model, I asked why no samples were taken at this stage (since my high-level model included a Sample entity). Later investigation showed that this was an oversight by the modeler, and I was congratulated on my knowledge of brewing! The other modelers had not noticed the omission, because without a high-level model, they were "too close to the problem" – unable to see the pattern for the detail.

4.14.5. Divide and Conquer

The structured approach to modeling gives us the ability to attack a model from the top down, the middle out, or the bottom up.

The top-down option is particularly important as it allows us to break a large modeling problem into manageable parts, then address the question: "What types of ... do we need to keep information about?" Our early analysis of a finance company might suggest the entities Customer and Loan (nothing terribly creative here!) We could then tackle the questions: "What types of loan are we interested in (and how do they differ)?" and "What type of customers are we interested in (and how do they differ)?" Alternatively, we might model the same business problem in terms of Agreements and Parties to Agreements. Again we can then proceed with more detailed analysis, *within the high-level framework we have established.*

In developing large models, we may allocate different areas to different modelers, with some confidence that the results will all fit together in the end. This is much harder to achieve if we divide the task based on function or company structure rather than data ("Let's model the data for commercial lending first, then retail lending"). Because data is frequently used by more than one function or area, it will be represented in more than one model, usually in different ways. Often the reconciliation takes much longer than the initial modeling!

From a creative modeling perspective, a top-down approach based on specialization allows us to put in place a set of key concepts at the supertype level, and fit the rest of our results into this framework. There is a good analogy with architecture here: the basic shape of the building determines how other needs will be accommodated.

4.15.   WHEN DO WE STOP SUPERTYPING AND SUBTYPING?

I once encountered a data model that contained more than 900 entities, and took up most of a sizeable wall. The modelers had adopted the rule of "keep subtyping until there are no optional attributes," and had in fact run out of wall space before they ran out of optional attributes.

There is no absolute limit to the number of levels of subtypes that we can use to represent a particular concept. We therefore need some guidelines as to when to stop subtyping. The problem of when to stop supertyping is easier. We can't go any higher than a single entity covering all the business data – the "Thing" entity. In practice, we'll often go as high as a model containing only five to ten entities, if only for the purpose of communicating broad concepts.

Very high levels of supertyping are actually implemented sometimes. As we should expect, they are used when flexibility is paramount. Data Dictionaries that allow users to define their own contents (or "meta models" as they are often called) are one example.

No single rule tells us when to stop subtyping, because we use subtypes for several different purposes. We may, for example, show subtypes that we have no intention of implementing as tables, in order to better explain the model. Instead, there are several guidelines. In practice, you will find that they seldom conflict. When in doubt, include the extra level(s).

4.15.1.   Differences in Keys

If an entity can be subtyped into entities that are identified by different keys, show the subtypes.

For example, we might subtype Equipment Item into Vehicle and Machine, because vehicles were identified by registration number and machines by serial number. Conversely, if we have two entities that are identified by the same key we should consider a common supertype.

Be careful of circular thinking here! I am not talking about keys you have allocated yourself, but keys that have some existing standing within or outside the organization.

4.15.2.   Different Attribute Groups

If an entity can be subtyped into entities that have different attributes, consider showing the subtypes.

In practice, optional attributes are so common that strict enforcement of this rule will result in a proliferation of subtypes – we shouldn't need to draw two boxes just to show that a particular attribute can take a null value. However, if *groups of attributes* are always null or nonnull together, show the corresponding subtypes.

4.15.3. Different Relationships

If an entity can be divided into subtypes such that one subtype may participate in a relationship while the other never participates, show the subtype.

Don't confuse this with a simple optional relationship. You need to look for groups that can never participate in the relationship. For example, a machine can never have a driver but a vehicle may have a driver (Figure 4-12).

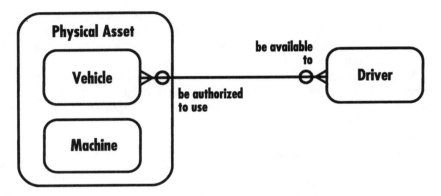

Figure 4-12. Subtyping Based on Relationship Participation

4.15.4. Different Processes

If some instances of an entity participate in important processes, while others don't, consider subtyping. Conversely, entities that participate in the same process are candidates for supertyping.

Be very wary of supertyping entities that are not treated in a similar way by the business, regardless of superficial similarity of attributes, relationships, or names. For example, a wholesaler might propose entities Supplier Order (placed by the wholesaler) and Customer Order (placed by the customer). The attributes of both types of order may be similar, but the business is likely to handle them in quite different ways. If so, it is unlikely that there will be much value in introducing an Order supertype.

4.15.5. Migration from one Subtype to Another

We do not usually subtype to a level where an entity occurrence may migrate from one subtype to another. For example, we would not subtype Account into Account-in-Credit and Overdrawn-Account, because an account could move back and forth from subtype to subtype.

If we were to implement a database based on such subtypes, we would need to transfer data from table to table each time the status changed. This would complicate processing, and make it difficult to keep track of accounts over time.

4.15.6. Communication

As mentioned earlier, we may add both subtypes and supertypes to help explain the model. Sometimes it is useful to show only two or three illustrative subtypes. To avoid breaking the completeness rule, we then need to add a "miscellaneous" entity. For example, we might show Merchant Event (in a credit card model) subtyped into Purchase Authorization, Voucher Deposit, Stationery Delivery, and Miscellaneous Merchant Event.

4.15.7. Capturing Meaning and Rules

In our discussions with users, we are often given information that can conveniently be represented in the data model, even though we would not plan to include it in the final level model. For example, the business specialist might tell us that "only management staff may take out staff loans." We can represent this rule by subtyping Staff Member into Manager and Non-Manager, and tying the relationship to Staff Loan to Manager only (Figure 4-13). We would anticipate that this subtyping would not be retained in the level model (the subtyping is likely to violate the "migration" rule), but we've captured an important rule to be included elsewhere in the system.

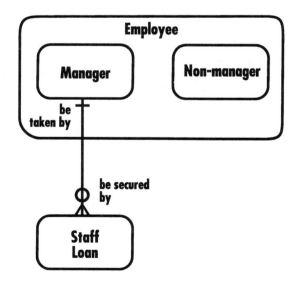

Figure 4-13. Using Subtypes to Represent Rules

4.15.8. Summary

Subtypes and supertypes are tools we use in the data modeling *process*, rather than structures that appear in the final model, at least as long as our database management systems are unable to implement them directly. Therefore, we use them whenever they can help us produce a better final product, rather than according to a rigid set of rules. No subtyping or supertyping is invalid if it achieves this aim, and obeys the very simple rules of completeness and overlap. In particular, there is nothing intrinsically wrong with subtypes or supertypes that do not have any attributes other than those inherited or rolled-up, if they contribute to some other objective, such as communicating the model.

4.16.   THEORETICAL BACKGROUND

In 1977 Smith and Smith published an important paper titled "Database Abstractions: Aggregation and Generalization,"[5] which recognized that the two key techniques in data modeling were aggregation/disaggregation and generalization/specialization.

Aggregation means "assembling component parts," and disaggregation means "breaking down into component parts." In data modeling terms, examples of disaggregation include breaking up Order into "Order Header" and "Ordered Item," or Customer into Name, Address, and Date of Birth. This is quite different from specialization and generalization, which are about classifying, rather than breaking down. I find it helpful to think of disaggregation as "widening" a model, and specialization as "deepening" it.

Most texts and papers on data modeling, focus on disaggregation, particularly through normalization. Decisions about the level of generalization are often hidden or dismissed as "common sense." We should be very suspicious of this; before the rules of normalization were formalized, that process too was regarded as just a matter of common sense.

In this book, and in day-to-day modeling, I try to give similar weight to the generalization/specialization and aggregation/disaggregation dimensions.

4.17.   SUMMARY

Subtypes and supertypes are used to represent different levels of entity generalization. They facilitate a top-down approach to the development and presentation of data models, and concise documentation of business rules about data. They support creativity by allowing alternative data models to be explored and compared.

---

[5] ACM *Transactions on Database Systems*, Vol. 2, No 2, (1977).

Subtypes and supertypes are not directly implemented by relational database management systems. The final data model therefore needs to be subtype-free. This can be achieved by selecting a single level of generalization from each subtype hierarchy, or by implementing both subtype and supertype entities, linked by one-to-one relationships.

By adopting the convention that subtypes are non overlapping and exhaustive, we can ensure that each level of generalization is a valid implementation option. The convention results in the loss of some representational power, but is widely used in practice.

5

Putting It All Together

The crux of creativity resides in the ability to manufacture variations on a theme.
– Douglas R. Hofstadter, *Metamagical Themas.*

5.1.   OVERVIEW OF THE DATA MODELING TASK

So far, we have established a set of diagramming conventions for documenting data models, and some basic rules of good design. We are in a position not unlike that of the budding architect who has learned only the drawing conventions and a few structural principles. The real challenge of taking a set of requirements and producing a sound data model to meet them is still in front of us.

In common with other design processes, development of a data model involves three main stages.

1. Identification of requirements
2. Design of solutions
3. Evaluation of the solutions

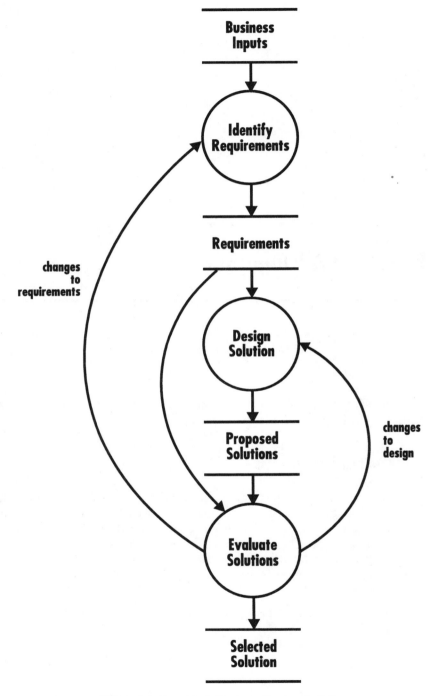

Figure 5-1. Data Modelling as a Design Activity

This is an iterative process (Figure 5-1). Initial requirements are never comprehensive or rigorous enough to constrain us to only one possible design. Draft designs will prompt further questions, which will in turn lead to new requirements being identified. The architecture analogy is again relevant: as users, we do not tell an architect the exact dimensions and orientation of each room. Rather we provide broader requirements such as "we need space for entertaining" and "we don't want to be disturbed by the children's play when listening to music." If the architect returns with a plan which includes a wine cellar, prompted perhaps by his or her assessment of our lifestyle, we may decide to include it in our requirements when evaluating any alternative designs.

In this chapter, we look at the overall organization of the data modeling task, and then at the three stages. The design stage is the most difficult to describe and to learn. Designing a candidate solution from first principles involves conceptualization, abstraction, and possibly creativity, skills which are hard to invoke on a day to day basis. So, like most designers, data modeling practitioners seldom work from first principles, but adapt solutions which have been used successfully in the past. The development and use of a repertoire of standard solutions is so much a part of the practice of data modeling, and so seldom addressed in texts, that I have devoted a large section of the chapter to it.

The chapter concludes with a summary of deliverables.

5.2.   ROLES AND RESPONSIBILITIES

There is some debate about how many and what sort of people should participate in the development of a data model. The extremes are the specialist data modeler working largely alone and gathering information from documentation and one-to-one interviews, and the joint applications development (JAD) style of session which brings business people, data modelers, and other systems staff together in facilitated workshops.

We need to keep in mind two key objectives: we want to produce the best possible model, and we need to have it accepted by all stakeholders. Both objectives suggest the involvement of a fairly large group of people, firstly to maximize the "brainstorming" power, and secondly to build commitment to the result. On the other hand, involvement need not mean *constant* involvement. Good ideas come not only from brainstorming sessions, but from reflection by individuals outside the sessions. Time outside group sessions is also required to ensure that models are properly checked for technical soundness (normalization, nonoverlapping subtypes, conformity to naming standards, etc). And some tasks are best delegated to one or two people, with the group being responsible for checking the result. These tasks include diagram production, detailed entity and attribute definition, and follow-up of business issues outside the expertise of the group.

One of the most important decisions in data modeling is the division of business rules amongst program logic, data content, and database design (covered in more detail in Chapter 11). Fairly obviously, this should not be decided by the data modeler in isolation, but jointly with the function modeler. Similarly, the physical database designer may be able to determine that one option has a strong performance advantage over another. However we organize the modeling task, we must ensure the involvement of these professionals.

My own preference is to nominate a small core team, usually consisting of a specialist data modeler, a senior function modeler (systems analyst) from the project team, and one of the system owners. If performance is likely to be a critical factor, I would consider including a member of the physical database design team. Another, larger team is made up of representatives of other stakeholders, always including further owner/user representatives, someone from the physical database design team, and at least one other specialist modeler. Other participants may include user representatives, subject area specialists (who may not actually be users of the system), the project manager(s), and a data administrator. The larger team meets regularly to discuss the model. In the initial stages, their focus is on generating ideas and exploring major alternatives. Later, the emphasis shifts to review and verification. The smaller team is responsible for managing the process, developing ideas into workable candidate models, ensuring that the models are technically sound, preparing material for review, and incorporating suggestions for change.

Support for the model by all stakeholders, particularly the function modelers and physical database designers, is critical. Many good data models have been the subject of long and acrimonious debate, and sometimes rejection, after being forced upon analysts and physical database designers who have not been involved in their development. This is particularly true of innovative models resulting from a creative modeling approach. Other stakeholders may not have shared in the flashes of insight which have progressively moved the model away from familiar concepts, nor be aware of the problems or limitations of those concepts. Taking all stakeholders along with the process stage by stage is the best way of overcoming this.

Be particularly careful in using methodologies which allow for stage by stage development of the model and logical database design with "hand-offs" from one group to another. Certainly there is value in having clear interim deliverables and responsibilities, but too often the serial involvement of different stakeholders results in a model which favors one group's requirements over another's. If control over change is tight, we find the later participants constrained in suggesting alternatives; if it is loose, the original set of requirements may be overridden. Follow the formal stages and sign-offs, but involve all the players.

5.3.   SEQUENCE

Larger applications are often partitioned and designed in stages.

There are essentially two approaches:

1. Design the functions which create entity instances before those which read, update, and delete them. Achieving this is not quite as simple as it might appear, as some entity instances cannot be created without referring to other entities. In the data model of Figure 5-2, we will not be able to create an instance of Contribution without checking Employee and Fund to ensure that the contribution refers to valid instances of these. We would therefore address these "reference" entities and associated functions first.

    Generally, this approach leads to us commencing at the top of the hierarchy and working down. In Figure 5-2 we would commence detailed modeling around Fund Type and Fund, Employer, or Account, at the top of the hierarchy, moving to Person only when Fund and Fund Type were completed, and Account Entry only when all the other entities were fully specified.

    The attraction of the approach is that it progressively builds on what is already in place and (hopefully) proven. If we follow the same sequence for *building* the system (as we will have to do if we are prototyping), we should avoid the problems of developing transactions which cannot be tested because the data which they read cannot be created.

2. Design core functions first, and put in place the necessary data structures to support them. In Figure 5-2, we might commence with the "Record Contribution" function, which could require virtually all of the entities in the model. This puts pressure on the data modeler to deliver quite a complete design early, but also provides considerable input on the workability of the high level model. If we follow the same sequence for development, we may have to use special programs (e.g., database utilities) to populate the reference tables for testing. While this approach is less elegant, it has the advantage of addressing the more critical issues first, leaving the more straightforward handling of reference data until later. As a result, re-work may be reduced.

There are as many variations on these broad options as there are systems development methodologies. Some rigorously enforce a sequence derived from "Create, Read, Update, Delete" dependencies, whilst others allow more flexibility to sequence development to meet business priorities. As a data modeler, my own preference is for the second approach, which tends to raise critical data modeling issues early in the process, before it is too late or expensive to address them properly. Whichever approach you use, the important thing is to be conscious of the quality and reliability of the data model at each stage, and to ensure that the function modeler understands the probability of change as later requirements are identified.

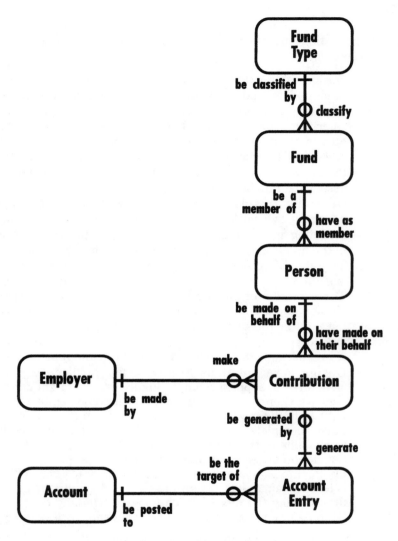

Figure 5-2. Pension Fund Model

5.4.   INPUTS TO THE MODELING TASK

We use a variety of sources to identify requirements. Interviews are essential, but should be used tactically, rather than as the sole input. Other important sources of information include existing systems and files, requests for system enhancements, system proposals and functional specifications, mission and job position statements, policy and procedure manuals, and the full variety of documentation which exists around any business function or existing system.

5.4.1.   Interviews

Interviews are an expensive and sometimes unreliable source of information. Be particularly wary of the "user representative" – the single person charged with answering all the modeler's questions about the business. One sometimes wonders why this all-knowledgable person is so freely available! The most valuable input usually comes from senior managers, who are best placed to paint a picture of future directions. Many a model has failed the stability test (which is a nice way of saying that the system has been rendered prematurely obsolete) because information known to senior management was not communicated to the modeler.

Getting to these people can be an organizational and political problem, but one which must be overcome. Keep time demands limited; if a consultancy is involved, bring in a senior partner for the occasion; explain in concise terms the importance of their contribution to the success of the system. Approach the interview with top management forearmed. Ensure that you are familiar with their area of business, and focus on future directions. What types of regulatory and competitive change does the business face? How does the business plan to respond to these challenges? What changes may be made to product range and organizational structure? What new systems are likely to be required in the future? By all means ask if their information needs are being met, but don't make this the focus of the interview. Most senior managers are far less driven by structured information than the vendors of executive information systems would have us believe. I recall one consultant being summarily thrown out by the chief executive of a major organization when he commenced an interview with the question: "What information do you need to run your business?"

Be very, very careful about drawing data models during interviews at any level. In fact, use anything *but* data models – plain text, data flow diagrams, event diagrams, functional hierarchies, report layouts, object models – unless you are very certain that the data model you draw will be incorporated in the final design. Data models are *not* a comfortable language for most business people, who tend to think more in terms of activities. And by drawing them in a session, you are making it harder (both cognitively and politically) to experiment with other options later.

Expressing the requirements in a form other than a data model provides a degree of *traceability*, and a basis for comparing alternative models. If only a data model is produced, the opportunity to experiment with other options is effectively lost: the initial data model effectively *becomes* the business requirement.

5.4.2.   Existing Systems & Reverse Engineering

One of the richest sources of raw material for the data modeler is existing systems, or, more specifically, existing file and database designs. Unfortunately, they are often disregarded by modelers determined to make a fresh start. Certainly, we should not incorporate earlier designs uncritically; after all, the usual reason for developing a new database is that the existing one no longer meets our requirements. But there are few things more frustrating to a user than a new system which lacks facilities provided by the old system.

Existing database designs provide both a "literal" starting point, as discussed later in this chapter, and a set of entities, relationships and attributes which we can use to ask the question "how does our new model support this?" This question is particularly useful when applied to attributes, and an excellent way of developing a first-cut attribute list for each entity. A sound knowledge of the existing system also provides common ground for interviews with users, who will frequently express their needs in terms of enhancements to the existing system.

The existing system may be manual or computerized. If you are very fortunate, the underlying data model will be properly documented. If not, you should produce at least an E-R diagram, short definitions, and attribute lists by "reverse engineering," a process analogous to an architect drawing the plan of an existing building.

The job of reverse engineering combines the diagram-drawing techniques which we discussed in Chapter 3 with a degree of detective work to determine the meaning of entities, attributes, and relationships. Assistance from someone familiar with the database is invaluable. The person most able to help is more likely to be a maintenance analyst or programmer than a database administrator.

You will need to adapt your approach to the quality of available documentation, but broadly the steps are as follows:

1. Represent existing files, segments, record types, tables, or equivalents as entities. Use subtypes to handle any redefinition (multiple record formats with substantially different meanings) within files.

2. Normalize. Recognize that here you are "improving" the system, and the resulting documentation will not show up any limitations due to lack of normalization. It will, however, provide a better view of data requirements as input to the new design. If your aim is purely to document the capabilities of the existing system, skip this step.

3. Identify relationships supported by "hard links." Nonrelational database management systems usually provide specific facilities ("sets," "pointers," etc) to support relationships. Finding these is usually straightforward; determining the meaning of the relationship and hence assigning a name is sometimes less so.

4. Identify relationships supported by foreign keys. In a relational database, all relationships will be supported in this way, but even where other methods for supporting relationships are available, foreign keys are often used to supplement them. Finding these is often the greatest challenge for the reverse engineer, primarily because data item (column) naming and documentation may be inconsistent. For example, the primary key of Employee may be Employee Number, but the data item Authorized By in another file may in fact be an employee number, and thus a foreign key to Employee. Common formats are sometimes a clue, but cannot be totally relied upon.

5. List the attributes for each entity and define each entity and attribute.

The resulting model should be used in the light of outstanding requests of system enhancement, and of known limitations. The proposal for the new system is usually a good source of such information.

5.4.3. Function Models

If you are using a function-driven approach to systems development, as outlined briefly in Section 1.9, you will have valuable input in the form of the data used by the processes. The data may be documented explicitly (e.g., as data stores) or implicitly within the function description (e.g., "Amend product price on invoice"). Even if you have adopted a data-driven approach, in which data modeling precedes function modeling, you should plan to verify the data model against the function model when it is available, and allow time for enhancement of the data model.

In any case, you should not go too far down the track in data modeling without some sort of function model, even if detailed development is not scheduled until later. I find a one or two level data flow diagram a valuable adjunct to data modeling, and in communicating the impact of different data models on the system as a whole. In particular, the processes in a highly generic system will look quite different from those in a more traditional system, and will require additional data inputs to support "table driven" logic. A data flow diagram shows the differences far better than a data model alone (Figures 5-3 and 5-4).

5.5. APPROACH TO DEVELOPING A DATA MODEL

Despite the availability of CASE tools, the early work in data modeling is usually done with whiteboard and pen. Most experienced data modelers initially draw only entities and partly annotated relationships. Crow's feet are usually shown, but optionality and names are only added where they serve to clarify an obviously difficult or ambiguous concept. The idea is to keep the focus on the big picture, rather than becoming bogged down in detail.

5.5.1. Identifying Entities

We cannot expect our users to have the data model already in their minds, ready to be extracted with a few well-directed questions ("What things do you want to keep data about?; what data do you want to keep about them?; how are they related?") Unfortunately, much that is written and taught about data modeling makes this very naive assumption. In practice, experienced data modelers do not try to solicit a data model directly, but take a holistic approach. They first establish a broad understanding of the client's requirements, then propose designs for data structures to meet them.

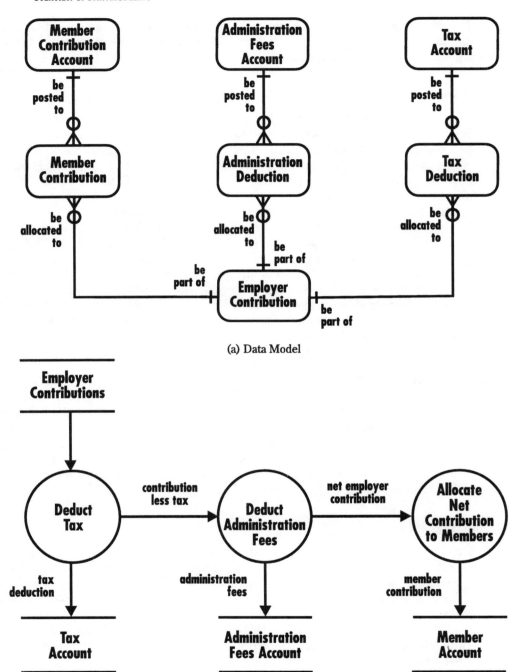

(a) Data Model

(b) Data Flow Diagram

Figure 5-3. Data Flow Diagrams Used to Supplement Data Models - OPTION 1.

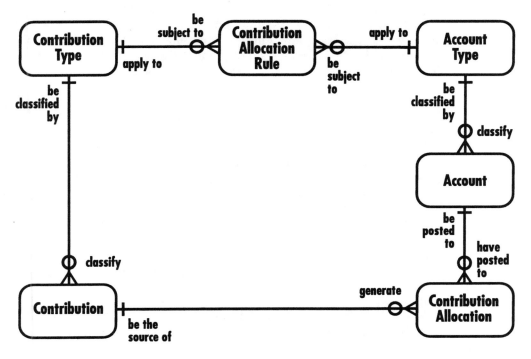

(a) Data Model

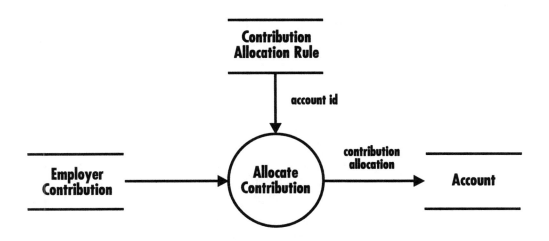

(b) Data Flow Diagram

Figure 5-4. Data Flow Diagrams Used to Supplement Data Models - OPTION 2

This puts the responsibility for coming up with the entities squarely on the data modeler's shoulders. In the last four chapters we've looked at a number of techniques which generate new entities: normalization produces new tables by disaggregating existing tables, and supertyping and subtyping produce new entities through generalizing and specializing existing entities. But we have to start with something!

To design a data model from "first principles," we generalize (more precisely, *classify*) instances of things of interest to the business into entities. We have a lot of choice as to how we do this, even given the constraint that we do not want the same fact to be represented by more than one entity type. Some classification schemes will be much more useful than others, but, not surprisingly, there is no rule for finding the *best* scheme, or even recognizing it if we do find it. Instead, we have a set of guidelines which are essentially the same as those we use for selecting good supertypes. The most important of these is that we group together things which the business handles in a similar manner (and will therefore need to keep similar data about).

This might seem a straightforward task. On the contrary, "similarity" can be a very subjective concept, often obscured by the organization's structure and procedures. For example, an insurance company may have assigned responsibility for handling personal accident and life insurance policies to separate divisions, which have then established quite different procedures and terminology for handling them. It may take a considerable amount of investigation to determine the underlying degree of similarity.

5.5.2. Using Patterns

Experienced data modelers rarely develop their designs from first principles. Like architects, they draw on a "library" of proven structures and structural components. We already have a few of these from the examples in earlier chapters. For example, we know the general way of representing a many-to-many relationship or a simple hierarchy.

It is worth distinguishing two types of patterns, which we use in different ways. A *standard structure* is a re-useable component of a data model. It may be application-independent, such as a hierarchy, or application-related, such as a standard way of modeling a chart of accounts. We use standard structures, modified if necessary, as building blocks for specific areas of a total model.

A *generic model* is a model covering a complete business or major business activity, usually at a high level of generalization. We might, for example, have a generic accounting or asset management model. Generic models provide a framework for more detailed modeling. They can also be useful in establishing the scope of a modeling exercise.

Developing the patterns requires *generalization*. Using them involves *specialization*.

5.6.   DEVELOPING AND USING GENERIC MODELS

5.6.1.   Using Existing Generic Models

In practice, we try to find a generic model which broadly meets the users' requirements, then tailor it to suit the particular application, drawing on standard structures as opportunities arise. For example, we may need to develop a data model to support human resource management. Suppose we have seen successful human resources models before, and generalized these to produce a generic model, shown in part in Figure 5-5.

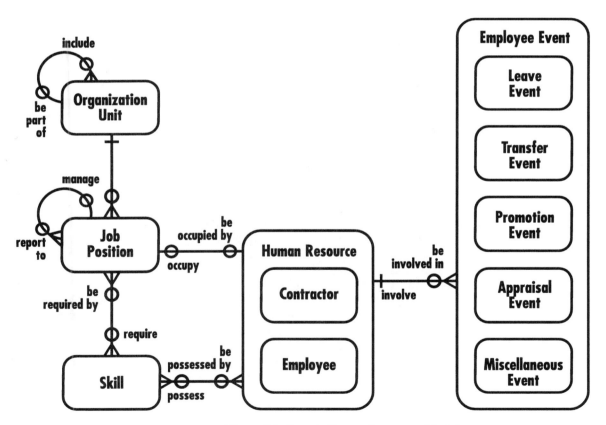

Figure 5-5. Generic Human Resources Model

The generic model suggests some questions, initially to establish scope (and our credibility as modelers knowledgeable about the data issues of human resource management). For example:

"Does your organization have a formally-defined hierarchy of job positions?" "Yes, but they're outside the scope of this project." We can remove this part of the model.

"Do you need to keep information about leave taken by employees?" "Yes, and one of our problems is to keep track of leave taken without approval, such as strikes." We will retain Leave Event, possibly subtyped, and add Leave Approval. Perhaps Leave Application – with a status of approved or not-approved would be better – or should this be an attribute of Leave Event? Some more focussed questions will help with this.

"Could Leave be approved but not taken?" "Certainly." *"Can one application cover multiple periods of leave?"* "Not currently – could our new system support this?"

And so on. Having a generic model in place as a starting point helps immensely, just as architects are helped by being familiar with some generic "family home" patterns. Incidentally, asking an experienced modeler for his or her set of generic models is likely to produce a blank response. Experienced modelers generally carry their generic models in their heads rather than on paper, and are often unaware that they use such models at all.

5.6.2.   Adapting Generic Models from Other Applications

Sometimes we don't have an explicit generic model available, but can draw an analogy with a model from a different field. Suppose we are developing a model to support the management of public housing. The users have provided some general background on the problem in their own terms. They are in the business of providing low cost accommodation, and their objectives include being able to move applicants through the waiting list quickly, providing accommodation appropriate to clients' needs, and ensuring that the rent is collected. We haven't worked in this field before, so we can't draw on a model specific to public housing. In looking for a suitable generic model, we might pick up on the central importance of the rental agreement. We recall an insurance model in which the central entity was Policy – an agreement of a different kind, but nevertheless one involving clients and the organization (Figure 5-6). This model suggests an analogous model for rental agreement management (Figure 5-7).

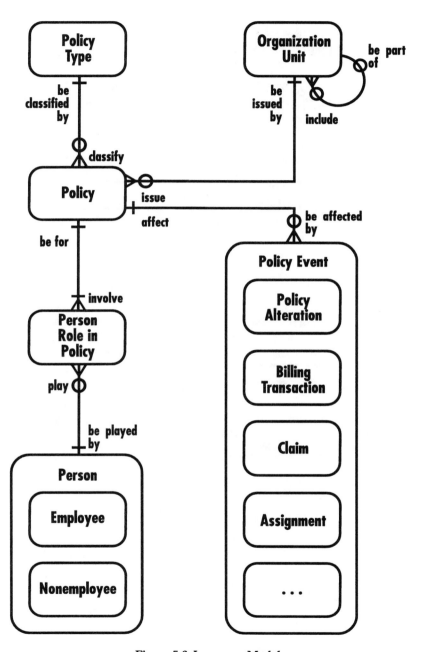

Figure 5-6. Insurance Model

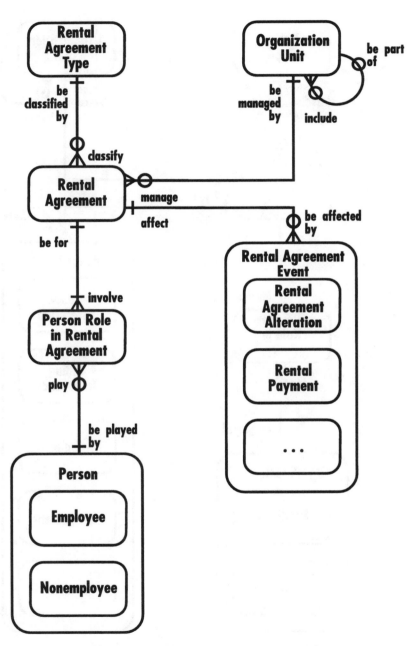

Figure 5-7. Rental Agreement Model based on Insurance Model

We proceed to test and flesh out the model with the business specialist:-

> *"Who are the parties to a rental agreement? Only persons? Or families, or organizations?"* "Only individuals (tenants) can be parties to a rental agreement, but other occupiers of the house are noted on the agreement. We don't need to keep track of family relationships."

> *"Are individual employees involved in rental agreements? In what role?"* "Yes, each agreement has to be authorized by one of our staff."

> *"How do we handle changes to rental agreements? Do we need to keep a history of changes?"* "Yes, it's particularly important that we keep a history of any changes to rent. Sometimes we establish a separate agreement for payment of arrears."

What do we do here? Can we treat a rental arrears agreement as a subtype of Agreement? We can certainly try the idea.

> *"How do rental arrears agreements differ from ordinary rental agreements?"* "They always relate back to a basic rental agreement. Otherwise, administration is much the same – sending the bill and collecting the scheduled repayments."

Let's check the cardinality of the relationship.

> *"Can we have more than one rental arrears agreement for a given basic rental agreement?"* "No, although we may modify the original rental arrears agreement later."

The answer provides some support for treating rental arrears agreements similarly to basic rental agreements. Now we can look for further similarities to test the value of our subtyping and refine the model.

> *"Do we have different types of rental arrears agreements? Are people directly involved in rental arrears agreements or are they always the same as those involved in the basic rental agreement?"*

And so on. Figure 5-8 shows an enhanced model including the rental arrears agreement concept.

5.6.3. Developing a Generic Model

As we gained experience with using this model in a variety of business situations, we would develop a generic "agreement" model, rather than drawing analogies, or going through the two stage process of generalizing from Policy to Agreement, then specializing to Rental Agreement.

With this model in mind, we can approach data modeling problems with the question: "What sort of agreements are we dealing with?" In some cases, the resulting model will be reasonably conventional, as with our housing example, where perhaps the only unusual feature is the handling of arrears repayment agreements. In other cases, approaching the problem from the perspective of agreements might lead to a new way of looking at the problem. The new perspective

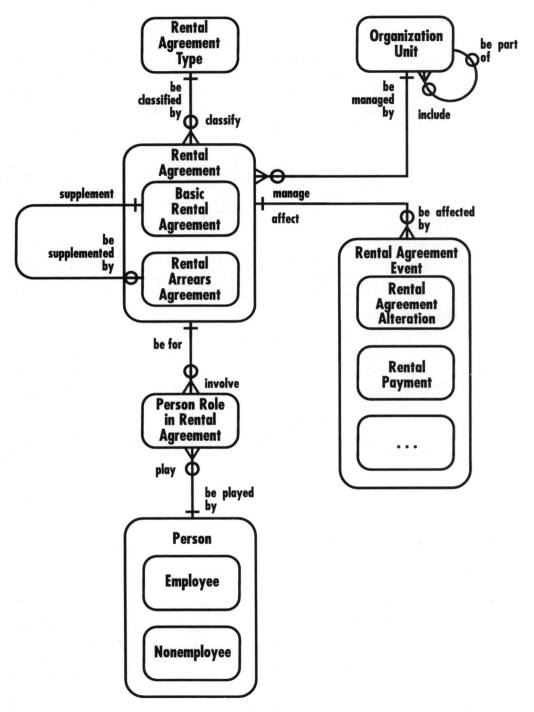

Figure 5-8. Inclusion of Rental Arrears Agreement

may offer an elegant approach; on the other hand, the result of "shoe-horning" a problem to fit the generic model may be inelegant, inflexible, and difficult to understand. For example, the "agreement" perspective could be useful in modeling foreign currency dealing, where deals could be modeled as Agreements, but less useful in a retail sales model. Certainly a sale constitutes an agreement to purchase, but the concepts of alterations, parties to agreements, etc. are less likely to be useful in this context.

Generic models can also be suggested by answers to the "what is our business?" type of question. Business people addressing the question are consciously trying to cut through the detail to the "essence" of the business, and the answers can be helpful in establishing a stable generic model. I recall the first time I attempted to model the complexities of money market dealing. A business specialist offered the explanation that the fundamental objective was to "trade cash flows." This very simple unifying idea suggested a generic model based on the entities Deal and Cash Flow, and ultimately provided the basis for a flexible and innovative system. Often these insights will come not from those who are close to the problem and burdened with details of current procedures, but from more senior managers, staff who have recently learned the business, consultants, and even textbooks.

Even amongst experienced modelers, there is a tendency to try to adopt an "all purpose" generic model. I have seen some particularly inelegant data models resulting from trying to force such a model to fit the problem. In our housing model, for example, there is unlikely to be much value in including Employment Agreement and Supplier Agreement under the Agreement supertype, unless we can establish that the business treats these entities in a common way.

Sometimes an organization will develop a generic model of its primary business activities, with the intention of coordinating data modeling at the project level (data models of this kind are discussed in Chapter 12). Such a model may be an excellent representation of the core business, but inappropriate for support functions such as personnel management or inventory control.

The best approach is to consciously build up your personal library of generic models, and to experiment with more than one alternative when tackling problems in practice. This is not only a good antidote to the "shoe-horning" problem; it also encourages exploration of different approaches, and often provides new insights into the problem. Frequently, the final model will be based primarily on one generic model, but will include ideas resulting from exploring others.

5.6.4. When There Isn't a Generic Model

From time to time, we encounter situations for which none of our generic models is a good fit. Such problems should be viewed as opportunities to develop new generic models. There are essentially two approaches, the first "bottom up" and the second "top down."

5.7.   BOTTOM-UP MODELING

With the bottom-up approach, you initially develop a very "literal" model, based on existing data structures and terminology, then use subtyping and supertyping to move towards other options.

We touched on this technique in Chapter 4, but it is so valuable that it's worth working through an example which is complex enough to illustrate it properly. Figure 5-9 shows a form containing information about products sold by an air conditioning systems retailer.

Product No.:	450TE	Volume	2-4		5%
Type:	Air Conditioning Unit – Indust.	Discount	5-10		10%
Unit Price:	$420		Over 10		12%
Sales Tax:	3% (except Vic/NSW: 2%)	Service	09	Install	$35
Delivery Charge:	$10	Charges	01	Yearly Service	$40
Remote Delivery:	$15		05	Safety Check	$10
Insurance:	5%				

Figure 5-9. Air Conditioning Product Form

Figure 5-10 is a straightforward model produced by normalizing the repeating groups contained in the form (note that we have already departed from strictly literal modeling by generalizing the specific types of tax, delivery, and service charges).

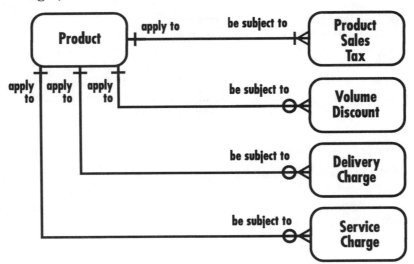

Figure 5-10. Literal Model of Air Conditioning Products

There is a reasonably obvious opportunity to generalize the various charges and discounts into a supertype entity "Additional Charge or Discount." In turn, this decision would suggest separating Insurance Charge from Product, even though it is not a repeating group, in order to represent all price variations consistently (Figure 5-11).

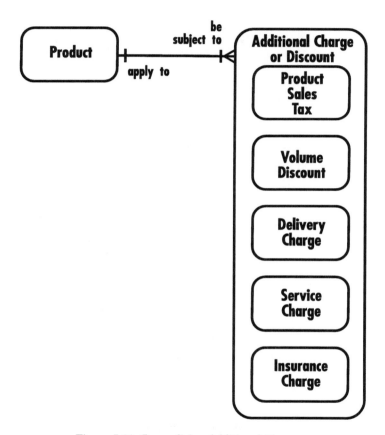

Figure 5-11. Generalizing Additional Charges

We could also consider including Unit Price, and renaming the supertype "Price Component," depending on how similarly the handling of Unit Price was to that of the price variations.

Looking at the subtypes of Additional Charge or Discount, we might consider an intermediate level of subtyping, to distinguish charges and discounts directly related to sale of the original product from stand-alone services (Figure 5-12).

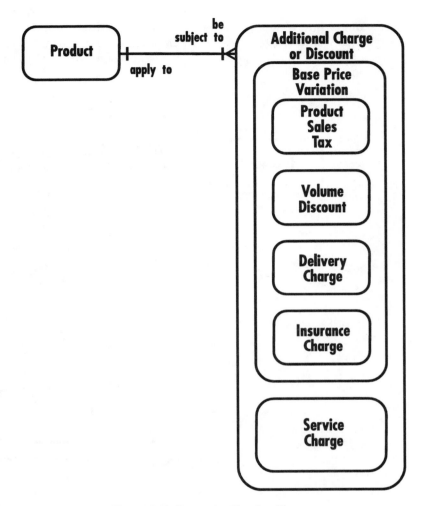

Figure 5-12. Separating Service Charges

This in turn might prompt a more adventurous generalization: why not broaden our definition of Product to embrace services as well? We would then need to change the name of the original Product entity to (say) Physical Product. Figure 5-13 shows the result.

Note that we started with a very straightforward model, based on the original form. This is the beauty of the technique – we don't need to be creative "on the fly," but can concentrate initially on getting a model which is complete and nonredundant, and clarifying how data is currently represented. Later we can break down the initial entities, and reassemble them to explore new ways of organizing the data. The approach is particularly useful if we are starting from existing data files.

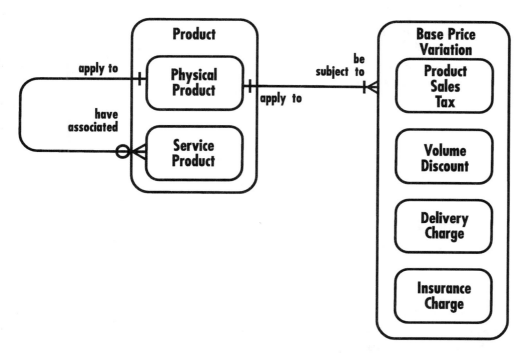

Figure 5-13. Redefining Product to Include Services

Note also that we ended up with a new definition of Product. Ideally, we would never give more than one meaning to the same word. However the desire to keep the model reasonably approachable through use of familiar terminology often means that a term will need to change meaning as we develop it. We could have encountered the same situation with Service, had we decided to regard delivery as a type of service. Just remember to keep the definitions up to date!

5.8.   TOP-DOWN MODELING

The top-down approach to an unfamiliar problem is an extreme version of the generic model approach; we simply use a model which is generic enough to cover at least the main entities in any business or organization. The ultimate extreme is that suggested in many texts: by asking "what 'things' are of interest to the business?" we are effectively starting from the single entity Thing, and looking for subtypes. We can usually be a little more specific than this!

I find the following high-level supertypes useful as a starting point:

Party – Who is involved in this business activity? Persons and organizations in various roles – suppliers, customers, internal organization units, employees, etc.

Contract or Agreement – What types of contracts or agreements do we enter into? Contracts for supply, purchase, employment, etc.

Product – What products or services do we provide? What does this business activity produce?

Resource – What resources do we need to manage? Physical, human, financial, etc.

Event – What events do we need to record? Customer transactions, internal activities, payments, receipts, etc.

Location – What geographic areas or points are we interested in? Regions, states, countries, nodes, delivery points etc.

Account – What type of accounts need to be set up or used to keep track of the financial position?

Be aware that using a first-cut classification like this is still only one step removed from asking "What things are we interested in?" and will produce a very literal and often incomplete picture if not used in conjunction with other techniques and views of the business. In particular, you should use these supertypes only as a starting point, and be prepared to re-group entities as the model develops.

5.9.   WHEN THE PROBLEM IS TOO COMPLEX

Sometimes it is possible to be overwhelmed by the complexity of the business problem. Perhaps we are attempting to model the network managed by a large and diverse telecommunications provider. Unless we are very experienced in the area, we will be quickly bogged down in technical detail, terminology, and traditional divisions of responsibilities. A useful strategy in these circumstances is to develop a first-cut generic model as a basis for classifying the detail.

Paradoxically, a good way to achieve this is by initially *narrowing* our view. We select a specific (and, as best as we can judge) typical area and model it in isolation. We then generalize this to produce a generic model which we use as a basis for investigating other areas. In this way we are able to focus on similarities and differences, and on modifying and fleshing out our base model.

Obviously the choice of initial area is important. We are looking for business activities which are representative of those in other areas – in other words we anticipate that when generalized they will produce a useful generic model. There is a certain amount of circular thinking here, but in practice, selection is not too difficult. Many organizations are structured around products, customer types or geographic locations. Often, each organization unit has developed its own procedures and terminology. Selecting an organizational unit, then generalizing out these factors is usually a good start. Often the *second* area which we examine will provide some good pointers on what can usefully be generalized.

In our telecommunications example, we might start by modeling the part of the network which links customers to local exchanges, or perhaps only that part administered by a particular local branch. Part of an initial model is shown in Figure 5-14.

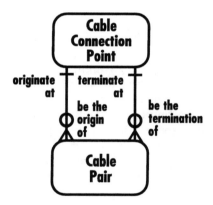

Figure 5-14. Local Exchange Network Model

Testing this model against the requirements of the Trunk Network Division, which has an interest in optical fibres and their termination points, suggests that Cable Pair can usefully be generalized to Physical Bearer, and Cable Connection Point generalized to Connection Point to take account of alternative technologies (Figure 5-15).

But we are now able to ask some pointed questions of the next division: "What sort of bearers do you use? How do they terminate or join?"

This is a very simple generic model, but no simpler than many which I have found invaluable in coming to grips with complex problems. And its use is not confined to telecommunications networks. What about other networks, such as electricity supply, railways, or electrical circuits? Or, more creatively, could the model be applied to a retail distribution network?

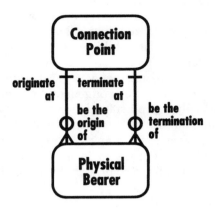

Figure 5-15. Generalized Network Model

5.10.   DEVELOPING ENTITY DEFINITIONS

Definitions, even if initially very rough, should be noted as entities are identified and written up more fully at the end of each session or day. It's surprising how much disagreement can arise overnight!

One useful way of getting to a first-cut definition is to write down a few candidate subtypes or examples, some of which are expected to fit the ultimate definition, and some of which are expected to be outside the definition or "borderline." Then take a vote of participants in the modeling session: "include" or "exclude." This is a very effective way of highlighting areas of agreement and disagreement, and often produces some surprises. For the entity Asset we might suggest Building, Vehicle, Consumable, Employee, Cash on Hand, and Bank Account Balance as potential subtypes. A vote might unanimously support inclusion of Building, Vehicle, Cash and Bank Account Balance and exclusion of Employee, but indicate disagreement on Consumable. Further discussion might indicate that some participants were assuming a strict accounting definition of asset, while others (perhaps unfamiliar with accounting!) had taken a more flexible view. Once any disagreements are resolved, the examples can be included permanently in the definition.

5.11.   HANDLING EXCEPTIONS

One of the frustrations of data modeling is to produce a model which seems to handle every case – except one or two. In general we should welcome these exceptions. Better to discover them now than to have them appear as new requirements after the database is built. Usually we face a choice between making the model more flexible, or adding new structures specifically to cope with the exceptions.

But sometimes the exceptions are historical, and unlikely to recur. In these situations, the best decision sometimes requires intervention at the business level. Perhaps those few unusual insurance policies can be paid out at less cost to the business than that of accommodating them in the information system. Another possibility is to handle them outside the system. This may be attractive from an operational, day-to-day processing perspective, but can play havoc with reporting and executive information as the exceptions have to be "added in." It is the data modeler's duty to suggest these options, rather than assuming that every problem requires a data modeling solution.

The option of deferring the exceptions to a later stage of systems development is usually unrealistic, though often proposed as an easy way of avoiding facing the problem; if the data model cannot accommodate the exceptions from the outset, we will not be able to handle them later without database changes, and probable disruption to existing programs.

5.12. TESTING THE MODEL

Having developed one or more candidate models, it remains to verify that they are workable, and to select the most appropriate option. We can employ several different approaches, and will usually use a combination of them. The hard work is usually in checking completeness and rule enforcement, which requires some fairly rigorous testing. Communication effectiveness, stability, and elegance can be more broadly and quickly assessed. Verification often involves people unfamiliar with the language of modeling. The critical factor then becomes communication, and you should work hard at presenting the model in the most effective way. Talk in terms of tables to database specialists, business concepts to business specialists, and program logic to programmers; bring in sample data, prototypes, and data flow diagrams – use every means at your disposal to get the message through.

5.12.1. Comparison with Function Model

One of the best means of verifying a data model is to ensure that it includes all the necessary data to support the function model. This is particularly effective if the function model has been developed relatively independently, as it makes available a second set of analysis results as a cross check. (This is not an argument in favor of data and function modelers working separately; if they work effectively together, the verification will take place progressively as the two models are developed.)

There will be little value in checking against the function model if an extreme form of data-driven approach has been taken, and functions mechanically derived from the data model.

There are a number of formal techniques for mapping function models against data models to ensure consistency, and to provide a more sophisticated version of the approach to sequencing development than that described earlier in this chapter. They include matrices of functions mapped against data entities, entity life histories, and state transition diagrams. Martin[1] describes an approach which is representative of those supported by popular methodologies and CASE products.

Remember however, that the final database may be required to support functions as yet undefined, and hence not included in the function model. Support for the function model is therefore a necessary but not sufficient criterion for accepting a data model.

5.12.2. Review with Users

Reviews with users and business specialists are an essential part of verifying a data model. But they need to be handled carefully and the results taken in the context of the users' level of understanding, which can be very difficult to assess. Several years ago, I spent some time walking through a relatively simple model with a quite sophisticated user – a recent MBA with exposure to formal systems design techniques, including data modeling. I was fully convinced that he understood the model, and it was only some years later that he confessed that his sign-off had been entirely due to his faith that I personally understood his requirements, rather than to his seeing them reflected in the data model.

This happens all too often, and many unworkable models have been duly signed off by users. I strongly counsel you to interpret the model in business terms to the user, rather than simply presenting the conventions and working through entity by entity. In particular, discuss design decisions and their rationale, instead of presenting your best solution without background.

For example: "This part of the model is based around the 'Right of Abode' concept rather than the various visas, passports, and special authorities. We've done this because we understand that new ways of authorizing immigrants to stay in the country may arise during the life of the system. Is this so? Here is how we've defined Right of Abode. Are there any ways of staying in the country which wouldn't fit this definition? We also thought of using a 'travel document' concept instead, but rejected it because an authority doesn't always tie to one document only. Did we understand that correctly?"

If the users don't find something wrong with the model, or at least prompt you to improve it in some way, you should be very suspicious about their level of understanding.

Reviews should be conducted throughout the modeling process rather than only at the end. Both the fully subtyped and the leveled model should be reviewed, as should any compromises required as physical design proceeds.

---

[1] *Information Engineering Trilogy*, Prentice Hall (1990).

5.12.3. Sample Data

If sample data is available, there are few better ways of communicating and verifying a data model than to work through where each item of data would be held. The approach is particularly appropriate when the data model represents a new and unfamiliar way of organizing data: fitting some existing data to the new model will provide a bridge for understanding, and may turn up some problems or oversights.

I recall a statistical analysis system which needed to be able to cope with a range of inputs in different formats. The model was necessarily highly generalized, and largely the work of one specialist modeler. Other participants in its development were at least a little uncomfortable with it. Half an hour walking through the model with some typical inputs was far more effective in communicating and verifying the design than the many hours previously spent on argument at a more abstract level (and it showed up some areas needing more work).

5.12.4. Prototypes

An excellent way of testing a sophisticated model, or part of a model, is to build a simple prototype. Useful results can often be achieved in a few days, and the exercise can be particularly valuable in winning support and input from function modelers – especially if they have the job of building the prototype.

One of the most sophisticated (and successful) models in which I have been involved was to support a product management database, and associated transaction processing. The success of the project owed much to the early production of a simple PC prototype, prior to the major task of developing a system to support fifteen million accounts. A similar design which was not prototyped failed at a competitor organization, arguably because of a lack of belief in its workability.

5.13.   PACKAGING IT UP

Having verified the model, it remains to assemble the deliverables. Their exact format will vary depending on the chosen methodology and/or CASE tool. However, they should include at least the following:

1.   A broad summary of requirements, covering scope, objectives, and future business directions. These should justify the overall approach taken – for example, highly generic, or customer-focused.
2.   Inputs to the model – interview summaries, reverse-engineered models, function models, etc. Normally these are appended to the main documentation, and referred to as necessary in definitions.
3.   A fully annotated entity-relationship diagram, including subtypes, as per Chapters 3 and 4.
4.   Entity definitions, attribute lists, and attribute definitions for every entity in the model.

5. A fully-normalized, subtype-free model suitable for direct implementation as a logical database design, produced by selecting levels of subtyping as discussed in Chapter 4.
6. Design notes covering decisions made in leveling the subtyped model, including choice of level of generalization, and removal of entities to be implemented elsewhere.
7. Cross-reference to the function model, proving that all functions are supported.
8. As necessary, higher level and local versions of the model to facilitate presentation.
9. Entity volumes. The data modeler is usually in the best position to collect this vital input to physical database design.

This is quite a lot of documentation – certainly more than a physical database designer needs to produce a default database design. Some of the additional documentation is aimed at function modelers and program designers, to ensure that they will understand the model and use it as intended. The documentation of source material provides some traceability of design decisions and allows proposals to change or compromise the model to be assessed in terms of the business requirements which they affect.

5.14. MAINTAINING THE MODEL

The data model as initially delivered is seldom the final version. Most data models are updated and tuned as further information comes to light in detailed function modeling, programming, physical database design, and testing. Too frequently, the data modeling team has been disbanded by this time, and alterations are made indiscriminately by non-specialists.

An effective way of managing change as a system is developed is for an "owner" of the data model, preferably one of its developers, to remain involved, and to coordinate any amendments to the model and resulting logical database design. The owner can also work with program designers and programmers to ensure that the design is properly understood and used. This is particularly important for innovative and very generalized models. Many generalized database designs are undermined by programmers writing specific logic which fails to take advantage of the higher level of generalization.

An additional benefit of the data modeler being involved is that he or she becomes more aware of the model's strengths and weaknesses from the systems development perspective, and will be able to bring the experience so gained to future projects.

After the system is implemented, there will be changes needed to support system maintenance and enhancement. The maintenance process should ensure that all of the original modeling deliverables are kept up to date. Complete and reliable documentation provides a base for future changes, facilitates use of the data for other purposes, and is likely to be valuable as a reference point when the system is eventually replaced.

5.15.   SUMMARY

The development of a data model is an iterative process, involving requirements analysis, design, and evaluation of candidate solutions. It is best performed by a small team, with input from and review by a larger group of stakeholders.

Sources of requirements and ideas include system users, business specialists, system inputs and outputs, existing databases, and the function model.

Data modelers tend to adapt generic models and standard structures, rather than work from first principles. Innovative solutions may result from employing generic models from other business areas. New problems can be tackled top-down from very generic supertypes, or bottom-up by modeling representative areas of the problem domain and generalizing.

The final data model should be supported by documentation which justifies design decisions, in particular the implementation of subtype hierarchies. The model may be verified through presentations, walkthroughs, testing against sample data, prototypes, and mapping against the function model.

Part II

ADVANCED DATA MODELING

6

More About Relationships and Foreign Keys

6.1.   INTRODUCTION

Relationships are one of the fundamental building blocks of entity-relationship models.

In Chapter 3, we covered the basics of relationship representation, concentrating on two-entity one-to-many and two-entity many-to-many relationships. We started by translating foreign keys into lines on a diagram, and interpreting these as relationships between entities. Later, we found that relationships could be proposed and verified directly from "business rules." In Chapter 4 we looked briefly at generalizing and specializing relationships in conjunction with entity supertyping and subtyping.

In this chapter we cover some of the issues raised in the earlier chapters in more detail.

We look first at the representation of relationships using foreign keys. Although the translation from a level (no subtypes) entity-relationship model to a relational model is generally a straightforward, mechanical process, there are some situations that require more detailed guidelines or decisions on a case-by-case basis.

We introduce the concept of *transferability*, to supplement the more widely used concepts of cardinality, optionality, and degree (number of entities participating in the relationship). Knowing whether a relationship is transferable or not is vital in making decisions about primary keys (Chapter 8), one-to-one relationships, and time-dependent data (Chapter 10).

We then look at three types of relationships that appear in most data models, but that we have so far not examined in any detail: one-to-one relationships, self-referencing relationships, and relationships involving three or more entities.

We discuss generalization of relationships in greater detail and introduce the "arc" convention for identifying mutually exclusive relationships, which may signal opportunities for generalization.

Finally, we examine some common myths and misunderstandings about relationships.

6.2.   TRANSLATING RELATIONSHIPS INTO FOREIGN KEYS

6.2.1.   The Basic Rule

In Section 3.2, we saw how to translate the links implied by primary and foreign keys in a relational model into lines representing one-to-many relationships on an E-R diagram. This is a useful technique when we have an existing database that has not been properly documented in diagrammatic form. The process of recovering the design in this all-too-frequent situation is called "reverse engineering," and is one of the less glamorous tasks of the data modeler (Section 5.4.2).

Normally, however, we work from the diagram to the tables, and apply the following rule:

A one-to-many relationship is supported by holding the primary key of the table representing the entity at the "one" end of the relationship as a foreign key in the table representing the entity at the "many" end of the relationship (Figure 6-1). Note the use of the asterisk convention to indicate that an attribute is a foreign key.

Unfortunately, we occasionally run into trouble with this simple rule. Usually, the problems are associated with multicolumn keys.

6.2.2.   Overlapping Foreign Keys

Figure 6-2 is a model for an insurance company that operates in several countries. Each agent works in a particular country, and sells only to customers in that country. Note that the E-R diagram *allows* for this situation, but does not *enforce* the rule.

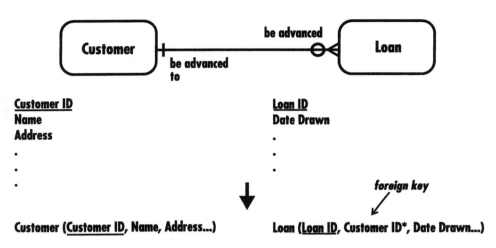

Figure 6-1. Deriving Foreign Keys from Relationships

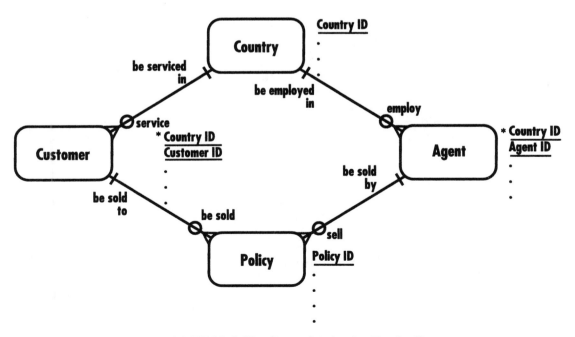

Figure 6-2. E-R Model Leading to Overlapping Foreign Keys

If we apply the rule for representing relationships by foreign keys, we find that the Country ID column appears twice in the Policy table – once to support the link to Agent, and once to support the link to Customer. We can distinguish the columns by naming one "Customer Country ID" and the other "Agent Country ID." But because of our rule that agents sell only to customers in their own country, both columns will always hold the same value. This seems a clear case of data redundancy, easily solved by combining the two columns into one. Yet there are arguments for keeping two separate columns.

The two column approach is more flexible: If we change the rule about selling only to customers in the same country, the two-column model will easily support the new situation. But here we have the familiar trade-off between flexibility and constraints; we can equally argue that the one-column model does a better job of enforcing an important business rule, if we are convinced that the rule will apply for the life of the database.

There is a more subtle flexibility issue: What if one or both of the relationships from Policy became optional? Perhaps it is possible for a policy to be issued without involving an agent. In such cases, we would need to hold a null value for the foreign key to Agent – but this involves "nulling out" the value for Country, part of the foreign key to Customer. We would end up losing our link to Customer. I've been involved in some long arguments about this one, the most common suggestion being that we only need to set the value of Agent ID to null, and can leave Country ID untouched. But this involves an inconsistency in the way we handle foreign keys. It might not be so bad if we only had to tell *programmers* to handle the situation as a special case ("Don't set the whole of the foreign key to null in this instance"), but these days program logic is likely to be generated automatically by a CASE product that is not so flexible about handling nonstandard situations. The database management system itself may recognize foreign keys, and rely on them not overlapping in order to support referential integrity (Section 2.7.6).

My advice is to hold both columns, and recognize that the rule about agents and customers being from the same country will be held elsewhere (for example, in the table definition as enforced by the database management system). Alternatively, use stand-alone keys for Customer and Agent, and the problem will not arise.

6.2.3.   Split Foreign Keys

The next structure has a similar flavor, but is a little more complex. You are likely to encounter it more often than the overlapping foreign key problem – once you know how to recognize it!

Figure 6-3 shows a model for an organization that takes orders from customers and dispatches them to the customers' branches. Note that the primary key of Branch is a combination of Customer No and Branch No, a choice that would be appropriate if we wanted to use the customers' own branch numbers rather than define new ones ourselves. In translating this model into relational tables, we need to carry two foreign keys in the Ordered Item table. The foreign key to Order is Order No, and the foreign key to Branch is Customer No + Branch No.

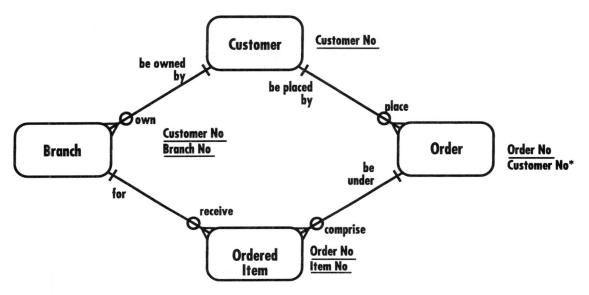

Figure 6-3. E-R Model Leading to Split Foreign Key

Our Ordered Item table, including foreign keys, is shown in Figure 6-4.

ORDERED ITEM (<u>Order No*</u>, <u>Item No</u>, Product, Customer No*, Branch No*)

Figure 6-4. Ordered Item Table

But let's assume the reasonable business rule that the customer who places the order is also the customer who receives the order. Then, since each order is placed and received by one customer, Order No is a determinant of Customer No. The Ordered Item table is therefore not fully normalized, as Order No is a determinant, but is not a candidate key of the table.

We already have a table with Order No as the key and Customer No as a nonkey item. Holding Customer No in the Ordered Item table tells us nothing new, and involves us in the usual problems of unnormalized structures. For example, if the Customer No for an order was entered incorrectly, it would need to be corrected for every Ordered Item on that order. The obvious solution seems to be to remove Customer No from the Ordered Item table. But this causes its own problems.

First, we have broken our rule for generating foreign keys from the diagram. If we were to draw a diagram from the tables, would we include a line from Ordered Item to Branch? Not according to our rules, but we started off by saying there *was* a relationship between the two. And what is Branch No doing in the Ordered Item table if not supporting a relationship to Branch?

But there is more to the problem than a diagramming nicety. Any CASE tool that generates foreign keys mechanically from relationships is going to include Customer No in the Ordered Item table. A program generator that makes the usual assumption that it can find the full primary key of Branch in the Ordered Item table will be in trouble if Customer No is excluded. Again, standard facilities for enforcing referential integrity are most unlikely to support the special situation that arises if Customer No is excluded.

Whether we include or exclude Customer No, we strike serious problems. When you encounter this situation – which you should pick up through a normalization check after generating the foreign keys – I strongly suggest you go back and select different primary keys. In this case, a stand-alone Branch No as the primary key of Branch will do the job. (The original Branch No and Customer No will become nonkey items, forming a second candidate key.) You will lose the constraint that the Customer who places the order receives the order. This will need to be enforced elsewhere in the system.

6.2.4.   Derivable Foreign Keys

Occasionally, you will model a relationship, and later discover that the foreign key values can be derived from attributes of the participating entities. The following two examples, illustrating derivable one-to-many and many-to-many relationships, are typical.

6.2.4.1.   Derivable One-to-Many Relationships

In Figure 6-5, we are modeling information about diseases and their groups (or categories), as might be required in a database for medical research.

During our analysis of attributes we discover that disease groups are identified by a range of numbers (Low No through High No), and that each disease in that group is assigned a number in the range. For example, 301 through 305 might represent "Depressive Illness" and "Post-Natal Depression" might be allocated the number 304. Decimals can be used to avoid running out of numbers. We see exactly this sort of structure in many classification schemes, including the Dewey decimal classification used in libraries. We can use either High No or Low No as the primary key: I've arbitrarily selected Low No.

Figure 6-5. Initial E-R Model of Diseases and Groups

Applying our rule to generate foreign keys, we arrive at the tables in Figure 6-6.

Disease (<u>Disease No</u>, Disease Group Low No*, Disease Name, ...)

Disease Group (<u>Disease Group Low No</u>, Disease Group High No ...)

Figure 6-6. Relational Model of Diseases and Groups

In this situation, the foreign key "Disease Group Low No" in the Disease table is derivable. We can determine which disease group a given disease belongs to by finding the disease group with the range containing its disease no.

To meet our objective of nonredundancy, we will need to remove Disease Group Low No from the Disease table. We will then also need to remove the relationship line from the diagram. Altering the diagram may seem a little unreasonable. Surely the relationship exists, regardless of the technique we use to implement it? Unfortunately, we can't adopt this view, unless we are prepared to lose the ability to move directly and mechanically from diagram to tables. In practical terms, if you describe a relationship to a CASE tool, it will generate the foreign key for you – whether you want it or not!

The alternative is to retain the relationship and the associated foreign key, and accept some redundancy as the price of consistency. As in the examples in the preceding section, carrying a derivable foreign key may be worthwhile if we are generating program logic, which is based on navigation using foreign keys. But carrying redundant data complicates update and introduces the risk of data inconsistency. In this example, we would need to ensure that if a disease moved from one group to another, the foreign key was updated. In fact this can happen only if the disease number changes (in which case we should regard it as a new disease – see Section 8.5) or if we change the boundaries of existing groups. We may well determine that neither of these changes are required by the business, in which case the derivable data option becomes more appealing.

The above situation also occurs commonly with dates and date ranges. For example, a bank statement might include all transactions for a given account between two dates. If the two dates were attributes of the Statement entity, the relationship between Transaction and Statement would be derivable by comparing these dates with the transaction dates. In this case, the boundaries of a future statement might well change, perhaps at the request of the customer, or because we wished to notify them that the account was overdrawn. If choosing the redundant foreign key approach, we would then need to ensure that the foreign key was updated in such cases.

6.2.4.2. *Derivable Many-to-Many Relationships*

A similar problem can occur with many-to-many relationships. Perhaps we have proposed Applicant and Welfare Benefit entities, and a many-to-many relationship between them (Figure 6-7).

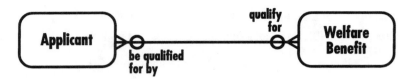

APPLICANT (<u>Applicant ID</u>, Name, Date of Birth...)

WELFARE BENEFIT (<u>Benefit ID</u>, Minimum Eligible Age, Maximum Eligible Age...)

Figure 6-7. Derivable Many-to-Many Relationship

On further analysis, we discover that eligibility for benefits is derivable by comparing attributes of the applicant with qualifying criteria for the benefit (e.g., Date of Birth compared with Eligible Age attributes).

In such cases, we should delete the relationship, on the basis that it is derivable (and hence redundant). We don't want to generate a resolution table that contains nothing but derivable data. If you look at any model closely, you will find numerous such many-to-many "relationships," derivable from inequalities ("greater than," "less than") or more complex formulae and rules. For example:

> Each Employee Absence may occur during one or more Strikes and
> Each Strike may occur during one or more Employee Absences
> (Derivable from comparison of dates).

> Each Aircraft Type may be able to land at one or more Airfields and
> Each Airfield may be able to support landing of one or more Aircraft Types
> (Derivable from airport services and runway facilities and aircraft type specifications).

What do we say to the users in these cases? Having presented them with a diagram, which they have approved, we have now removed a relationship. One option is to surreptitiously amend the model on the basis that "we know better." A more formal and controllable approach that achieves the same end is to introduce another stage of modeling, to distinguish the "user model" from the "implementation model." I'm strongly opposed to either of these approaches, as they lead almost invariably to important decisions being taken without user participation, as well as further complicating modeling for little gain. I've found that the simplest and most effective approach is to explain the problem to the user. Show how the relationship is derivable from other data, and demonstrate, using sample transactions, that including the derivable relationship will add redundancy and complexity to the system.

6.3.   TRANSFERABILITY

An important property of relationships that we have not discussed so far is *transferability*. There are two reasons for not including it in the presentation of the basics:

First, it does not directly affect the design of a relational database (although some facilities provided by the DBMS, such as management of "delete" operations, may need to know whether a relationship is transferable). Changing a relationship from transferable to nontransferable will not alter the set of tables and columns that result from the conversion to a relational model. Transferability is of interest primarily to function modelers and to data modelers themselves.

Second, most CASE tools do not support a symbol to indicate transferability. However, some do provide for it to be recorded in supporting documentation, and some support the closely related concept of weak entities (Section 8.6.3).

6.3.1.   The Concept of Transferability

Figure 6-8 illustrates the distinction between transferable and nontransferable relationships.

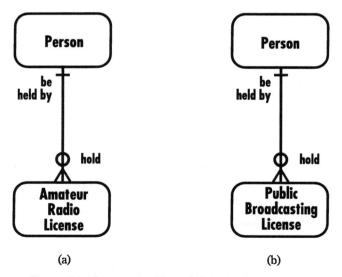

(a)   (b)

Figure 6-8. Nontransferable and Transferable Licenses

The two models appear identical in structure. However, let's impose the reasonable rule that public broadcasting licenses may be transferred from one person to another, while amateur licenses are nontransferable. Every time someone wants an amateur license, a new one is issued.

6.3.2.   Importance of Transferability

The difference in transferability has some important consequences. For example, we could choose to identify amateur licenses with a two-column key of Person ID + License No, where License No was not unique in itself. We would expect the value of the key for a particular license to be stable, because the Person ID associated with a license could not change. But if we used this key for public broadcasting licenses, it would not be stable, because the Person ID *would* change if the license were transferred. The role of transferability in defining primary keys is discussed in some detail in Section 8.6.3.

Another difference is in handling historical data. If we wanted to keep an "audit trail" of changes to the data, we would need to provide for an ownership history of public broadcasting licenses, but not of amateur licenses. Later in this chapter, we will see that transferability is an important criterion when deciding whether entities participating in a one-to-one relationship should be combined.

6.3.3.   Documenting Transferability

So transferability is an important concept in modeling, which we will use elsewhere in this book. I've found it very useful to be able to show on E-R diagrams whether or not a relationship is transferable. Unfortunately, as previously mentioned, most CASE tools do not support a transferability symbol.

Richard Barker[1] suggests a symbol for nontransferability (the less common situation) and, rather than invent another, I recommend you use the adaptation shown in Figure 6-9. As Barker is the architect of the Oracle CASE Designer tool, there must be a reasonable chance that at least this product will eventually support the symbol. I have not suggested a separate symbol to indicate that a relationship is *transferable* (nor does Barker) – this is the default.

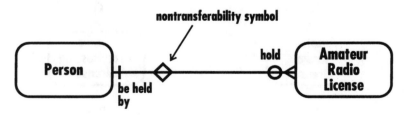

Figure 6-9. Nontransferability Symbol

---

[1] *CASE Method Entity Relationship Modelling,* Addison Wesley (1990).

Note that transferability, unlike optionality and cardinality, is *non directional.* Transferring a public broadcasting license from one person to another can equally be viewed as transferring the persons from one license to another. It is usually more natural and useful to view a transfer in terms of the entity at the many end of the relationship being transferable. In relational model terms, this translates into a change in the value of the foreign key.

Non transferable one-to-many relationships are usually, but not always, mandatory in the "one" direction. An example of an *optional,* non transferable relationship is shown in Figure 6-10. An insurance policy need not be sold by an agent (optionality,) but if it is sold by an agent it cannot be transferred to another (non transferability.)

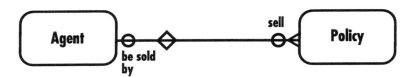

Figure 6-10. Optional Nontransferable Relationship

Many-to-many relationships are usually transferable. The transferability of one-to-one relationships, as discussed later in this chapter, is critical in making decisions about whether to consolidate the participating entities into a single entity, and should therefore always be documented.

A point of definition: we regard establishment or deletion of a relationship instance without adding or deleting entity instances as a transfer. (The terms "connect" and "disconnect" are sometimes used to describe these situations.) For example, if we could connect an agent to an existing policy that did not have an associated agent, or disconnect an agent from the policy, the relationship would be considered transferable. Obviously these types of transfers are only relevant to *optional* relationships.

Transferability can easily be incorporated in the business sentences we generate from relationships:

> Each public broadcasting license must be owned by one person *who may change over time.*

> Each amateur radio license must be owned by one person *who must not change over time.*

> I generally use the nontransferability symbol only where it is relevant to a design decision, and follow the same practice in this book.

6.4.   ONE-TO-ONE RELATIONSHIPS

One-to-one relationships occur far less frequently than one-to-many and many-to-many relationships. Nevertheless, along with supertypes and subtypes, they are one of the most important tools in creative modeling, allowing us to "break up" traditional entities and reassemble them in new ways. They also present some special problems in implementation.

6.4.1.   One-to-One Relationships and Creativity

The value of one-to-one relationships in fostering creativity is best illustrated by an example. Figure 6-11 shows a simple banking model, including provision for regular transfers of funds from one account to another.

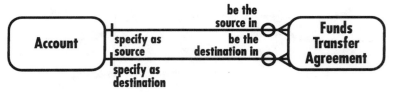

Figure 6-11. Funds Transfer Model

There doesn't appear to be much scope for generalization or specialization here. But there is an opportunity to break Account into two parts – the "accounting part," which is basically the balance, and the "contractual part," which covers interest rates, fees, etc. – giving us the model in Figure 6-12. We now have some more material for generalization. We might choose to regard both Account Operating Contract and Funds Transfer Agreement as *agreements* between the bank and the customer (Figure 6-13) – and we're on our way to exploring a new view of data. Many banks have, in fact, implemented systems based on this new view, usually after a far longer and more painful creative process than described here!

Of course, you don't need to use one-to-one relationships to arrive at a new view. But they often provide a starting point, and can be particularly useful "after the event" in showing how a new model relates to the old. But on what basis do we decide to break an entity into two entities linked by a one-to-one relationship? Or, conversely, on what basis do we combine the entities participating in a one-to-one relationship?

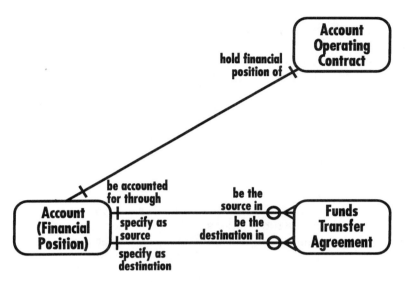

Figure 6-12. Separating Components of Account

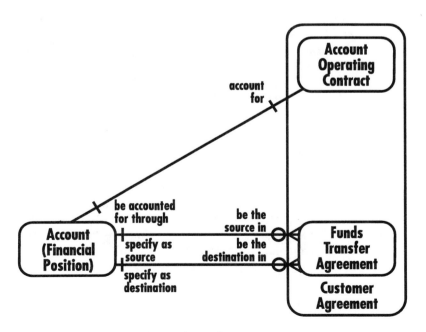

Figure 6-13. Generalizing Customer Agreements

6.4.2. When to Use One-to-One Relationships

There is little to stop us from taking any entity and splitting it into two or more entities, each identified by a candidate key of the original entity – provided, for the sake of nonredundancy, that each nonkey attribute appears in only one of the new entities.

The main consequence of splitting an entity in this way is that inserting and deleting full rows in the resulting database becomes a little more complicated. We now have to update two or more tables instead of one. The sacrifice in simplicity and elegance means that we should have a good reason for introducing one-to-one relationships. Once again, there are few absolute rules, but several useful guidelines.

6.4.2.1. *Distinct Real World Concepts*

Be very wary of combining entities that represent concepts commonly accepted as distinct, just because the relationship between them appears to be one-to-one (e.g., Person and Passport, Country and Currency, Driver and Racing Car), particularly in the earlier stages of modeling. Closer examination may suggest supertypes in which only one of the pair participates, or even that the relationship is actually one-to-many or many-to-many. Combining the entities will hide these possibilities.

In the bank account example of Figures 6-11 through 6-13, we worked in the opposite direction, splitting a single entity into two entities that had value in their own right. The entity Telephone Exchange provides another nice example: closer examination usually shows that it can be broken into entities representing location, node, switching equipment, and the building that houses them.

In many of these cases, transferability (as discussed below) will dictate that the entities remain separate. Relationships that are optional in both directions suggest entities that are independently important. And look also at the cardinality: could we envisage a change to the business that would make the relationship one-to-many or many-to-many?

6.4.2.2. *Support for Creativity*

If splitting an entity or combining entities linked by a one-to-one relationship helps to develop a new and potentially useful model of the business area, then there is no need for further justification. (Of course, the professional modeler will try to look behind his or her intuition to understand the original motivation for proposing the split – e.g., are there really two concepts that the business handles differently? Chances are the same situation will appear again.)

6.4.2.3. *Separating Attribute Groups*

In Section 4.15.2, we discussed the situation in which a *group* of attributes would be either applicable or not applicable to a particular entity instance. For example, in a Client entity, the attributes Date of Incorporation, Company Registration No, and Number of Employees might only be applicable if the client was a company rather than a person. We saw that this situation suggested a subtyping strategy – in this case, subtyping Client into Company Client and Personal Client to represent the "all applicable or none applicable" rule.

But sometimes we can better handle an attribute group by removing it to a separate entity. For example, we might have a number of attributes associated with a Client's credit rating – perhaps Rating, Source, Date Last Updated, Reason for Checking. If these were recorded for only some clients, we could model two subtypes: Client with Credit Rating and Client without Credit Rating. But this seems less satisfactory than the previous example. For a start, a given client could migrate from one entity to another where a credit rating was acquired. An alternative is to model a separate Credit Rating entity, linked to the Client entity through a one-to-one relationship (Figure 6-14). Note the optional and mandatory symbols, showing that a Client *may* have a Credit Rating.

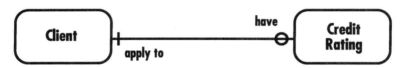

Figure 6-14. Separate Entity for Credit Rating Attributes

Which is the better approach? The subtyping approach is based on specialization, the one-to-one relationship on disaggregation, so they are fundamentally different. But both allow us to represent the constraint that the attribute group applies to only certain instances. A few guidelines will help.

Look at the name of the attribute group. Does it suggest an entity in its own right (e.g., Credit Rating) or a set of data that applies only to certain stable subtypes (e.g., Additional Company Data?) In the first case we would prefer a one-to-one relationship, in the second, subtypes.

In Section 4.15.5, we introduced the guideline that real world instances should not migrate from one subtype to another – or at least that such subtypes would not remain as entities in the final (level) model. A company will not become a person, but a client may acquire a credit rating. So the "never applicable to this instance" situation suggests subtyping; the "not currently applicable to this instance" situation suggests the one-to-one approach.

Remember also that our subtyping rules restrict us to nonoverlapping subtypes. If there is more than one relevant attribute group, we will have trouble with the subtyping approach. But there is no limit to the number of one-to-one relationships that an entity can participate in. This is a good technique to bear in mind when faced with alternative useful breakdowns into subtypes based on attribute groups.

6.4.2.4. Transferable One-to-One Relationships

Transferable one-to-one relationships should always be modeled as such, and never combined into a single entity. Figure 6-15 shows a transferable one-to-one relationship between parts and bins. If we were to combine the two entities, then transferring parts from one bin to another would involve not only updating the Bin No, but all other attributes "belonging to" the bin.

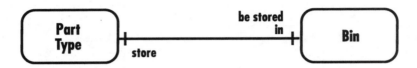

Figure 6-15. Transferable One-to-One Relationship

Another way of looking at transferability is that the relationship will be many-to-many over time.

Figure 6-15 is an excellent counterexample to the popular view that one-to-one relationships that are mandatory in both directions should always be reduced to a single entity. In fact, we may want to model *three* entities. Suppose that Bin Capacity was defined as the number of parts that could be stored in a bin. Should we now hold Bin Capacity as an attribute of Part or of Bin? Updating the attribute when a part moves from one bin to another is untidy. We might want to consider modeling a separate entity with a key of Part No + Bin No as the most elegant solution to the problem.

We discuss this same example from a normalization perspective in Section 7.5.

6.4.2.5. Self Referencing One-to-One Relationships

Self-referencing one-to-one relationships can not be collapsed into a single entity. These are discussed in Section 6.5.

6.4.3.   Implementing One-to-One Relationships

A one-to-one relationship can be supported in a relational database by implementing both entities as tables, and using the same primary key for both. This strategy ensures that the relationship is indeed one-to-one, and is the preferred option.

But we can't use this approach for transferable relationships. If we used Part No to identify both Part and Bin in our earlier example, it would not be stable as a key of Bin (whenever a new part was moved to a bin, the key of that bin would change.)

In this situation, we would identify Bin by Bin No and Part by Part No, and support the relationship with a foreign key: either Bin No in the Part table or Part No in the Bin table. Of course, what we are really supporting here is not a one-to-one relationship any more, but a one-to-many relationship. We have flexibility whether we like it or not! We will need to enforce the one-to-one rule outside the model. Some database management systems will allow you to specify that each value of the foreign key appears only once in the table, providing a simple practical solution. Since we have a choice as to the direction of the one-to-many relationship, we will need to consider other factors, such as performance and flexibility. Will we be more likely to relax the "one part per bin" or the "one bin per part" rule?

Incidentally, I once struck exactly this situation in practice. The database designer had implemented a single table, with a key of Bin No Parts that were then effectively identified by their bin no, causing real problems when parts were moved from one bin to another. In the end, they "solved" the problem by relabeling the bins each time a part was moved!

6.5.   SELF-REFERENCING RELATIONSHIPS

We use the terms "self-referencing," "recursive," or "involuted" to describe a relationship that has the same entity at both ends. Such relationships are an important part of the data modeler's tool kit, and appear in most data models. Self-referencing relationships are used to represent three types of structure: hierarchies, networks, and chains (Figure 6-16).

6.5.1.   Hierarchies (One-to-Many Relationships)

Hierarchies are characterized by each instance of the entity having any number of subordinates but only one superior of the same entity type. Accordingly we use one-to-many relationships to represent them.

Examples of the types of hierarchies we need to model in practice are:

> "Contains" – e.g., System may contain (component) Systems, Location may contain (smaller) Locations.

> "Classifies" – e.g., Equipment Type may classify (more specific) Equipment Types, Employee Type may classify (more specific) Employee Types.

> "Controls" – e.g., Organization Unit may control (subordinate) Organization Units, Network Node may control (subordinate) Network Nodes.

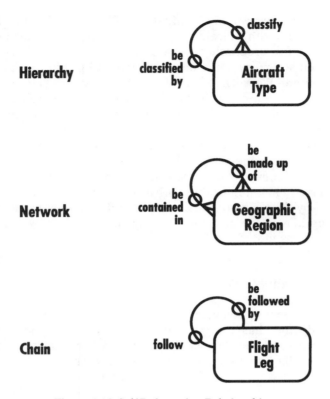

Hierarchy — classify / be classified by — **Aircraft Type**

Network — be made up of / be contained in — **Geographic Region**

Chain — be followed by / follow — **Flight Leg**

Figure 6-16. Self-Referencing Relationships

The more we generalize our entities, the more these structures appear. Figure 6-17 shows an organization structure at two levels of generalization. If we choose to implement the model using Branch, Department, and Section entities, we do not require any self-referencing relationships. But if we choose the higher level of generalization, the relationships between branches, departments, and sections become self-referencing relationships between organization units.

Implementation of one-to-many self-referencing relationships is straightforward, and was covered in Sections 2.7.5 and 3.5.4. (Basically, we hold a foreign key such as "Superior Organization Unit.")

Programming against such structures is less straightforward, if we want to retain the full flexibility of the structure, in particular the unlimited number of levels. Some languages (e.g., COBOL, SQL) do not provide good support for recursion. Screen and report design is also more difficult, if we want to allow for a variable number of levels.

I have found data modelers to be a little cavalier in their use of self-referencing relationships, sometimes to represent quite stable two or three level hierarchies. The important thing here, as always, is to make the options clear by showing the subtypes and their explicit relationships as well as the more general entity. One way of limiting the number of levels is to use a structured primary key, as discussed in Section 8.8.

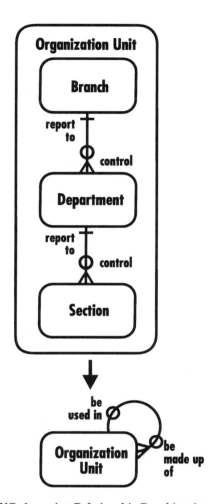

Figure 6-17. Self-Referencing Relationship Resulting from Generalization

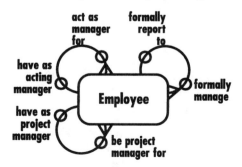

Figure 6-18. Multiple Hierarchies

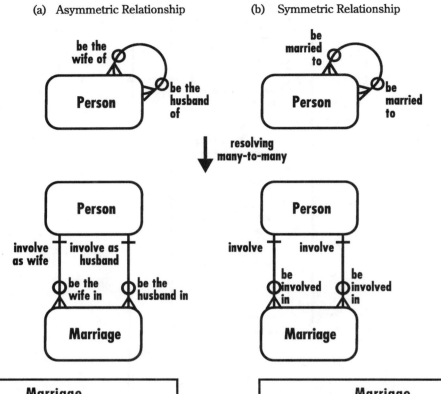

(a) Asymmetric Relationship   (b) Symmetric Relationship

Marriage		
Husband	Wife	Date
Bill	Mary	2 June 1953
Fred	Sue	8 Mar 1982
Bill	Jane	5 Jul 1965

Marriage		
Person 1	Person 2	Date
Bill	Mary	2 Jun 1953
Fred	Sue	8 Mar 1982
Bill	Jane	5 Jul 1965
Mary	Bill	2 Jun 1953
Sue	Fred	8 Mar 1982
Jane	Bill	5 Jul 1965

Figure 6-19. Symmetry Leading to Duplication

6.5.2.   Networks (Many-to-Many Relationships)

Networks differ from hierarchies in that each entity instance may have more than one superior of the same entity type. We therefore model them using many-to-many relationships (which can be resolved as discussed in Section 3.5.4.)

Like hierarchical structures, they are easy to draw, and not too difficult to implement, but can provide plenty of headaches for programmers. Again, modelers frequently fail to recognize underlying structures that could lead to a simpler system. In particular, multiple hierarchies are often generalized to networks without adequate consideration. For example, it might be possible for an employee to have more than one superior, which suggests a network structure. But further investigation might show that individual employees could report to at most three superiors – their manager as defined in the organization hierarchy, a project manager, and a technical mentor. This structure could be more accurately represented by three hierarchies (Figure 6-18) leaving us the option of direct implementation using three foreign keys, or generalization to a many-to-many relationship.

Be careful in defining self-referencing many-to-many relationships to ensure that they are asymmetric: the relationship must have a different name in each direction. Figure 6-19 shows the reason.

If we name the relationship "married to," we will end up recording each marriage twice. Sometimes we need to impose this asymmetry on a symmetric world, as in Figure 6-20. Here, we deliberately make the "associated with" relationship asymmetric, using the primary key as a means of determining which role each entity instance plays. The primary key is a good choice, because it should be stable (as discussed in Section 8.5.) If we selected an unstable attribute as the basis of ordering the relationship, we would be faced with a complicated update problem when the value changed.

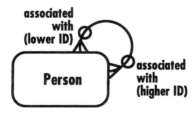

Figure 6-20. Deliberate Creation of Asymmetry

6.5.3.   Chains (One-to-One Relationships)

Chains (sometimes called *linked lists*) occur far less frequently than hierarchies and networks. In a chain, each entity instance is associated with a maximum of one other entity of the same type in either direction. Chains are therefore modeled using one-to-one relationships. Implementation using a foreign key presents us with the same problem as for transferable one-to-one relationships: we end up implementing a one-to-*many* relationship whether we like it or not. Other mechanisms, such as unique indexes on the foreign key attribute (not always possible if the attribute can be null) will be needed to enforce the one-to-one constraint.

A frequently used alternative is to group the participants in each chain and introduce a sequence number to record the order (Figure 6-21).

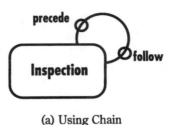

(a) Using Chain

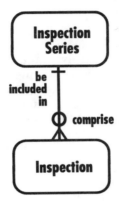

INSPECTION (Inspection Series ID, Inspection ID, Sequence...)

(b) Using Group and Sequence Number

Figure 6-21. Chaining and Grouping

This is another example of deviating from the conventional implementation of relationships; but, unlike some of the other variations we have looked at, it is usually well supported by database management systems. But inserting a new instance in the chain will involve resequencing, an inelegant option.

6.6.   RELATIONSHIPS INVOLVING THREE OR MORE ENTITIES

We saw in Section 3.5.5 that relationships involving three or more entities – sometimes described as "ternary" (3), "quaternary" (4), etc. – are handled by introducing a resolution entity to represent the relationship, in much the same way that many-to-many relationships between two entities can be represented with a resolution entity.

We begin to encounter problems if we start talking about the cardinality and optionality of these higher degree relationships prior to their resolution. The concepts are certainly applicable,[2] but difficult to come to grips with for most data modelers, let alone business specialists asked to verify the model. Nor do we have a diagramming convention to represent the unresolved relationships. My advice is to resolve the relationships, then work with the familiar two-entity relationships that result.

Whenever you encounter what appears to be a higher degree relationship, you should check that it is not in fact made up of individual many-to-many relationships among the participating entities. The two situations are not equivalent, and choosing the wrong representation may lead to normalization problems. This is discussed in some detail in Section 7.4.

Figure 6-22 shows a number of legitimate structures, with different cardinality and optionality.

6.7. GENERALIZATION OF RELATIONSHIPS

In Section 4.9.4, I referred briefly to generalizing relationships as well as entities and attributes. Choosing the right level of generalization for relationships is important, and involves the same trade-off between enforcement of constraints and stability in the face of change.

However, our options for generalizing or specializing relationships are far more limited, because we are only interested in relationships between the same pair of entities. Much of the time we have only one to play with! For that reason, we don't have a separate convention for "subtyping" relationships.

But as we generalize entities, we find that the number of relationships between them increases, as a result of "rolling up" from the subtypes (Figure 6-23). Much of the time, we generalize relationships of the same name almost automatically, and this very seldom causes any problems. Most of us would not bother about the intermediate stage of Figure 6-23(b) but would move directly to Figure 6-23(c). I recommend you review the level of relationship generalization at the time of leveling the model for translation into relational form.

As with entities, our decision needs to be based on commonality of use, stability, and enforcement of constraints. Are the individual relationships used in a similar way? Can we anticipate further relationships? Are the rules that are enforced by the relationships stable?

Let's look briefly at the two main types of relationship generalization.

---

[2] See, for example, Ferg, S., "Cardinality Concepts in Entity-Relationship Modeling," *Proceedings of the 10th International Conference on the Entity Relationship Approach*, San Mateo (1991).

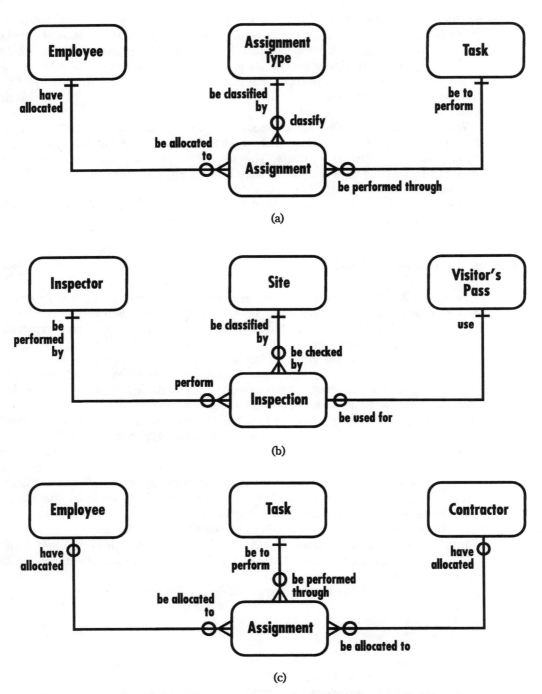

Figure 6-22. Structures Interpretable as Three-Way Relationships

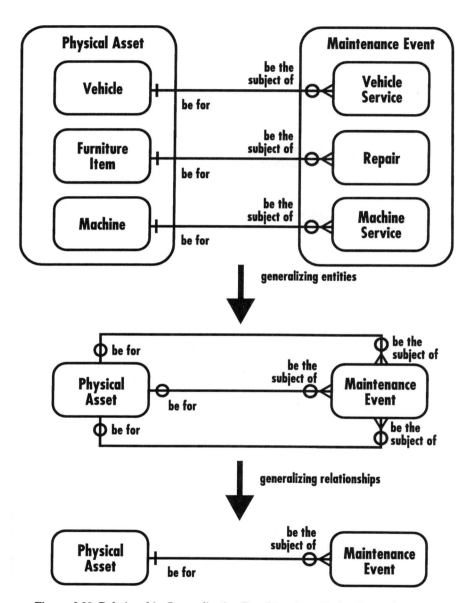

Figure 6-23. Relationship Generalization Resulting from Entity Generalization

6.7.1.   Multiple One-to-Many Relationships to Many-to-Many

Figure 6-24 shows several one-to-many relationships between Customers and Insurance Policies. These can easily be generalized to a single many-to-many relationship.

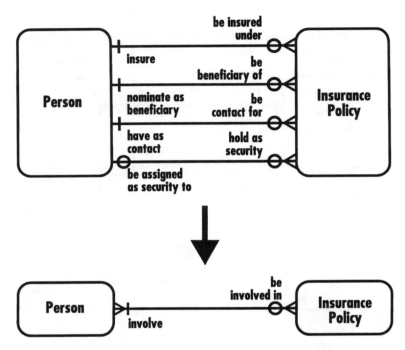

Figure 6-24. Generalization of One-to-Many Relationships

Bear in mind the option of generalizing only some of the one-to-many relationships, and leaving the remainder in place. This may be appropriate if one or two relationships are fundamental to the business, while the others are "extras." For example, we might choose to generalize the "beneficiary," "contact," and "security" relationships, but leave the "insure" relationship as it stands. This apparently untidy solution may in fact be more elegant from a programming point of view if many programs must navigate only the most fundamental relationship.

6.7.2.   Multiple One-to-Many Relationships to Single One-to-Many

Generalization of multiple one-to-many relationships to form a single many-to-many relationship is appropriate if the individual one-to-many relationships are *mutually exclusive,* a more common situation than you might suspect. We can indicate this with an *exclusivity arc* (Figure 6-25).

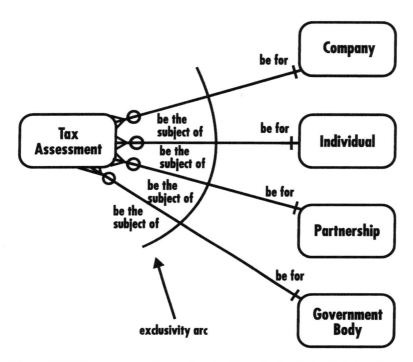

Figure 6-25. Diagramming Convention for Mutually Exclusive Relationships

In Chapter 4, I warned against introducing too many additional conventions and symbols. However, the exclusivity arc is useful enough to justify the extra complexity, and is even supported by some CASE tools.[3] As well as highlighting opportunities to generalize relationships, the exclusivity arc can suggest potential entity supertypes. In Figure 6-25, we are prompted to supertype Company, Individual, Partnership, and Government Body, perhaps to Taxpayer (Figure 6-26).

I find that I use exclusivity arcs quite frequently during the modeling process, but seldom have many in the final model. In most cases, they end up being replaced by supertypes.

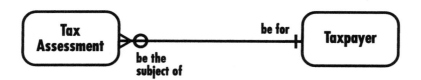

Figure 6-26. Entity Generalization Prompted by Mutually Exclusive Relationships

---

[3] Notably Oracle CASE Designer from Oracle Corporation.

6.8.   MYTHS AND FOLKLORE

As with any relatively new discipline, data modeling has acquired its own folklore of "guidelines" and "rules." Some of these can be traced to genuine attempts at encouraging good and consistent practice. Barker[4] labels a number of situations "impossible," when a more accurate description would be "possible but very uncommon." The sensible data modeler will be alerted by such situations, but will not reject a model *solely* on the basis that it violates some such edict.

Here are a few pieces of advice, including some of Barker's "impossible" relationships, which should be treated as warnings rather than prohibitions.

6.8.1.   Entities without Relationships

"Every entity must participate in at least one relationship." It is perfectly possible, though not common, to have an entity that is not related to any other entity. A trivial case that arises occasionally is a single entity model. Other counter examples appear in models to support management information systems, which may require data from disparate sources; for example, Economic Forecast and Competitor Profile. Entities representing rules among types may be stand-alone if the types themselves are not represented by entities (see Section 11.3.3).

6.8.2.   Allowed Combinations of Cardinality and Optionality

Figure 6-27 shows examples of relationships with combinations of cardinality and optionality I have seen described as impossible.

The problem with relationships that are mandatory in both directions may be the "chicken and egg" question – which comes first? We can't record a customer without an account and we can't record an account without a customer. In fact, the problem is illusory, as we create both the customer and the account within one transaction. The database meets the stated constraints both at the beginning and the end of the transaction.

Remember also that self-referencing relationships need not only represent simple hierarchies, but may model loops.

6.9.   SUMMARY

The translation from relationships to foreign keys is not always straightforward. Problems may arise with overlapping foreign keys, foreign keys split across two tables, and "relationships" supported by comparison of attribute values. Selection of the best approach may involve trade-offs between consistency and rule enforcement.

---

4 Barker, R., *CASE Method Entity Relationship Modelling*, Addison Wesley (1990).

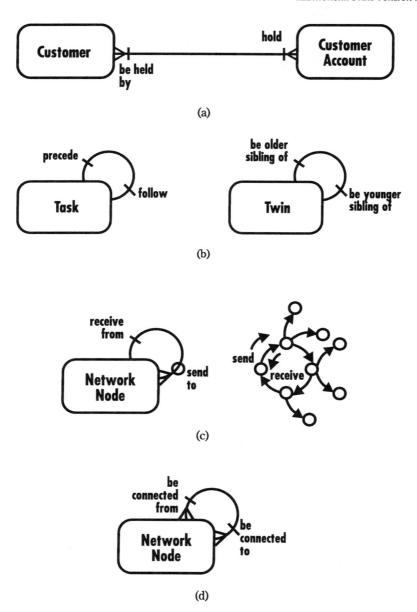

Figure 6-27. Examples of Unusual but Legitimate Relationships

Transferability is an important property of relationships, but most CASE products do not provide a means of representing it. It is important in constructing primary keys: the key of an entity at the "many" end of a transferable relationship should not include the key of the entity at the "one" end.

One-to-one relationships are useful in fostering creativity, by allowing an entity to be split into components, which may then be generalized separately. The two entities participating in a transferable one-to-one relationship should not be consolidated into a single entity.

Business relationships involving three or more entities are modeled using a resolution entity. The resulting two-entity relationships should then be checked individually for cardinality and optionality.

Much folklore surrounds relationships. Most combinations of optionality, cardinality, transferability, and recursion are possible in some context. The modeler should be alert for unusual combinations, but examine each case from first principles.

7

Advanced Normalization

7.1.   INTRODUCTION

In Chapter 2 we looked at normalization, a formal technique for eliminating certain problems from data models. Our focus was on situations in which the same facts were carried in more than one row of a table, causing the usual problems associated with redundancy: wasted space, more complex update logic, and the risk of inconsistency. In data structures that are not fully normalized, it can also be difficult to store certain types of data independently of other types of data. For example, we might be unable to store details of customers unless they currently held accounts with us.

The normalization techniques presented in Chapter 2 enable us to put data into third normal form (3NF). However, it is possible for a set of tables to be in 3NF and still not be *fully* normalized; they can still contain the sort of problems that we expect normalization to remove.

In this chapter, we look at three further stages of normalization: Boyce-Codd normal form (BCNF), fourth normal form (4NF), and fifth normal form (5NF).

We then discuss in more detail a number of issues that were mentioned only briefly in Chapter 2. In particular, we look further at the limitations of normalization in eliminating redundancy and allowing us to store data independently, and at some of the pitfalls of failing to follow the rules of normalization strictly.

7.2.   INTRODUCTION TO THE HIGHER NORMAL FORMS

I have left the discussion of the normal forms beyond 3NF until this chapter, not because the problems they address are unimportant, but because they occur much less frequently. Most tables in 3NF are already in BCNF, 4NF, and 5NF. The other reason for handling the higher normal forms separately is that they are a little more difficult to understand, particularly if we use only the relational notation, as in Chapter 2. Diagrams, which were not introduced until Chapter 3, make understanding much easier.

If you are a practicing data modeler, you are bound to encounter normalization problems beyond 3NF from time to time. Recognizing the patterns will save a lot of effort. And, because each higher normal form includes all the lower normal forms, you only need to be able to prove that a structure is in 5NF to be certain that it is also in 1NF through 4NF.

7.2.1.   Common Misconceptions

Before we start on the specifics of each of the higher normal forms, it is worth clearing up a few common misconceptions.

Practitioners are frequently advised to normalize "only as far as third normal form," on the basis that further normalization offers little benefit or that it incurs serious performance costs. Let's look at these two issues in turn.

The argument that normalization beyond 3NF is not useful is only true in the sense that normalization to 3NF will remove most, and *usually* all, of the problems associated with unnormalized data. In other words, once we have put our data in 3NF, it is very often already in 5NF. But those data structures that are in 3NF but not in 5NF still exhibit serious problems, of very much the same sort we address in the earlier stages of normalization: redundancy; insertion, update, and deletion complexity; and difficulty in storing facts independently.

The performance argument is no more valid for the higher normal forms than it is for 3NF. As with the other normal forms, and good design practices in general, we may ultimately need to make compromises to achieve adequate performance, but our starting point should always be fully normalized structures. Denormalization is usually a last resort because the resulting redundancy, complexity, and incompleteness is expensive to manage.

The most common reason for not looking beyond 3NF is plain ignorance: not knowing how to proceed any further! Indeed, the general lack of understanding of the higher normal forms among practitioners has led to all sorts of data modeling advice and decisions, both good and bad, being paraded under the banner of 4NF and 5NF. Many an unsound data structure has been defended on the basis that it was required to achieve someone's spurious definition of 4NF or 5NF. And I have even seen perfectly sound design practices rejected on the basis that they lead to (incorrectly defined) 4NF or 5NF structures, which in turn are seen to be academic or detrimental to performance. If nothing else, an understanding of the higher normal forms will ensure that you are not swayed by these sorts of arguments.

7.3.   BOYCE-CODD NORMAL FORM

7.3.1.   Example of Structure in 3NF but not BCNF

Look at the model in Figure 7-1, representing data about an organization's branches, and how each branch services its customers.

Figure 7-2 shows the Branch-Customer Relationship table.

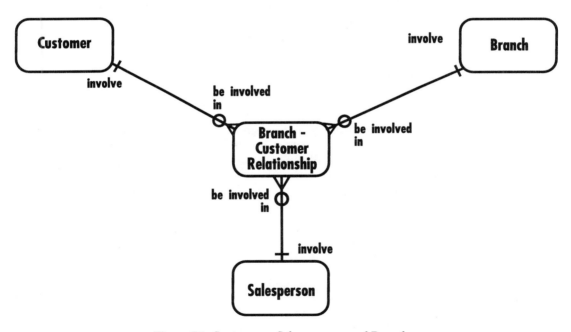

Figure 7-1. Customers, Salespersons, and Branches

BRANCH-CUSTOMER RELATIONSHIP (<u>Customer No</u>, <u>Branch No</u>, Visiting Frequency, Date Relationship Established, Salesperson No)

Figure 7-2. Branch-Customer Relationship Table

We should note three things about this table:

1. The table enforces the rule that each branch will serve a customer through only one salesperson, as there is only one Salesperson No for each combination of Customer No and Branch No. Note that this cannot be deduced from the E-R diagram alone. We need the additional information that Customer No and Branch No form the primary key of the table (hence each combination can occur only once).
2. The table is in 3NF: there are no repeating groups and every determinant of a nonkey item is a candidate key.
3. If we are told that each salesperson works for one branch only, the table still has some normalization problems. The fact that a particular salesperson belongs to a particular branch can appear in more than one row. In fact, it will appear in every row for that salesperson.

The underlying reason for the normalization problems is that we have a dependency between Salesperson No and Branch No: Salesperson No is a *determinant* of Branch No. (A reminder on the terminology – this means that for every Salesperson No, there is only one corresponding Branch No). The unusual feature here is that Branch No is part of the key. In all our examples so far, we have dealt with determinants of *nonkey* items. We now have a real problem. What we would like to do is set up a look-up table with Salesperson No as the key (Figure 7-3).

SALESPERSON (<u>Salesperson No</u>, Branch No)

Figure 7-3. Salesperson Look-up Table

But this doesn't really help. Although we can now record which branch a salesperson belongs to, regardless of whether he or she is serving any customers, we cannot take anything out of the original table. We would like to remove Branch No, but that would mean destroying the key.

The trick is to recognize that the original table has another candidate key. We could just as well have used a combination of Salesperson No and Customer No as the primary key (Figure 7-4).

CUSTOMER-SALESPERSON RELATIONSHIP (<u>Customer No</u>, <u>Salesperson No</u>, Visiting Frequency, Date Relationship Established, Branch No)

Figure 7-4 . Changing the Primary Key

The new key suggests a new name for the table. But now we are not even in 2NF. Salesperson No is a determinant of Branch No, so we need to split these off to another table (Figure 7-5).

CUSTOMER-SALESPERSON RELATIONSHIP (<u>Customer No</u>, <u>Salesperson No</u>, Visiting Frequency, Date Relationship Established)

SALESPERSON (<u>Salesperson No</u>, Branch No)

Figure 7-5. Normalized Tables

We now have our Salesperson look-up table, including the foreign key to Branch, and have eliminated the problem of repeated data. Technically, we have resolved a situation in which the tables were in 3NF but not BCNF.

7.3.2.   Definition of BCNF

For a table to be in BCNF, we require that the following rule be satisfied:

Every determinant must be a candidate key.

In our example, Salesperson No was a determinant of Branch No, but was not a candidate key of Branch-Customer Relationship. Compare this with the definition of 3NF: "Every determinant of a *non key column* must be a candidate key." From the two definitions is should be clear that BCNF is stronger than 3NF in the sense that any table in BCNF will also be in 3NF.

Situations in which tables may be in 3NF but not BCNF can only occur when we have more than one candidate key – to be more precise, *overlapping* candidate keys. We can often spot them more quickly in diagrammatic form. In Figure 7-1, the Branch-Customer-Relationship box indicates a three-way relationship between Branch, Customer, and Salesperson. Approaching the problem from an Entity-Relationship perspective, we would normally draw the diagram as in Figure 7-6, recognizing the direct relationship between Salesperson and Branch. Any proposed relationship between Customer-Salesperson Relationship and Branch would then be seen as derivable from the separate relationships between Customer-Salesperson Relationship and Salesperson, and Salesperson and Branch. Taking this top-down approach, we would not have considered holding Branch No as an attribute of Customer-Salesperson Relationship, and the BCNF problem would not have arisen.

You may find it interesting to experiment with different choices of keys for the various entities in the flawed model of Figure 7-1. In each case, you will find that a normalization rule is violated or a basic business requirement not supported.

7.3.3.   Enforcement of Rules Versus BCNF

There are some important issues about rules here, which can easily be lost in our rather technical focus on dependencies and normalization. In the original table we enforced the rule that a given customer was only served by one salesperson from each branch. Our new model no longer enforces that rule. It is now possible for a customer to be supported by several salespersons from the same branch. We have traded the enforcement of a rule for the advantages of normalization. It is almost certainly a good trade, because it is likely to be easier to enforce the rule within program logic than to live with the problems of redundant data, update complexity, and unwanted data dependencies.

But do not lose sight of the fact that changing data structure, for whatever reason, changes the rules that it enforces. For example, in Figure 7-6, we enforce the rule that each salesperson is employed by a single branch; in the original example, the rule is only implicit in our description.

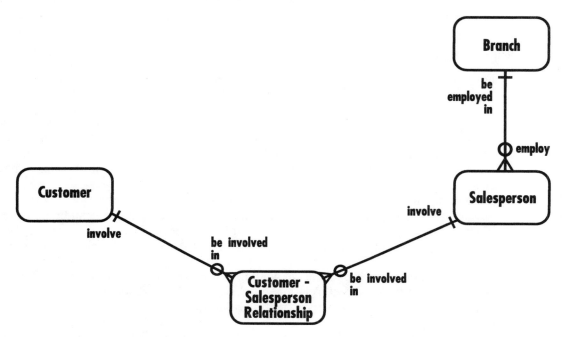

Figure 7-6. Revised E-R Model for Customer-Salesperson-Branch

7.3.4.   A Note on Domain Key Normal Form

Finally, a slightly academic aside. You may occasionally see references to Domain Key Normal Form (DKNF), which requires that "All constraints are a consequence of domains or keys."[1] The idea of a constraint being a consequence of a domain (set of allowed values – see Section 9.5) is a familiar one – if we say that the value of Gender must be drawn from a domain containing only the values "M" and "F," then Gender is constrained to those two values. The idea of a constraint being a consequence of the choice of keys is less obvious, but our example nicely illustrates it: If we choose a combination of Branch No and Customer No as the key of Branch-Customer Relationship in Figure 7-1, we are able to enforce the constraint that each customer is served by only one salesperson from each branch, but if we choose a combination of Customer No and Salesperson No as the key, we do not enforce the constraint.

---

[1] Fagin, R., "A Normal Form for Relational Databases That Is Based on Domains and Keys," *ACM Transactions on Database Systems* (September 1981).

7.4.   FOURTH NORMAL FORM (4NF) AND FIFTH NORMAL FORM (5NF)

Let's start our discussion of fourth and fifth normal forms with some good news. Once data structures are in BCNF, all remaining normalization problems come up only when we are dealing with "key only" tables; that is, tables in which every column is part of the key. Even then, they only apply to tables with three or more columns (and hence a three-or-more-part key). I will discuss 4NF and 5NF together, because the reason these two forms are defined separately has more to do with the timing of their discovery than anything else. We will not bother too much about a formal definition of 4NF, because the 5NF definition is simpler, and covers 4NF as well. (As mentioned earlier, any structure in 5NF is automatically in 4NF and all the lower normal forms).

7.4.1.   Data in BCNF but Not in 4NF

Suppose we want to record data about financial market dealers, the instruments they are authorized to trade, and the locations at which they are allowed to operate. For example, Smith might be authorized to deal in stocks in New York, and in Government Bonds in London.

Let's suppose for the moment that:

> Each instrument can be traded only at a specified set of locations; and
> Each dealer is allowed to trade in a specified set of instruments.

So, if we wanted to know whether Smith could deal in Government Bonds in Sydney, we would ask:

> Can Government Bonds be traded in Sydney?
> Can Smith deal in Government Bonds?

If the answer to both questions was yes, then we would deduce that Smith could indeed deal in Government Bonds in Sydney. Figures 7-7(a) and (b) show data models for this situation. In (b), the many-to-many relationships shown in (a) are resolved using all-key tables.

If we wanted to know all of the authorized combinations of dealer, location, and instrument, we could *derive* a list by combining (joining) the two tables to produce the single table in Figure 7-8.

But what if this derived table was offered up as a solution in itself? It should be reasonably clear that it suffers from normalization-type problems of redundancy and nonindependence of facts. Any authorized combination of instrument and location (e.g., the fact that Government Bonds can be traded in New York) will have to be repeated for each dealer permitted to trade in that instrument. This is the familiar normalization problem of the same fact being held in more than one row. Adding or deleting a combination will then involve updating multiple rows. A similar problem applies to combinations of dealer and instrument. Note that the derived table carries more attribute values than the two original tables. This is hardly surprising, considering that it contains duplicated data, but I have often seen derived tables offered up on the basis that they will save space.

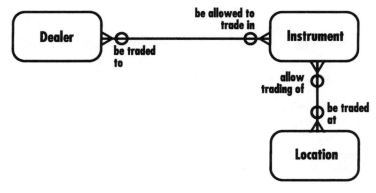

(a) Using Many-to-Many Relationships

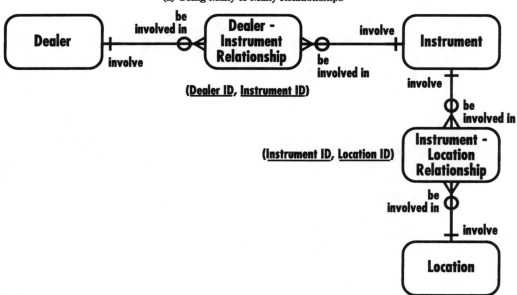

(b) Many-to-Many Relationships Resolved

Dealer ID	Instrument ID
Smith	Ordinary Stocks
Smith	Government Bonds
Bruce	Futures
Bruce	Government Bonds

Instrument ID	Location ID
Government Bonds	New York
Government Bonds	London
Government Bonds	Sydney
Futures	Singapore
Futures	Tokyo
Options	Tokyo

Figure 7-7. Dealing Model with Sample Data

Dealer	Instrument ID	Location ID
Smith	Government Bonds	New York
Smith	Government Bonds	London
Smith	Government Bonds	Sydney
Bruce	Futures	Singapore
Bruce	Futures	Tokyo
Bruce	Government Bonds	New York
Bruce	Government Bonds	London
Bruce	Government Bonds	Sydney

Figure 7-8. Allowed Combinations of Dealer, Instrument, and Location

Using the three-column table, we cannot record the fact that an instrument is allowed to be traded at a particular location unless there is at least one dealer who can trade in that instrument. Options can be traded in Tokyo, but this fact is not reflected in the derived table. Nor can we record the fact that the dealer can trade in a particular instrument unless that instrument can be traded at a minimum of one location. The derived table does not show that Smith is authorized to trade in ordinary stocks.

So our derived table appears to be unnormalized, but on checking, we find that it is in BCNF. Technically, our normalization problem is the result of a *multivalued dependency* (MVD)[2] and our table is not in 4NF (which specifies, roughly speaking, that we shouldn't have any non trivial multivalued dependencies).

Rather than get sidetracked by more formal definitions of 4NF and multi valued dependencies, let's refer back to the E-R diagrams. In our one-table solution, we have tried to resolve two many-to-many relationships with a single table, rather than with two separate tables. The simple message is *not* to do this! Another way of looking at it is that we should record *underlying* rules rather than *derived* rules. This is a basic principle of data modeling we have encountered before when eliminating derivable attributes and relationships. It also provides a good starting point for understanding 5NF.

7.4.2.   Fifth Normal Form (5NF)

Throughout the various stages of normalization, at least one thing has remained constant: each new stage involves splitting a table into two or more new tables. As my colleague Graham Witt says, "Normalization is like marriage – you always end up with more relations."

---

2 Instrument ID is said to *multidetermine* Location ID and Dealer ID, and conversely, these *multidetermine* Instrument No.

We have taken care not to lose anything in splitting a table: we could always reconstruct the original table by *joining* (matching values in) the new tables. In essence, normalization splits each table into underlying tables from which the original table can be derived, if necessary.

The definition of 5NF picks up on this idea, and essentially tells us to keep up this splitting process until we can go no further. We only stop splitting when:

1. any further splitting would lead to tables that could not be joined to produce the original table, or

2. the only splits left to us are trivial.

"Trivial" splits are defined as being splits based on candidate keys, such as those shown in Figure 7-9. A *nontrivial* split results in two or more tables with different keys, none of which is a candidate key of any other table.

EMPLOYEE (<u>Employee Number</u>, Name, Date of Birth)

can be trivially split into:

EMPLOYEE-NAME (<u>Employee Number</u>, Name)

EMPLOYEE-BIRTH (<u>Employee Number</u>, Date of Birth)

(a) Split Based on Primary Key

DEPARTMENT (<u>Department Number</u>, Department Name, Location, Manager Employee Number)

Assuming Department Name is a candidate key, can be trivially split into:

DEPARTMENT-LOCATION (<u>Department Number</u>, Department Name, Location)

DEPARTMENT-MANAGER (<u>Department Name</u>, Manager Employee Number)

(b) Split Based on Non-primary Candidate Key

Figure 7-9. Table Splits Based on Primary Key and Candidate Keys

The definition of 5NF differs in style from our definitions for earlier stages in normalization. Rather than picking on a certain type of anomaly to be removed, 5NF defines an end-point after which any further "normalization" would cause us to lose information. Applying the definition to the dealing authority problem, we have shown that the three-key table can be split into two without losing information; hence we perform the split.

The 5NF definition enables us to tackle a more complex version of the dealing authority problem. Suppose we introduce an additional rule: Each dealer can only operate at a specified set of locations. The new model is shown in Figure 7-10 (a) and (b).

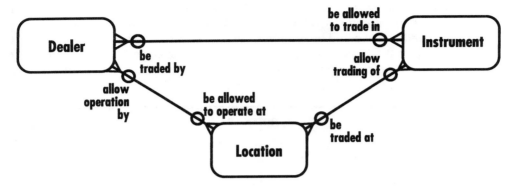

(a) Using Many-to-Many Relationships

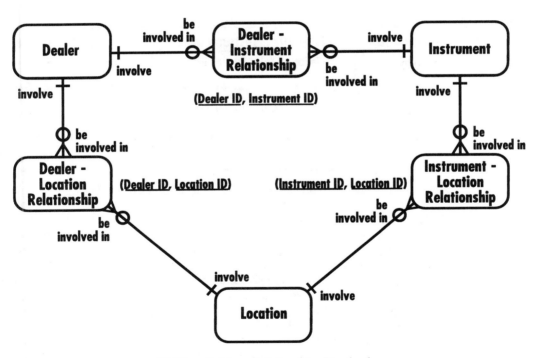

(b) Many-to-Many Relationships Resolved

Figure 7-10. Dealing Model with Three Many-to-Many Relationships

Now that we have *three* separate relationships, could we resolve them all with one entity? I hope your intuitive answer based on the preceding discussion is no. The resulting three column table would have to be equivalent to the three separate tables, and hence could be broken down into them. Figure 7-11 shows the combined table, which still exhibits normalization problems. Changing one of the underlying rules may require multiple rows to be added or deleted, and we cannot record rules that do not currently lead to any valid combinations.

Dealer ID	Location ID	Instrument ID
Smith	Sydney	90-Day Bills
Smith	Sydney	180-Day Bills
Smith	Tokyo	90-Day Bills
Smith	Tokyo	10-Year Bonds
Philip	Sydney	180-Day Bills
Philip	Perth	180-Day Bills

Is derivable from

Dealer ID	Location ID
Smith	Sydney
Smith	Tokyo
Philip	Sydney
Philip	Perth

Dealer ID	Instrument ID
Smith	90-Day Bills
Smith	180-Day Bills
Smith	10-Year Bonds
Philip	180-Day Bills

Location ID	Instrument ID
Sydney	90-Day Bills
Sydney	180-Day Bills
Tokyo	90-Day Bills
Tokyo	10-Year Bonds
Perth	180-Day Bills

Figure 7-11. Allowed Combinations Derivable from Underlying Rules

For example, deleting the rule that Smith can trade in Tokyo requires only one row to be removed from the underlying tables, but two from the derived table. As populations are increased from a few sample rows to hundreds or thousands of rows, the differences become correspondingly greater.

Technically, the three-column derived table is in 4NF, as there are no multivalued dependencies. (You may have to take my word on this!) But because we can split the table into three new tables and reconstruct it, it is not yet in 5NF. Splitting the table into three solves the problem.

In simple terms, then, the definition of 4NF effectively says that two many-to-many relationships cannot be resolved with one table. Satisfying 5NF requires that two *or more* many-to-many relationships are not resolved by a single table.

7.4.3.   Recognizing 4NF and 5NF Situations

The first step in handling 4NF and 5NF problems is recognizing them. At the relational level, we can spot all-key tables with three or more columns; at the E-R diagram level, we look for three (or more)-way resolution entities. Figure 7-12 shows some variations on the theme.

Any of these structures may exhibit 4NF or 5NF problems. Of course, some three-way relationships are perfectly legitimate. The problems arise only when they are derivable from simpler, more fundamental relationships.

If, in our dealer authority example, authorities were decided on a case-by-case basis, independent of underlying rules, then the three-way relationship entity would be valid. Figure 7-13 shows a table of values assigned in this way. You may find it an interesting exercise to try to break the table down into "underlying" tables – it can't be done because there are no underlying rules beyond "any combination may be independently deemed to be allowed." Any set of two-column tables will either fail to cover some permitted combinations, or generate combinations that are not permitted. For example, our "underlying" tables would need to record that:

1.   Smith can deal in Sydney (first row of table).
2.   Smith can deal in 180-day Bills (third row of table).
3.   180-day bills can be traded in Sydney (fourth row of table).

With these three facts we would derive a three-column table which recorded that Smith can deal in 180-day bills in Sydney – which, as we can see from the original table, is not true.

We have gone as far as we can in table splitting, and our tables are therefore in 5NF.

7.4.4.   Checking for 4NF and 5NF with the Business Specialist

In determining whether all-key tables are in 4NF and 5NF, I suggest that you do not bother with the multivalued dependency concept. It's not an easy idea to grasp, and certainly not a good starting point for dialogue with a nontechnical business specialist. And at the end of the day, you've only established 4NF, with 5NF still in front of you! Move straight to the 5NF definition, and look to see if there are simpler business rules underlying those represented by the multiway relationship. Ask the following questions: On what (business) basis do we add a row to this table? On what basis do we delete rows? Do we apply any rules? Understanding the business reasons behind changes to the table is the best way of discovering whether it can be split further.

Don't expect the answers to these business questions to come easily. Often the business rules themselves are not well understood or even well defined. I've found it helpful to present business specialists with pairs of attribute values, or, equivalently, with a null value in one of the columns of a three-column table, and ask "Does this mean anything by itself?" Another useful technique is to look for possible nonkey attributes. Remember that 4NF and 5NF problems only occur with all-key tables.

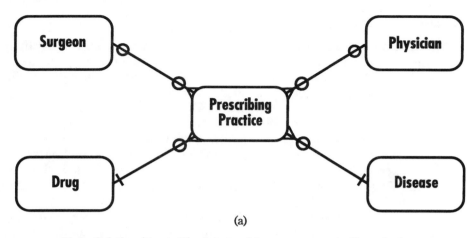

(a)

Note: Relationships to Physician and Surgeon are mutually exclusive. Structure emerges clearly if we use the "mutually exclusive relationships" arc described in Chapter 6, or generalize Surgeon and Physician to Medical Practitioner.

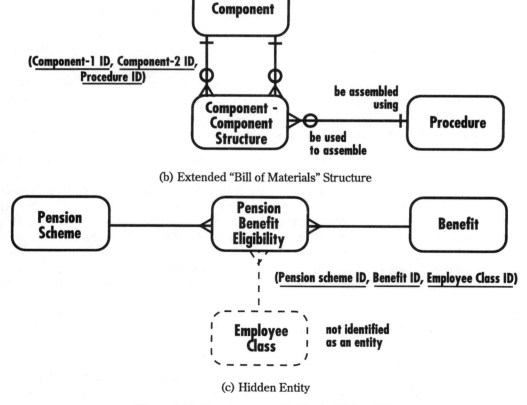

(b) Extended "Bill of Materials" Structure

(c) Hidden Entity

Figure 7-12. Structure Possibly Not in 4NF or 5NF

Dealer ID	Location ID	Instrument ID
Smith	Sydney	90-Day Bills
Smith	Tokyo	90-Day Bills
Smith	Tokyo	180-Day Bills
Philip	Sydney	180-Day Bills

Figure 7-13. Nonderivable Combinations

7.4.5. Further Reading on Higher Normal Forms

You will have little trouble finding texts and papers covering the higher normal forms with far more theoretical detail than presented here.[3] Most authors stick strictly with the relational notation, and don't offer a lot of context. For example, 4NF and 5NF problems usually show only one table to start with; this is technically adequate, but it can be hard coming to grips with the problem unless you imagine the attributes as foreign keys to "context" tables. If you have trouble following such examples, you are not alone! I suggest you draw an E-R diagram of the problem and add extra entities as we did in our 4NF and 5NF examples to show context.

7.5. BEYOND 5NF – SPLITTING TABLES BASED ON CANDIDATE KEYS

In defining 5NF, we indicated that the task of normalization was complete when the only ways of further splitting tables either resulted in our losing information or were based on candidate keys. 5NF is usually considered synonymous with "fully normalized."

However, as we saw in Section 6-4 in our discussion of one-to-one relationships, sometimes we *do* want to split tables based on candidate keys. We looked at an example of a manufacturing business that stored parts in bins according to the following rules:

1. Each type of part is stored in one bin only.
2. Each bin contains one type of part only.

It is interesting to reexamine this example from a normalization perspective. We might be offered the following table to represent data about parts and bins (Figure 7-14):

PART (<u>Part No</u>, Bin No, Bin Capacity, Part Name, Quantity)

Figure 7-14. Parts and Bins

---

[3] Kent, W., "A Simple Guide to the Five Normal Forms of Relational Database Theory," *Communications of the ACM* (February 1983) is a very readable paper at a similar level to this chapter.

In checking normalization, our first reaction is likely to be that Bin No determines Bin Capacity. But Bin No is a candidate key, so technically we don't have a problem. Nevertheless, most experienced data modelers would still feel uncomfortable about this structure, and with good reason. Think about the problem of moving parts from one bin to another. Suppose, for example, we want to swap the parts stored in two bins. We would expect this to involve changing only the Bin Nos for the relevant Parts. But with this structure, we will also need to update (swap) the values for Bin Capacity, and of any other attributes that "belong to" bins rather than parts. If we split Bin and Part data into separate tables, we can avoid this problem, and this is indeed the best approach.

But what distinguishes the trivial Employee example in the previous section where we didn't split the original table? The difference is basically that Bin Nos and Part Nos represent different things in the real world, *and the relationship between them is transferable* i.e., a part may move from one bin to another and vice versa. Although the 5NF rule does not *require* us to split the data into separate tables, it does not prohibit us from doing so. The two resulting tables are still in 5NF.

This issue is seldom discussed in texts on normalization, and you need to be aware of it, if only to back up your intuition when a database designer argues that the two tables should be combined. In practice, if you start with an E-R diagram, you will almost certainly identify separate entities, with a one-to-one relationship between them, rather than a single entity.

7.6.   OTHER NORMALIZATION ISSUES

In this section, we look more closely at some normalization issues I have mentioned only in passing so far. We start by examining some common misconceptions about what is achieved by normalization. We then look at some of the less usual situations that may arise when applying the standard rules of normalization.

7.6.1.   Normalization and Redundancy

Normalization plays such an important role in reducing data redundancy that it is easy to forget that a model can be fully normalized and still contain redundant information. The most common situations are:

7.6.1.1.   Overlapping Tables

Normalization does not address data redundancy resulting from overlapping classifications of data. If we recognize Teacher Number and Student Number as keys when normalizing data, we will build a Teacher table and a Student table. But if a teacher can also be a student, we will end up holding the values of any common attributes (such as Address) in both tables.

7.6.1.2. *Derivable Data*

If the value of one column can be calculated from others, normalization by itself will not eliminate the redundancy. If the underlying column values and the result are all within one row, normalization will remove the calculated value to a separate table (Figure 7-15), but we will still need to observe that the table itself is redundant and remove it.

ORDER ITEM (<u>Order No</u>, <u>Item No</u>, Quantity Ordered, Quantity Delivered, Quantity Outstanding)

Quantity Outstanding = Quantity Ordered *less* Quantity Delivered

Hence (Quantity Ordered, Quantity Delivered) determines Quantity Outstanding

Normalizing:

ORDER ITEM (<u>Order No</u>, <u>Item No</u>, Quantity Ordered, Quantity Delivered)

OUTSTANDING ORDER (<u>Quantity Ordered</u>, <u>Quantity Delivered</u>, Quantity Outstanding)

Outstanding Order table contains no useful information and can be removed on this basis

Figure 7-15 Removing Derivable Data

Better to remove the derivable item at the outset rather than going through this procedure! Normalization will not help at all with values calculated from multiple rows (possibly from more than one table), such as "Total Quantity of this Item Outstanding," or Total Charge on an Invoice Header.

Another example of data derivable across multiple rows is a table used to translate contiguous numeric ranges – for example zip code ranges to States – and including columns First Number and Last Number. The value of Last Number is incremented by 1 to derive the next First Number; hence, if the Last Number column was lost, we could recreate it by substracting 1 from the next highest First Number (Figure 7-16). (We do *not* need to have the rows sequenced to achieve this.) This is, however, hardly elegant programming. And can we rely on the organization that defines the ranges to maintain the convention that they are contiguous?

Repeated data of this kind does not show up as the simple dependencies we tackle with normalization. As discussed in Chapter 2, the best approach is to remove columns representing *derivable* data (as distinct from dependent data), prior to starting normalization. But sometimes the distinction may be hard to make. And, as in the example of Figure 7-16, the sacrifice in programming simplicity and stability may not justify the reduction in redundancy. If in doubt, leave the questionable columns in, then review again after normalization is complete.

AUSTRALIAN POSTCODE TABLE		
FIRST NUMBER	**LAST NUMBER**	**STATE**
.	.	.
5000	5999	South Australia
3000	3999	Victoria
4000	4999	Queensland
etc		

Figure 7-16. Data Derivable across Rows

7.6.2.   Look-Up Tables Produced by Normalization

Each stage in normalization beyond 1NF involves the creation of "look-up" tables, insofar as some data is removed from the original table to another table where it can be "looked up" by citing the relevant value of the primary key. As well as reducing data redundancy, these tables allow us to record instances of the look-up data that do not currently appear in the unnormalized table. For example, we could record a hospital for which there were no operations or a customer who did not hold any accounts with us. We become so used to these look-up tables appearing during the normalization process that it is easy to miss the fact that normalization alone will not always generate all the look-up tables we require.

Imagine we have the table of employee information shown in Figure 7-17.

SKILL HELD (<u>Employee No</u>, <u>Skill Name</u>, Skill Description, Employee Name)

Normalizing:

SKILL HELD (<u>Employee No</u>, <u>Skill Name</u>)

EMPLOYEE (<u>Employee No</u>, Employee Name)

SKILL (<u>Skill Name</u>, Skill Description)

Figure 7-17. Normalization Producing Look-Up Table

Normalization gives us a table of all the employees and their names and another table of all the skill names and their descriptions. We have not only eliminated duplicate rows, but are now able to record a skill even though no employee has that skill. But, if we remove Skill Description from the problem, normalization will no longer give us a Skill table (which would contain the single attribute Skill Name). If we want such a list, we can certainly specify an all-key table consisting of Skill Name only. But normalization won't do it for us.

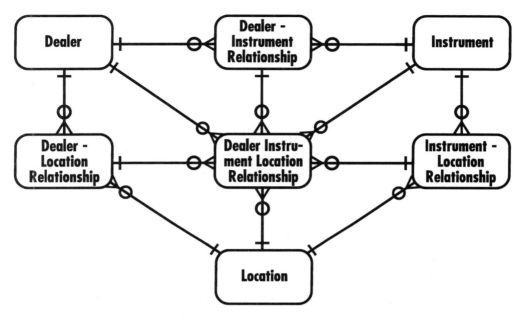

(a) All Foreign Key Links Shown

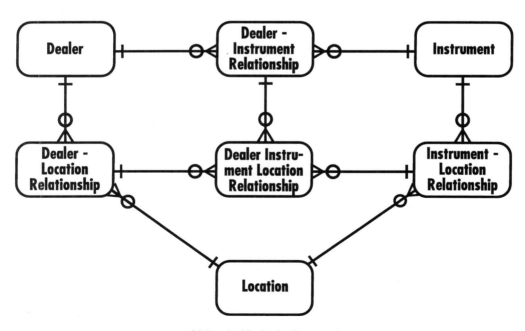

(b) Derivable Links Removed

Figure 7-18. Dealing Model Including Dealer-Location-Relationship Entity

In discussing 4NF and 5NF situations, we raised the possibility of finding a nonkey attribute. If such an attribute, dependent on the full key, was added, our 4NF and 5NF problems would disappear. So why not just introduce a dummy attribute? The problem is much the same as that we encountered with employees and skills: Normalization will provide an internally consistent model, but will not generate the look-up tables we require.

Suppose, for example, we found that there was a limit on the size of any deal for each combination of Dealer, Location, and Instrument. We now need the three-key table to hold the limit, even if our underlying rules are as in Figure 7-10, giving us the model in Figure 7-18. (This one can be a bit tricky to draw. Modelers often show relationships from the base entities rather than the intersection entities. I've shown it first with *all* foreign-key relationships, including redundant relationships, then with redundant relationships removed. I've also left off relationship names in the interest of minimizing clutter.)

Can we now eliminate the three outside intersection entities, giving us the model in Figure 7-19?

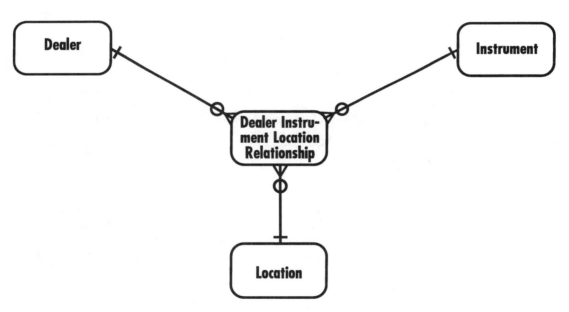

Figure 7-19. Dealing Model with Two-Way Intersection Entities Removed

At first glance, the answer may appear to be "yes." It would seem that we could find all allowable combinations of, say, dealer and location just by searching the relevant columns of the three-column Authority table. The problem is that some of the underlying (two-column) rules may not have given rise to any rows in the Authority table. For example, a dealer may be authorized to deal in New York, but may not yet be authorized to deal in any of the instruments available in that city.

In this example, if we started with just the Authority table, including Limit, no rule of normalization would lead us to the two-column intersection tables – the "look-up" tables. This is because they contain separate and additional facts to the information in the original table. But it is also the sort of thing that is easily missed.

The message here is that normalization is an adjunct to E-R modeling, not a substitute. In the two examples discussed here, we need to identify the look-up tables as entities during the E-R modeling phase.

7.6.3.   Selecting the Primary Key after Removing Repeating Groups

In Chapter 2, we highlighted the importance of correctly identifying primary keys at each stage of the normalization process. Once the tables are in 1NF, this is usually straightforward: In progressing to BCNF, we identify determinants that become primary keys, and the new tables we create in moving beyond BCNF are "all key."

The point, therefore, at which mistakes in primary key identification are most often made is in moving from unnormalized structures to 1NF. We should already have a key for the original file (I don't use the word table here, as tables don't have repeating groups); the problem is to identify a key for the new table that represents the repeating group. The simplest approach is to look at the repeating group before removing it, and ask: What identifies one occurrence in the group, within the context of a given record in the file? Then, ask whether the context is necessary at all; in other words, do we need to add the primary key of the original file or not?

On most occasions, we *do* need to include the primary key of the original file. But this is not always so, and you will eventually get into trouble if you do so unthinkingly. Figure 7-20 shows normalization of a simple file of insurance agents and the policies they have sold.

AGENT (<u>Agent No</u>, Name, {Policy No, Customer ID, Amount Insured})

Policy No uniquely identifies Policy

Each policy is sold by only one agent

Normalizing :

AGENT (<u>Agent No</u>, Agent Name)

POLICY (<u>Policy No</u>, Customer ID, Amount Insured, Agent No*)

Figure 7-20 Repeating Group Table with Stand-Alone Key

The key of Policy is Policy No alone. Although Agent No must be included in the Policy table as a foreign key, it is not part of the primary key. Note that the result depends on the two business rules stated underneath the original model in Figure 7-20.

Surprisingly, a number of texts and papers do not recognize this possibility, or through choice of examples encourage a view that it does not occur.

7.6.4. Sequence of Normalization, and Cross-Table Anomalies

We conclude this chapter with an example that illustrates the importance of rigorously following the rules of normalization, and of developing a sound E-R model at the outset.

Let's go back to the Customer-Salesperson example we used to illustrate BCNF earlier in this chapter (shown again in Figure 7-21):

CUSTOMER-SALESPERSON RELATIONSHIP (<u>Customer No</u>, <u>Salesperson No</u>, Visiting Frequency, Date Relationship Established)

SALESPERSON (<u>Salesperson No</u>, Branch No)

Figure 7-21. Customer-Salesperson Model

Recall that we ended up with two tables, and observed that the structure did not appear to enforce our original business rule that each branch serviced a customer through one salesperson only.

But think about the consequences of relaxing the rule. Let's assume that Date Relationship Established is the date that the *branch* established a relationship with the customer. Then, for a given customer, we will end up carrying that same date for each salesperson within the branch – exactly the sort of redundancy that we would expect normalization to eliminate. But both tables are fully normalized.

We can see the problem more clearly if we go back to our original single table (Figure 7-22).

CUSTOMER-SALESPERSON RELATIONSHIP (<u>Customer No</u>, <u>Salesperson No</u>, Visiting Frequency, Date Relationship Established, Branch No)

Figure 7-22. Original Customer-Branch-Salesperson Model (Not Fully Normalized)

If we now normalize, taking into account the revised rule, we see that Customer No + Branch No is a determinant of Date Relationship Established, and is no longer a candidate key. We therefore need to set up a separate table for these items, removing Date Relationship Established from the original table. Salesperson No is still a determinant of Branch No, so we set up another table for these items, removing Branch No from the original table. The result is shown in Figure 7-23.

CUSTOMER-SALESPERSON RELATIONSHIP (<u>Customer No</u>, <u>Salesperson No</u>, Visiting Frequency)
CUSTOMER-BRANCH RELATIONSHIP (<u>Customer No</u>, <u>Branch No</u>, Date Relationship Established)

SALESPERSON (<u>Salesperson No</u>, Branch No)

Figure 7-23. Fully Normalized Customer-Branch-Salesperson Model

There are at least three lessons here:

1. If you find during normalization that assumptions you have relied on are incorrect, go back to the beginning – be very careful about "patching" the model.
2. Normalization alone is not completely reliable if you start with data already divided into more than one table. In practice, this is what we do virtually all of the time. So we need to analyze our E-R diagrams for problems as well as going through the steps of normalization.
3. Try to identify all the determinants at the start, and don't remove any part of them until all the columns they determine have first been removed. In this example, if we had removed Branch No first, we would have missed the "Branch No + Customer No determines Date Relationship Established" dependency.

7.7.   ADVANCED NORMALIZATION IN PERSPECTIVE

In teaching the higher normal forms and some of the more subtle aspects of normalization, I am frequently challenged by experienced data modelers as to the value of normalization in practice. Their usual argument is that most of the problems that normalization addresses are more easily seen and resolved in the context of an E-R diagram. As we have seen in this chapter, there is a lot of truth in this.

But much of data modeling is about understanding, recognizing, and reusing patterns. The real value of the normalization to practitioners is in increasing their store of patterns, and backing it up with a deep understanding of the advantages and disadvantages of those patterns. When I see a three-way resolution entity, I automatically know to ask whether it can be derived from underlying relationships. If it is derivable, I can quote exactly the types of problems that will occur if it is not broken down into individual tables. (If I have forgotten, I need only look up a text on 4NF or 5NF, having classified the problem.)

These patterns are useful enough that every professional data modeler needs to have them in his or her armory.

7.8.   SUMMARY

Tables in third normal form may not be in Boyce Codd, fourth, and fifth normal forms. Such tables will have problems with redundancy and incompleteness. The higher normal forms are frequently misunderstood by practitioners and hence ignored, or cited to support unsound modeling practices.

Boyce Codd Normal Form requires that every determinant be a candidate key. A table in 3NF will be in BCNF unless a key item is determined by a nonkey item. This will only occur if the table has multiple overlapping candidate keys. The problem is fixed by replacing the primary key with another candidate key and renormalizing.

A table in BCNF will only exhibit 4NF and 5NF problems if it has three or more columns, all of which are part of the key, and can be derived from "underlying" tables. In entity-relationship terms, 4NF and 5NF problems arise when two or more many-to-many relationships are (incorrectly) resolved using a single entity.

To use normalization as the prime modeling technique, we need to start with all data in a single table. In practice, we commence with an E-R model, which will embody numerous assumptions. Normalization will not challenge these.

Normalization by itself does not remove all redundancy from a model nor guarantee completeness.

8

Primary Keys and Identity

No entity without identity.
– Slogan cited by P. F. Strawson in *Contemporary British Philosophy.*

8.1. INTRODUCTION – BASIC REQUIREMENTS AND TRADE-OFFS

There is no area of data modeling in which mistakes are more frequently made, and with more impact, than the selection of primary keys. On the surface, the job is straightforward. For each entity, we need to select or create a set of attributes that will have a different combination of values for each entity instance.

Navigation around a relational database relies on being able to refer unambiguously to a specific row of a table by specifying the values of the primary key columns. Relationships are supported by foreign keys that need to point to one row only. Imagine the problems if we had an insurance policy referring to customer number "12345," but found two or more rows with that value in the Customer table.

So we require that a primary key be *unique*. Even more fundamentally, we require that it be *applicable* to all instances of an entity (and hence to all rows in the table). It isn't much good using Registration Number to identify vehicles if we need to keep track of unregistered vehicles. We require that a key be *minimal:* we shouldn't add more columns beyond those necessary for uniqueness. A key should also be *stable:* it should not change value over time. The stability requirement is frequently overlooked in data modeling texts and training courses, but by observing it we can avoid the often complex program logic needed to cater to changes in key values.

A very simple way of meeting all of the requirements is to invent a new attribute for each entity, specifically to serve as the key, and to assign a different, system-generated value to each entity instance. We refer to such an attribute as a *surrogate key*. Familiar examples are simple customer numbers, employee numbers, and account numbers allocated sequentially or from predefined ranges.

But there are reasons for preferring a more "natural" identifier as the primary key. In the real world, we specify individual entity instances by using familiar identifiers such as names. When retrieving data from a computerized database, the natural identifier is often the most convenient starting point. Customers cannot always be expected to quote a customer number, and applicants for visas will nominate the name of their country of origin rather than our locally defined country number. In these cases the physical designer will need to provide for efficient access to the relevant table using the natural identifier, as well as the primary key. If the two are the same, we can get away with only one access mechanism, and a consequent payoff in performance. Using a natural identifier for the primary key can also simplify programming logic by reducing the need to access look-up tables: if the primary key of Country is Country Name, it will have immediate meaning wherever it appears as a foreign key; but if we use a Country Number of our own invention, we will need to look up the country name in the Country table.

So we have an argument for using a natural identifier as the primary key. Unfortunately, many natural identifiers fall short of meeting the requirement for applicability, uniqueness, and stability. Outside a database, these deficiencies may not cause any serious problems, because we are often working with only a subset of all of the instances (i.e., there is an implicit *context*) and can seek clarification if ambiguity arises. People's names are the obvious example: within the context of the people we know personally, names are *almost* unique, and on the odd occasion when two or more people have the same name, we resolve any ambiguity by specifying another distinguishing characteristic. But in navigating within a database, possibly containing millions of rows, we do not have the ability to seek clarification; we rely entirely on the uniqueness of primary keys.

Most arguments about primary keys come back to the choice between surrogate and natural keys. At the one extreme we have the argument that only surrogate keys should be used; at the other, a view that the natural key should always be the starting point, even if it needs to be modified or augmented to provide uniqueness. Not surprisingly, the former options tend to be preferred by data modelers, and the latter by physical database designers concerned with performance. Most serious mistakes in primary key selection are the result of ill-considered decisions to use natural keys without reference to whether or not they meet the basic requirements.

Going back to these basic requirements can also help us resolve the majority of questions about primary keys that arise in practice. In this chapter, we look first at the basics of primary key selection, then draw on these to examine some specific issues that arise frequently in practice: surrogate keys, structured keys, partially null keys, and alternative candidate keys.

8.2.   APPLICABILITY

We must be able to determine a value for the primary key for every entity instance. Watch for the following traps when attempting to use natural keys.

8.2.1.   Special Cases

Often our understanding of a business area is based on a few examples that may not be adequately representative. It is worth adopting the discipline of asking the business specialists, "Are there any cases in which we would not have a value for any of these (primary key) attributes?" Do we ever encounter persons without a Social Security number? Or flights without a flight number? Or sound recordings without a catalogue number? Surprisingly often, such special cases emerge. We are then faced with a choice of:

1. setting up a mechanism to allocate key values to these cases;
2. excluding them from the entity definition altogether; or
3. rejecting the proposed primary key, usually in favor of a surrogate key.

Selecting option 2 will lead to a change in the model at the entity level, as a new entity is added to cater to the special cases, or the overall scope of the model modified to exclude them.

8.2.2.   Data Unavailable at Time of Entry

All components of a primary key need to be available at the time a row is first stored in the database. This can sometimes be a problem if we are building up data progressively. For example, we may propose Customer Number plus Departure Date as the primary key of Travel Itinerary. But will we always know the departure date at the time we first record information about an itinerary? Are we happy to hold off recording the travel plans until that date is available? Again, a surrogate key is often the simplest solution.

8.2.3.   Broadening of Scope

One of the most common causes of problems with keys is a broadening of the original scope of a system, resulting in tables being used to hold data beyond that originally intended. Frequently, the primary key is not applicable to some of the instances embraced by the more general definition. For example, we may decide to market our products to individual persons, where in the past we only dealt with companies. In this case, a government-assigned Company Number will no longer be suitable as a primary key for Customer. Or our book-selling business may broaden its product range to include stationery, and International Standard Book Number will no longer be an appropriate key for Product.

One way of reducing the likelihood of being caught by scope changes is to be as precise as possible in entity naming and definition: name the original entity Company rather than Customer, or Book Title rather than Product. Then use supertyping to explore different levels of generalization, such as Customer and Product. The resulting model will prompt questions such as "Are we potentially interested in customers who are not companies?" It now comes back to the familiar task of choosing a level of generalization, and a corresponding key, that will accommodate business change. We can't expect to get it right every time, but most problems which arise in this area are a result of not having addressed the generalization issue at all, rather than coming up with the wrong answer.

8.3.   UNIQUENESS

Uniqueness is the most commonly cited requirement of primary keys. To reiterate: *you can't build a relational database without unique primary keys*. Indeed, the term "unique primary key" is a tautology – if a combination of attributes is not unique, it does not qualify to be called a primary key. There are three ways you can be reasonably sure that a key will be unique.

The first is that it is intrinsically unique, as a result of the nature of the real world. A finger print or signature qualifies on this criterion, as do coordinates of a location, if sufficiently precise. Such keys occur only rarely in practice.

The second is that you, as the designer, control the allocation of key values, and can therefore ensure that no value is allocated more than once. Surrogate keys, such as computer-generated sequential Customer Numbers, are the obvious examples. Another possibility is a *tie-breaker* – a (usually sequential) number added to an "almost unique" set of attributes. A common example is a numeric suffix added to a person's or organization's name, or part of the name ("Drummond 0043"). Why use a tie-breaker when it would seem at least as easy to use a sequential number for the whole key? Performance, real or imagined, is usually the reason. The designer aims to be able to use a single index to provide access on both the primary key and a natural key (the first part of the primary key). In keeping with the "one fact per attribute" rule introduced in Section 2.4 (and discussed in detail in Section 9.3), a tie-breaker should be handled as a separate attribute, rather than simply appended to the natural key. And, as always with natural keys, you need to make sure that the stability requirement is met.

The third possibility is that someone else with the same intention as you has allocated the key values. A vehicle registration number is allocated by a state authority with the intention that it be unique in the issuing state. In these cases, the most common problem is a difference between our scope of interest and theirs. For example, we may be interested in vehicles in more than one state. We can address this problem by including in the key an attribute to identify the issuer of the number – e.g., State of Registration. Again, we need to think about possible extensions to the scope of the system. Racehorse names may be unique within a country, but what happens if we want to extend our register to cover overseas events, or greyhounds?

The advantage of using someone else's scheme, particularly if it is widely accepted, is that the primary key will be useful in communicating with the world outside the system. Customers will be able to quote and verify registration numbers, and we avoid singularity problems (discussed below). But there is an element of faith in tying our primary key to another's decisions. We need to be reasonably confident that the key issuer's entity definition will remain in line with our own, and that the key also meets basic standards of soundness. Many a system has been severely disrupted by an external decision to change a numbering scheme or to reuse old numbers.

If you are not using one of these three schemes, you need to ask yourself, "How can I *guarantee* that the key will be unique?" A common mistake is to use a "statistical reduction" approach, best illustrated by the problem of choosing a primary key for persons (customers, employees, etc.). The modeler starts with a desire to use Person Name as the key, prompted by its obvious real world significance as an identifier. We all know that names are not unique – but what about Name plus Date of Birth? Or Name plus Date of Birth plus Zip Code plus ...? The problem is that while we can reduce the possibility of duplicates, we can never actually eliminate it, and it takes only one exception to destroy the integrity of the database. And don't forget that human beings are remarkably good at deliberately causing odd situations, including duplicates, if doing so isn't actually impossible or illegal!

8.4.   MINIMALITY

A primary key should not include attributes beyond those required to ensure uniqueness. Having decided that Customer Number uniquely identifies a customer, we should not append Customer Name to the key. Whenever such an overlarge primary key appears as a foreign key, we will have normalization problems, as the extra attribute will be determined by the "real" key. For example, if we held both Customer Number and Customer Name in a Purchase table, we would be carrying Customer Name redundantly for each purchase made by the customer. A change of name would require a complex update procedure. Minimality problems don't often occur, and are usually a result of simple errors in modeling or documentation rather than an attempt to achieve any particular objective such as performance. They should be picked up by normalization, and there should be no argument about correcting them.

8.5.   STABILITY

Stability is the most subtle of the design considerations for primary keys, and the one least discussed in the literature on data modeling and relational database – hence the one most often violated. The idea is that a given real world entity instance should keep the same value of the primary key for as long as it is recorded in the database. For example, a given customer should retain the same customer number for as long as he or she is a customer.

The first reason for using stable primary keys is that they are used elsewhere as foreign keys. Changing the value of a primary key is therefore not a simple process, because all of the foreign key references will also need to be updated. We will need to write program logic to cater to this, and maintain it whenever another table carrying the relevant foreign key is added to the database design. An even more serious problem arises with archived and other external data – data that is not in the database proper, but held on microfiche, tape, paper, or other backup media. What do we do with the foreign key references there? How do we find old versions of a table row whose primary key has changed?

The foreign key maintenance problem is usually the most effective method of convincing programmers and physical database designers of the need for stable primary keys. But there is an even more fundamental reason for not allowing changes to primary key values. Think about our customer example again. The customer may, over time, change his/her name, address, or even date of birth if it was misstated or entered incorrectly. To match historical data with the current picture, we require some attribute or combination of attributes that is not only unique, but does not change over time. The requirement for uniqueness points us to the primary key; to be able to conveniently match current and historical data, we require that it be stable.

Another way of looking at the issue is this: In a relational database, all of the nonkey columns hold data *about* real world entity instances; but the key represents the *existence* of real world entity instances. In other words, a new primary key value corresponds to a new entity instance being recorded in the database, while deletion of a primary key value corresponds to the record of an entity instance being deleted from the database. Without this discipline it is difficult to distinguish a change of key value from the deletion of one entity instance and the addition of another.

Admittedly, it is possible to build workable databases without stable primary keys, and much complicated program logic has been written to support key changes. But the *simplest* approach is to adhere rigidly to the discipline of stable primary keys. Stability can always be achieved by using surrogate keys if necessary. There is invariably a payoff in terms of simpler, more elegant databases and systems. *In all of the examples in this book, I assume that the primary keys are stable.* If you require further convincing that unstable primary keys cause complexity, I suggest you try modifying some of the time-dependent models in Chapter 10 to accomodate primary key changes.

A final illustration: In the insurance business, there are many options that we may want to add to or delete from a policy in order to provide the cover required by the client over the years. At some point, however, the business may decide that a particular change should not be accommodated under the original policy, and a replacement policy should be issued. It is important for the business to distinguish between changes and replacements to allow consistent compliance with legislation and management reporting ("How many new policies did we issue this month? What is the average cost of issuing a new policy?") The supporting information systems need to reflect the distinction, and the primary key of Policy provides the mechanism. We can change virtually every nonkey attribute of a policy, but if the key value remains the same, we interpret the table row as representing the same policy. Conversely, we can leave all other attribute values unchanged, but if the key value changes, we interpret it as a new policy being recorded with identical characteristics to the old.

Stability, then, is tied very closely to the idea of identity. In some cases, such as persons, the definition of identity is so well entrenched that we would have to be creative modelers indeed to propose alternatives (although it is worth thinking about how a database would handle the situation of a police informer being given a "new identity," or even an employee who resigns and is later reemployed). In others, such as insurance policies, products, and organization units, a variety of definitions may be workable. The data modeler needs to capture in entity definitions the essence of what distinguishes one instance from another, and define the primary key accordingly.

8.6.   STRUCTURED KEYS AND WEAK ENTITIES

8.6.1.   Problems with Structured Keys

A structured key is simply a key made up of more than one attribute. Because of this, structured keys are sometimes also called "concatenated keys" or "composite keys." The term also covers the situation in which several distinct attributes have been combined to form a single-column key, in contravention of the one-fact-per-column rule introduced in Section 2.4. Structured keys often cause problems, but not because there is anything inherently wrong with multiattribute keys. Rather, the problem keys usually fail to meet one or more of the basic requirements discussed above, in particular stability.

Structured keys are particularly prone to a special kind of stability problem – running out of numbers – which can ultimately require that we reallocate *all* key values. The more parts to a key, the more likely we are to exhaust all possible values for one of them. This is where the problems really start, for rather than tackling a complete redefinition of the key, we will be tempted to add new data and meaning to other parts of the key in order to keep the overall value unique. In turn, we now have to write program logic to extract the meaning of the values held in these parts.

Most experienced data modelers have a horror story to tell in this area. I recall one organization that had a team of four staff members working full time on allocating location codes, and another that had to completely redevelop a system because they ran out of insurance agent identifiers (the agent identifier consisted of a State Code, Branch Code within state, and Agent Number within state and branch; when all agent numbers for a particular branch had been allocated, new numbers were assigned by creating phantom branches and states). As a result of problems of this kind, it is often suggested that structured keys be avoided altogether. However, a structured key should involve no more risk than a single-column key, as long as we make adequate provision for growth of each component, and do not break the basic rules of column definition and key design.

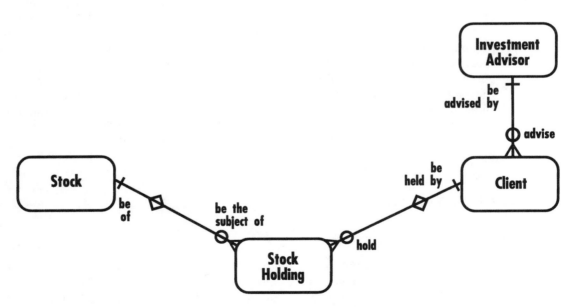

Figure 8-1. Transferability Influencing Key Choice

8.6.2. Using Structured Keys to Control Transferability

Look at Figure 8-1 and note the use of the nontransferability symbol introduced in Chapter 6. Most data modelers would automatically propose a key for Stock Holding which included the primary keys of Stock and Client (e.g., Stock ID + Client ID + Effective Date). But few data modelers would suggest that the primary key of Client should include the primary key of Investment Adviser. And rightly so. The difference in the two situations is that the structured key of Stock Holding will be stable, because the Stock ID and Client ID associated with a given Stock Holding will never change (the Stock Holding cannot be transferred). On the other hand, a client may be transferred to a new Investment Adviser – hence a key that contained the primary key of Investment Adviser would not be stable.

To summarize the rule: We only include the key of another entity in a primary key if that other entity is at the "one" end of a mandatory,[1] non transferable relationship.

We can look at this rule from another perspective. If we are rigorous in obeying the rule that primary keys be stable, then a decision to use a concatenated key is a way of *enforcing* nontransferability. In the example, we cannot record a transfer of a Stock Holding from one Client to another, because that would mean changing the value of the key, which we are not allowed to do. The most common examples of nontransferable relationships are those arising from resolving many-to-many or multi-entity real world relationships. The resulting relationships are intrinsically nontransferable, as each resolution entity instance represents a real world relationship between two specific entity instances: changing one or both of those instances would be seen as deleting the old real world relationship and establishing a new one.

8.6.3. Weak Entities

Chen[2] introduced the concept of a *weak entity,* an entity that relies on another for its identification. In our example, Stock Holding would be a weak entity, *if we decided to use Client ID and/or Stock ID in constructing its primary key.* An entity with a stand-alone key (i.e., a nonweak entity) is called a *regular* entity. The primary key of a weak entity is sometimes called a *weak key.* These are useful terms to have in our vocabulary for describing models and common structures (for example, the split foreign key situation covered in Chapter 6). Chen introduced special diagramming symbols to distinguish weak entities (Figure 8-2), but I find the non-transferability concept more useful at the E-R modeling stage, when we may have yet to identify or design attributes and keys. Of course, if you stick strictly to the practice of always enforcing nontransferability by using appropriately structured keys, then nontransferability and weakness will be one and the same.

---

[1] An exception to the mandatory requirements is discussed in Section 8.8.
[2] "The Entity Relationship Model – Toward a Unified View of Data," *ACM Transactions on Database Systems* (March 1976).

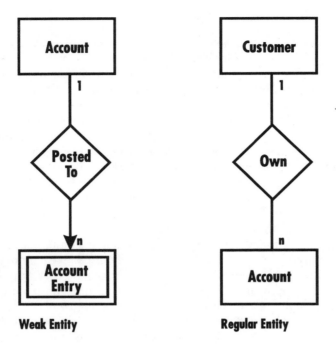

Figure 8-2. Chen's Weak Entity Convention

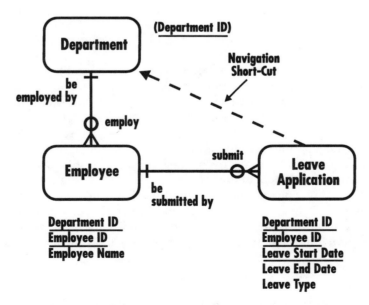

Figure 8-3. Navigation Short Cut Supported by Structured Key

We can usually come close to consistently using weak keys for nontransferable entities, but will sometimes find that a nontransferable entity has an excellent stand-alone key available. We may then choose to trade enforcement of non-transferability for the convenience of using an available "natural" key. For example, it may not be possible for a visa to be transferred from one person to another; hence we could include the key of Person in the key of Visa, but we may prefer to use a well-established stand-alone Visa Number.

8.6.4.   Programming and Structured Keys

Structured keys may simplify programming and improve performance by providing more data items in a table row without violating normalization rules. In Figure 8-3, we are able to determine which department a leave application comes from without needing to access the Employee table. But can an employee transfer from one department to another? If so, the primary key of Employee will be unstable – almost certainly an unacceptable price to pay for a little programming convenience and performance. If performance was critically affected by the decision, it would probably be better to carry Department ID redundantly as a nonprimary key item in the Leave Application table.

8.6.5.   Performance Issues with Structured Keys

Although performance is not our first concern as data modelers, it can be an important factor in deciding between alternatives that rate similarly against other criteria. In some cases, performance issues are paramount, and we should not leave it to the physical database designer to find models that are of similar utility to ours but perform better. Structured keys may affect performance in three principal ways:

First, they may reduce the number of tables that need to be accessed by some transactions, as in Figure 8-3, discussed above.

Second, they may reduce the number of access mechanisms that need to be supported. Take the Stock Holding example from Figure 8-1. If we proposed a stand-alone surrogate key for Stock Holding, it is likely that the physical database designer would need to construct three indexes – one for the surrogate key, and one for each of the foreign keys to Client and Stock. But if we used Client ID + Stock ID + Date, the designer could probably get by with two indexes, resulting in a saving in space and update time.

Third, as the number of attributes in a structured key increases, so does the size of table and index records. It is not unknown for a table at the bottom of a deep hierarchy to have seven or more attributes in its key. Indeed, I recall a key for insurance risk that reflected the following hierarchy: State; Branch; District; Agent; Client; Policy Class; Original Issuer; Policy; Risk – a nine part key, used throughout the organization. In this case, the key had been constructed in the days of serial files, and reflected neither a true hierarchy nor nontransferable relationships.

When we encounter large keys, we have the option of introducing a stand-alone surrogate key at any point(s) in the hierarchy, reducing the size of the primary keys from that point downwards. Doing so will prevent us from fully enforcing non-transferability and will cost us an extra access mechanism. In the record library model of Figure 8-4, we can add a surrogate key Track ID to Track, as the primary key, and use this to replace the large foreign key in Performer Role. The primary key of Performer Role would then become Track ID + Performer ID. However, the model would no longer enforce the fact that a track could not be transferred from one record to another.

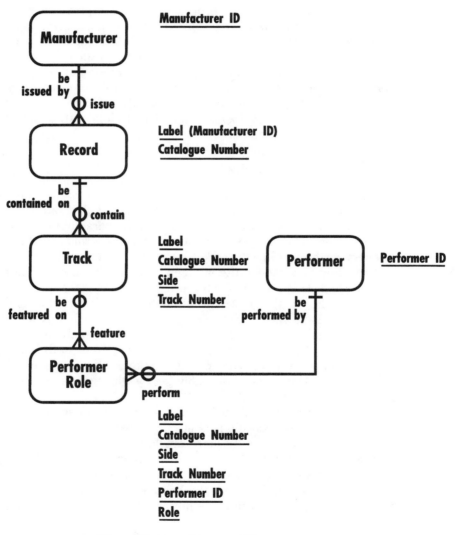

Figure 8-4. Large Structured Keys

8.7.   SURROGATE KEYS

The requirements of applicability, uniqueness, minimality, and stability seem to have a simple answer: just create a single primary key attribute for each entity, and use the system to generate a unique value for each occurrence. For example, we could specify Branch ID as the primary key of Branch, and number the first Branch "1," the second "2," and so forth. I refer to all such attributes as *surrogate keys,* although some modelers reserve the term for keys that are not only system-generated, but are kept invisible to system users.

8.7.1.   When to Use Surrogate Keys

The two major arguments against surrogate keys are programming complexity and performance. As discussed in the introduction to this chapter, whenever a surrogate key appears as a foreign key, we need to access a look-up table to find the corresponding natural identifier. This situation occurs often enough that programmers are frequently opponents of surrogate keys. Performance is not usually a problem if the look-up tables are small and can reside in primary storage.

The more common performance-related issue with surrogate keys is the need for additional access mechanisms such as indexes to support access on both the surrogate and natural keys. In databases handling high volumes of new data, problems may also arise with contention for "next available numbers." Some database management systems now provide sophisticated mechanisms specifically to address this problem.

A sensible general approach is to use:

1. natural identifiers when they are available *always subject to the basic requirements of applicability, uniqueness, and stability*
2. weak keys when the relevant entity is nontransferable,
3. stand-alone surrogate keys if no suitable natural identifier is available, and the entity is transferable.

But remember when specifying surrogate keys that simply specifying "Customer ID" as the key of Customer does not solve the problem of matching real world customers with rows in a database table. However, in many cases we are able to "change the world" by making the surrogate key values available and suggesting or insisting that they be used when data is to be retrieved. This is easier to insist upon if the keys are used only within our organization, rather than externally, or if there is some incentive for using them. In general it's relatively easy to get employees and suppliers to play by our rules; customers can be more difficult!

8.7.2.   Should Surrogate Keys Be Visible?

Theoreticians often suggest that surrogate keys be hidden from system users, and used only as a mechanism for navigation within the database. The usual arguments are:

1. If the surrogate keys are visible, users will begin to attribute meaning to them ("the Contract Number is between 5000 and 6000 – hence it is managed in London"). This meaning may not be reliable.
2. We may wish to change the keys, perhaps as a result of not making adequate provision for growth or to consolidate existing databases.

I have seen the problem described in 1 above, and it usually arises when specific ranges of numbers are allocated to different locations, subtypes, or organization units. In these cases we *can* place a meaning on the code, but the meaning is "issued by," which is not always equivalent to "permanently responsible for." The problem can be avoided by making it more difficult or impossible for the users to interpret the numbers, by allocating multiple small ranges, or assigning available numbers randomly to sites. At the same time, we need to make sure the real information is available where it is required so the user doesn't need to resort to interpreting the code.

The problem described in 2 above, should not often arise. Changing primary keys is a painful process even if the keys are hidden. We can insure against running out of numbers by allowing an extra digit or two. When designing the system, we should look at the likelihood of other databases being incorporated, and plan accordingly: simply adding a Source attribute to the primary key to identify the original database will usually solve the problem. If we have not made this provision, one of the simpler solutions is to assign new surrogate keys to one set of data, and to provide a secondary access mechanism based on the old key, which is held as a nonkey item.

In my experience, the disadvantages of a visible key are usually outweighed by the advantage of being able to specify simply the row we want in a table. One example of surrogate keys that is in common use throughout the world is the booking number used in airline reservation systems (sometimes called a "record locator"). If a customer provides his/her record locator, access is available quickly and unambiguously to the relevant data. If the customer doesn't have the number available, the booking can be accessed by a combination of other attributes, but this is intrinsically a more involved process.

CRIMINAL CASE		CIVIL CASE	
Case ID	Date Scheduled	Case ID	Date Scheduled
000001	01/02/93	000001	01/02/93
000002	01/03/93	000002	01/03/93
000003	01/04/93	000003	01/05/93
000004	01/06/93	000004	01/07/93

(a) Primary Keys allocated independently

CRIMINAL CASE		CIVIL CASE	
Case ID	Date Scheduled	Case ID	Date Scheduled
000001	01/02/93	000002	01/02/93
000005	01/03/93	000003	01/03/93
000006	01/04/93	000004	01/05/93
000008	01/06/93	000007	01/07/93

(b) Primary Keys Allocated from Common Source

Figure 8-5. Allcoation of Key Values to Subtypes

8.7.3.   Surrogate Keys and Subtypes

If we decide to define a surrogate key at the supertype level, that key will be applicable to all of the subtypes. An interesting question then arises if we choose to implement at the subtype level: Should we allow instances belonging to different subtypes to take the same key value? For example, if we implement Criminal Case and Civil Case tables, having previously defined a supertype Legal Case, should we allocate numbers as in Figure 8-5 (a) or as in 8-5(b)? If contention for "next available number," as described earlier in this section, is not a serious problem, I recommend you choose option (b). This provides some recognition of the supertype in our relational design. A supertype table can then be constructed using the "union" operator, and easily related ("joined") to tables that hold Legal Case numbers as foreign keys (Figure 8-6).

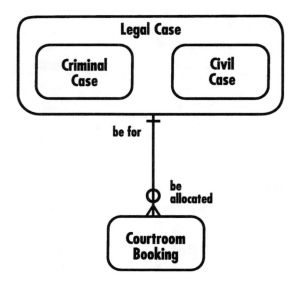

Original Tables:

CRIMINAL CASE (<u>Case ID</u>, Date Scheduled...)

CIVIL CASE (<u>Case ID</u>, Date Scheduled...)

COURTROOM BOOKING (<u>Courtroom ID</u>, <u>Date</u>, <u>Period</u>, Case ID*...)

<u>**After Union of Criminal Case and Civil Case Tables:**</u>

LEGAL CASE (<u>Case ID</u>, Date Scheduled...)

COURTROOM BOOKING (<u>Courtroom ID</u>, <u>Date</u>, <u>Period</u>, Case ID*)

Figure 8-6. Combining Subtypes

8.7.4.   Singularity

Finally, one of the most difficult problems with surrogate keys is the possibility of allocating more than one value to the same real world object, a violation of *singularity*, which requires that each real world object have only one key value, and hence only one row in the relevant database table. This happens with natural keys as well as surrogate keys – for example, a person may have aliases – but less commonly. Merging two or more rows once the problem has been discovered can be a complicated business, especially if foreign keys also have to be consolidated.

The only real solution is good design of data capture procedures, to ensure that duplicates are picked up at data entry time. For example, a company might ask a "new" customer: "Do you already have business with us?" and back this up with a check for matching names, addresses, etc. Making the employee who captures the details responsible for fixing any duplicates has proved a useful approach to improving the quality of checking.

8.8.   **NULL AND PARTIALLY NULL KEYS**

There are plenty of good reasons why primary keys should never be allowed to take a null value. One of the most obvious is the problem of interpreting foreign keys – does null mean "no corresponding row" or is it a pointer to the row with the null primary key?

But conventional wisdom also dictates that no *part* (i.e., no column) of a primary key should ever hold a null value. Some of the arguments are to do with sophisticated handling of different types of nulls, which is currently of more academic than practical relevance, since the null handling of most database management systems is very basic. For the sake of simplicity, and practicality, I'll simply use "null" here to mean blank or "spaces." On this basis, it's hard to sustain the argument that part-null keys are invalid.

The issue often arises when implementing a supertype whose subtypes have distinct primary keys. For example, an airline may want to implement a Service entity whose subtypes are Flight Service (identified by an Flight Number) and Accommodation Service (identified by an alphabetic Accommodation Service ID). The key for Service could be Flight Service No + Accommodation Service ID, where one value would always be null. This is a workable, if inelegant, alternative to generalizing the two to produce a single alphanumeric attribute.

A variant of this situation is shown in Figure 8-7. The weak keys for Branch and Department are legitimate as long as branches cannot be transferred from one division to another and departments cannot be transferred from one branch to another.

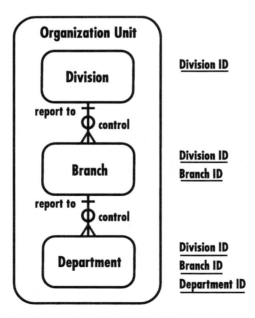

Figure 8-7. Model Allowing Partially Null Key Values for Organization Unit

But if we decide to implement at the Organization Unit level, giving us a simple hierarchy, can we generalize the primary keys of the subtypes into a primary key for Organization Unit? The proposed key would be Division ID + Branch ID + Department ID. For divisions, Branch ID and Department ID would be null, and for branches Department ID would be null. Again we have null values in the primary key, and again we have a solution that is workable, which I have seen employed successfully in practice.

The choice of key in this example has some interesting implications. The foreign key, which points to the next level up the hierarchy, is contained in the primary key (e.g., Branch ID "0219" contains the key of Division "02"). This limits us to three levels of hierarchy; our choice of primary key has imposed a constraint on the number of levels and their relationships. With a surrogate key, any such limits would need to be enforced outside the data structure. This is another example of a structured key imposing constraints that we may or may not want to enforce for the life of the system.

Figure 8-8 shows another situation in which partially null primary keys may be useful. A null value of Date Returned would indicate that the loan was outstanding. The alternative in this case is to use Date Borrowed, which should always have a nonnull value. However the first approach could offer performance advantages if a single access mechanism on the primary key also allowed outstanding loans to be efficiently selected for retrieval. Note, that the stability criterion will be violated unless we regard returned books and outstanding loans as different instances, rather than stages in the life of the same loan.

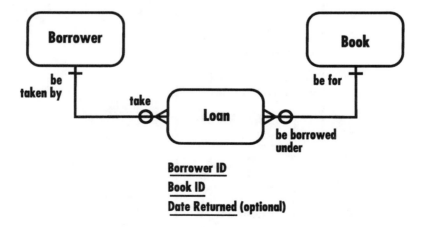

Figure 8-8. Use of Part-Null Primary Key

8.9. MULTIPLE CANDIDATE KEYS

8.9.1. Candidate Keys

Quite frequently we encounter tables in which there are two or more columns (or combinations of columns) that could serve as the primary key. There may be two or more natural keys or, more often, a natural and a surrogate key. We refer to each possible key as a *candidate key*. There are a few rules we need to observe, and some traps to watch out for when there is more than one candidate key.

8.9.2. Choosing a Primary Key

We must always nominate a single primary key for each entity. One of the most important reasons for doing so is to specify how relationships will be supported: the foreign key needs to be a copy of the primary key, not just any candidate key.

Selection should be based on the requirements and issues discussed earlier in this chapter. In addition to comparing applicability, stability, structure, and meaningfulness, we should ask, "Does each candidate key represent the same thing for all time?" As discussed in Chapters 6 and 7, the presence of multiple candidate keys may be a clue that an entity should be split into two entities linked by a one-to-one transferable relationship.

8.9.3. Normalization Issues

We saw in Section 7.3 that multiple candidate keys can result in tables that are in third normal form but not Boyce Codd normal form. Tables with two or more candidate keys can be also be a source of confusion in earlier stages of normalization. Some informal definitions of 3NF imply that a nonkey column is not allowed to be a determinant of another nonkey column (e.g., "Each nonkey item must depend on the key, the whole key, and *nothing but the key*").

Look at the table in Figure 8-9:

CUSTOMER (<u>Customer No</u>, Tax File No, Name, Address, ...)

Figure 8-9. Table with Two Candidate Keys

Let's assume that every customer has a Tax File No, and that no two customers have the same Tax File No. A bit of thought will show that Tax File No (a nonkey item) is a determinant of Name, Address, and indeed every other column in the table. On the basis of our informal definition of 3NF, we would conclude that the table is not in third normal form, and remove Name, Address, etc. to another table, with Tax File No copied across as the key.

We *don't* want to do this! It doesn't achieve anything useful. Remember our definition of 3NF in Chapter 2: Every determinant of a nonkey item must be a candidate key. Our table satisfies this – it's only the "rough and ready" definition of 3NF that leads us astray.

8.10.   SUMMARY

Primary keys must be applicable to all instances, unique, minimal, and stable. Stability is frequently overlooked, but stable keys lead to simpler system designs. "Natural" keys may offer performance advantages, but are often unstable.

Structured keys consist of two or more attributes. Provided they satisfy the basic criteria of soundness, they can contribute to enforcing nontransferability, and may offer better performance. An entity that includes the key of another entity in its key is called a *weak* entity.

Surrogate keys are system-generated, meaningless keys, and can be managed to ensure uniqueness and stability. They do not guarantee singularity (one key value per real world entity instance), and may introduce a performance bottleneck. Surrogate keys may be made visible to users, but no meaning that is not constant over time for each instance should be attached to them.

Primary keys must not be allowed to take a null value, but individual components may be allowed to do so.

9

Attributes

Real Data Modelers don't do attributes.
– Misguided Data Modeler

9.1.   INTRODUCTION

Attribute definition does not always receive the attention it deserves from data modelers.

One reason is the emphasis on diagrams as the primary means of presenting a model. While they are invaluable in communicating the overall shape, they hide the detail of attributes. It is not uncommon for many of the participants in the development and review of a model to see only the diagrams, and remain unaware of the underlying attributes.

A second reason is that data models are developed progressively, with the full requirements for attributes becoming clear only towards the end of the analysis task. By this time the specialist data modeler may have departed, leaving the supposedly straightforward and noncreative job of attribute definition to database administrators, function modelers, and even programmers. I have encountered many data modelers who believe that their job is finished when a reasonably stable framework of entities, relationships, and primary keys is in place.

On the contrary, the data modeler who remains involved in the development of a data model right through to implementation will be in a good position to ensure not only that attributes are soundly modeled as the need for them arises, but to intercept "improvements" to the model before they become entrenched.

In this chapter we look at the main issues that arise in modeling attributes. Not surprisingly, decision making centers around the two fundamental modeling techniques of aggregation and generalization. As with entity modeling, we have some quite firm rules for aggregation, whereas generalization decisions often involve trade-offs among conflicting objectives. This is similar to the situation that we encounter at the entity and relationship level. As always, there is room for choice and sometimes creativity.

We also look at *domains* – sets of allowed values for attributes – and the use of look-up tables as one technique for enforcing these.

Finally, I suggest some guidelines for constructing attribute names. Naming of attributes is far more of an issue than naming of entities and relationships, if only because the number of attributes in a model is so much greater.

9.2.   ATTRIBUTE DEFINITION

Proper definitions are an essential starting point for detailed modeling of attributes. In the early stages of modeling, we propose and record attributes even before entities are fully defined, but our final model must include an unambiguous definition of each attribute. If we fail to do this, we are likely to overlook the more subtle issues discussed in this chapter, and run the risk that the resulting columns in the database will be used inappropriately by programmers. Definitions need not be long. A single line is often enough if the parent entity is well defined.

A complete definition includes formatting and editing rules along with optionality (are null values allowed?) and key status (primary, foreign, candidate).

9.3.   ATTRIBUTE DISAGGREGATION – ONE FACT PER ATTRIBUTE

In Chapter 2 we introduced the basic rule for attribute disaggregation – one fact per attribute. It is almost never technically difficult to achieve this, and it generally leads to simpler programming, greater reuseability of data, and easier implementation of change.

Normalization relies on the rule being observed; otherwise we may find "dependencies," which are really dependencies on only part of an attribute. (For example, Bank Name may be determined by a three-part Bank-State-Branch Number, but closer examination might show that the dependency is only on the "Bank" part of the Number).

Why, then, is the rule so often broken in practice? Violations may occur for a variety of reasons, including:

1. failing to identify that an attribute can be decomposed into more fundamental attributes *that are of value to the business;*
2. attempting to achieve greater efficiency through data compression;
3. reflecting the fact that the compound attribute is more often used by the business than are its components;
4. relying on database management system or programming facilities to perform "trivial" decomposition when required;
5. confusing the way data is presented with the way it is stored;
6. difficulties with handling variable length and semistructured attributes (e.g., addresses);
7. changing the definition of attributes after the database is implemented as an alternative to changing the database design;
8. complying with external standards or practices; and
9. perpetuating past practices, which may have resulted originally from (1) through (8) above.

In my experience, most problems occur as a result of attribute definition being left to programmers or analysts with little knowledge of data modeling. In virtually all cases, a solution can be found that meets requirements without compromising the "one-fact-per-attribute" rule. Compliance with external standards or user wishes is likely to require little more than a translation table or some simple data formatting and unpacking between screen and database. However, as in most areas of data modeling, rigid adherence to the rule will occasionally compromise other objectives. For example, dividing a date attribute into components of Year, Month, and Day may make it difficult to use standard date manipulation routines. When conflicts arise, we need to go back to first principles and look at the total impact of each option.

The most common types of violation are:

9.3.1.   Simple Aggregation

An example of simple aggregation is an attribute Quantity Ordered which includes both the numeric quantity and the unit of measure (e.g., "12 cases"). Quite obviously, this aggregation of two different facts restricts our ability to compare quantities and perform arithmetic without having to "unpack" the data. Of course, if the business was only interested in Quantity Ordered as, for example, text to print on a label, we would have a good argument for treating it as a single attribute. A good test as to whether an attribute is fully decomposed is to ask:

1. Does the attribute correspond to a single business fact? (Answer should be yes.)
2. Can the attribute be further decomposed into attributes that themselves correspond to meaningful business facts? (Answer should be no.)
3. Are there business processes that update only part of the attribute? (Answer should be no.) We should also look at processes that read the attribute (e.g., for display or printing). However, if the reason for using only part of the attribute is merely to provide an abbreviation of the same fact as represented by the whole, there is little point in decomposing the attribute to reflect this.
4. Are there dependencies (potentially affecting normalization) that apply to only part of the attribute? (Answer should be no.)

Let's look at a more complex example in this light. A Person Name attribute might be a concatenation of salutation (Ms), family name (Deng), given names (Chan, Wei), and post nominals (MB BS, FRACP). Will the business want to treat given names individually (in which case we will regard them as forming a repeating group and normalize them out to separate entities)? Or will it be sufficient to separate "First Given Name" from "Other Given Names?" Should we separate the different qualifications represented by the postnominals? It depends on whether the business is genuinely interested in individual qualifications, or simply wants to address letters correctly. To answer these questions, we need to consider the needs of all potential users of the database, and employ some judgment as to likely future requirements.

Experienced data modelers are inclined to err on the side of disaggregation, even if familiar attributes are broken up in the process. The situation has parallels with normalization, in which familiar concepts (Invoice) are broken into less obvious components (Invoice Header, Invoice Line) to achieve a technically better structure. But most of us would not split First Given Name into Initial and Remainder of Name, even if there was a need to deal with the initials separately. We can verify this decision by using the questions suggested earlier:

"Does First Given Name correspond to a single business fact?" (Most people would agree that it does. This provides a strong argument that we are already at a "one-fact-per-attribute" level.)

"Can First Given Name be meaningfully decomposed?" (Initial has some real world significance, but only as an abbreviation for another fact. Rest of Name is unlikely to have any value to the business in itself.)

"Are there business processes that change the initial or the rest of the name independently?" (We would not expect this to be so; a change of name is a common business transaction, but we are unlikely to provide for "change of initial" or "change of rest of name" as distinct processes.)

"Are there likely to be any other attributes determined by (i.e., dependent on) Initial or Rest of Name?" (Probably no.)

On this basis, we would accept First Given Name as a "single fact" attribute.

9.3.2.   Complex Codes

We encountered a complex code in Chapter 2 with the Hospital Type attribute, which carried two pieces of information (whether the hospital was public or private, and whether it offered teaching services or not). Codes of this kind are not as easy to spot as simple aggregations, but they lead to more awkward programming and stability problems.

The problems arise when we want to deal with one of the underlying facts in isolation. Values may end up being included in program logic ("If Hospital Code equals 'T' or 'P' then ...") making change more difficult.

One apparent justification for complex codes is their value in enforcing data integrity. Only certain combinations of the component facts may be allowable, and we can easily enforce this by only defining codes for those combinations. (For example, private hospitals may not be allowed to have teaching facilities, so we simply do not define a code for "Private & Teaching.") This is a legitimate approach, but the data model should then specify a separate table (see section 9.5) to translate the codes into their components, in order to avoid the sort of programming mentioned earlier.

The constraint on allowed combinations can also be enforced by holding the attributes individually, and maintaining a look-up table of allowed combinations. Enforcement now requires that programmers follow the discipline of checking the look-up table. Note also that such a look-up table will not be produced by mechanical normalization (see Chapter 7).

9.3.3.   Meaningful Ranges

A special case of the complex codes situation results from assigning meaning not only to the value of the attribute, but to the (usually numeric) range in which it falls. For example, we may specify an attribute Status Code for an immigration application, then decide that values 10 through 50 are reserved for applications requiring special exemptions. What we actually have here is a hierarchy, with status codes subordinate to special exemption categories. In this example the hierarchy is two levels deep, but if we were to allocate meaning to subranges, subsubranges, and so on, the hierarchy would grow accordingly. The obvious, and correct, approach is to model the hierarchy explicitly.

Sometimes, ranges are allocated as a means of ensuring uniqueness of a primary key. This is a legitimate approach, often used when data is captured by independent, perhaps geographically scattered systems for later consolidation ("Policy Numbers 800,000 to 850,000 are reserved for the Northern Territory branch"). The important thing is not to attach meaning to the ranges when using the data. This problem is discussed further in Chapter 8.

Variants of the "meaningful range" problem occur from time to time, and should be treated in the same way. An example is a "meaningful lengths"; in one database I worked with, a four-character job number identified a permanent job while a five-character job number indicated a job of fixed duration.

9.3.4.   Inappropriate Generalization

Every COBOL programmer can cite cases where data items have been inappropriately redefined, often to save a few bytes of space, or to avoid reorganizing a file to make room for a new item. The same occurs under other file management and database management systems, often even less elegantly. (COBOL at least provides an explicit facility for redefinition; relational databases allow only one column name.)

The result is usually a data item that has no overall meaning except in terms of its specialized parts: for example, an attribute of Client, which means "Gender" for personal clients and "Industry Category" for company clients. Such a generalized item is unlikely to be used anywhere in the system without some program logic to determine which of its two meanings is appropriate.

Again, we complicate programming, in exchange for a notional space saving, and enforcement of the constraint that the attributes are mutually exclusive. These are seldom adequate compensation. In fact, data compression at the physical level may allow most of the "wasted" space to be retrieved in any case. On the other hand, few would argue with the value of generalizing, say, Assembly Price and Component Price if we had already decided to generalize the entities Assembly and Component to Product.

But not all attribute generalization decisions are so straightforward. In the next section, we look at the factors that contribute to making the most appropriate choice.

9.4.   ATTRIBUTE GENERALIZATION

9.4.1.   Options and Trade-Offs

In Chapter 4, we looked at entity generalization (and its converse, specialization), and the use of supertypes and subtypes to represent the results. Recall that higher levels of generalization meant fewer entities, fewer rules within the data structure, and greater resilience to change. On the other hand, specialization provided a more detailed picture of data and enforcement of more business rules, but less stability in the face of changes to these rules.

The best design was necessarily a trade-off among these different features. Making the best choice started with being aware of the different possibilities (by showing them as subtypes and supertypes on the model), rather than merely recording the first or most obvious option.

Much the same trade-offs apply to attribute definition. In some cases, the decision is largely predetermined by decisions taken at the entity level – we generalize two or more entities, then review their attributes to look for opportunities for generalization. In other cases, the discovery that attributes belonging to different entities are used in the same way may prompt us to consider generalizing their parent entities.

Alternatively, close examination of the attributes of a single entity may suggest that the entity could usefully be subtyped. One or more attributes may have a distinct meaning for a specific subset of entity instances (e.g., Ranking, Last Review Date, and Special Agreement Number apply only to those Suppliers who have *Preferred Supplier* status). Often a set of attributes will be null under certain conditions. We need to look at the conditions, and decide whether they provide a basis for entity subtyping.

Generalizing attributes *within* an entity can also affect the overall shape of the model. For example, we might generalize Standard Price, Trade Price, and Preferred Customer Price to Price. The generalized attributes will then become a repeating group, requiring us to separate them out in order to preserve first normal form (as discussed in Chapter 2).

Finally, at the attribute level, *consistency* of format, coding, naming, etc., is an important consideration, particularly when we are dealing with a large number of attributes. The starting point for consistency is generalization: Without recognizing that several attributes are in some sense similar, we cannot recognize the need to handle them consistently. In turn, consistent naming practiCes may highlight opportunities for generalization.

Some examples will illustrate these ideas.

9.4.2. Attribute Generalization Resulting From Entity Generalization

Figure 9-1 shows a simple example of entity generalization/specialization. The generalization of Company and Person to Client may have been suggested by their common attributes; equally it may have resulted from our knowledge that the two are handled similarly. Alternatively, we may have worked top-down, starting with the Client entity and looking for subtypes. The subtyping may have been prompted by noting that some of the attributes of Client were applicable only to people, and others only to companies.

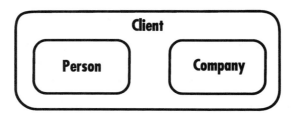

CLIENT (<u>Client ID</u>, Name, Title, Address, Responsible Salesperson, Date of Birth, Gross Income, Annual Turnover, Date of Incorporation, Occupation, Industry Code)

Figure 9-1. Allocating Attributes among Subtypes

Our initial task is to allocate attributes among the three entities. We have three options for each attribute:

1. Allocate the attribute to one of the subtypes only. We do this if the attribute can apply only to that subtype. For example, we may allocate Date of Birth to Person only.

2. Allocate the attribute to the supertype only. We do this if the attribute can apply to all of the subtypes, and has essentially the same meaning wherever it is used. For example, Address might be allocated to Client.

3. Hedge our bets! Allocate the attribute to the supertype *and* the relevant subtypes. Indicate that the attributes are related in the documentation. We do this if the attribute has a different meaning in each case, but not so different that we cannot see any value in generalization. For example, we might allocate Name to all three entities, on the basis that some processes will handle the names of both persons and companies in the same way (e.g., "display client details") while others will be specific to company or person names (e.g., "print envelope for person, including title").

If we are thorough about this, handling of attributes when we level the model (by selecting the final level of generalization for each entity) will be reasonably straightforward. If we follow the largely intuitive "inheritance" and "roll up" rules in Chapter 4, the only issue in leveling the model will be what to do in situation (3) if we implement at the supertype level. We will then have to decide whether to specify a single generalized attribute, or retain the distinct attributes as rolled up from the subtypes.

A good guide is to look closely at the reasons for selecting the higher level of generalization for the entity. Are we anticipating further, as yet unidentified, subtypes? If so, will they require a corresponding attribute? Have we decided that the subtypes are subject to common processes? How do these processes use the attribute in question? In practice, I tend to carry through the entity generalization to the attribute more often than not.

I also find frequently that I haven't been as thorough as I should have been in spotting possible attribute generalizations. Once the entity level has been decided upon, it's worth reviewing all of the attributes "rolled up" from subtype entities to ensure that opportunities for generalization have not been overlooked.

9.4.3. Attribute Generalization Within Entities

Opportunities for attribute generalization can arise quite independently of entity generalization.

The Financial Performance table in Figure 9-2 represents data about budgeted and annual expenditure on a quarterly basis.

FINANCIAL PERFORMANCE

(Department No.
Year
Approved By
Budget First Quarter Material
Budget Second Quarter Material
Budget Third Quarter Material
Budget Last Quarter Material
Actual First Quarter Material
Actual Second Quarter Material
Actual Third Quarter Material
Actual Total Material
Budget First Quarter Labor
Budget Second Quarter Labor
Budget Third Quarter Labor
Budget Last Quarter Labor
Actual First Quarter Labor
Actual Second Quarter Labor
Actual Third Quarter Labor
Actual Total Labor
Budget Other
Actual Other
Discretionary Spending Limit)

Figure 9-2. Financial Performance Table Prior to Attribute Generalization

The opportunities for attribute generalization here are sufficiently obvious that it's worth pointing out that the structure as it stands *is* a legitimate option, usable without further generalization. In particular, it is in, at least, first normal form. Technically, there are no repeating groups in the structure, despite the temptation to view, for example, the four material budget items as a repeating group. Doing this requires that we bring to bear our knowledge of the problem domain, and recognize the items as representing *at some level of generalization*, the "same thing."

Having conceded that the structure is at least workable, we can be a bit more critical, and note some problems with resilience to change. Suppose we were to make a business decision to move to monthly rather than quarterly reporting, or to include some other budget category besides "labor," "material," and "other" – perhaps "external subcontracts." Changing the table structures and corresponding programs would be a major task, particularly if the possible generalizations had not been recognized even at the program level; in other words, if we had written separate program logic to handle each quarter, or to handle labor figures in contrast to material figures. Perhaps this seems an unlikely scenario; on the contrary, I have seen very similar structures on many occasions in practice.

Let's start our generalization with the four material budget attributes. We make two decisions here.

First, we confirm that there is value in treating all four in a similar way; that there are business processes that handle first, second, third, and last quarter budgets in much the same way. If this is so, we make the generalization to Material Quarterly Budget Amount, noting that the new attribute occurs four times. We flag this as a repeating group to be normalized out. Because sequence within the group is important, we need to add a new attribute Quarter Number. Another way of looking at this is that we have removed some information from the data structure (the words first, second, third, and last) and need to provide a new place to store that information; hence the additional attribute.

Second, we relax the upper limit of four. We know that normalization is going to remove the constraint in any case, so we might as well recognize the situation explicitly and consider its consequences. In this example, the effect is that we are no longer constrained to quarterly budgets, so we need to change the name of the attributes accordingly – "Material Budget Amount" and "Period Number."

We can now remove the repeating group, creating a new table Material Budget Item (Figure 9-3).

MATERIAL BUDGET ITEM (<u>Department No</u>, <u>Year</u>, <u>Period Number</u>, Material Budget Amount)

Figure 9-3. Material Budget Table

The example thus far has illustrated the main results of attribute generalization within an entity:

1. The increased flexibility obtainable through sensible generalization.
2. The need to add data items to hold information taken out of the data structure by generalization.
3. The creation of new entities to normalize out the repeating groups resulting from generalization.

Continuing with the financial results example, we could apply the same process to labor and other budget items, and to material, labor, and other actual items, producing a total of seven tables as in Figure 9-4.

In doing this, we would notice that there was no attribute named Actual Fourth Quarter Material. Instead we have Actual Total Material. This does break any data modeling rules, since one value could be derived from the others. But if we choose to generalize, we will have to replace the "total" attribute with a "fourth quarter" attribute to make generalization possible. Even if we decide not to model the more generalized structure, we are likely to change the attribute anyway, for the sake of consistency. It is important to recognize that this "common sense" move to consistency *relies on our having seen the possibility of generalization in the first place*. To achieve consistency, we need to recognize first that the attributes have something in common.

There is a flavor of creative data modeling here too. We deliberately choose a particular attribute representation in order to provide an opportunity for generalization.

FINANCIAL PERFORMANCE (<u>Department No</u>, <u>Year</u>, Approved By, Discretionary Spending Limit)
MATERIAL BUDGET ITEM (<u>Department No</u>, <u>Year</u>, <u>Period Number</u>, Material Budget Amount)
LABOR BUDGET ITEM (<u>Department No</u>, Year, <u>Period Number</u>, Labor Budget Amount)
OTHER BUDGET ITEM (<u>Department No</u>, <u>Year</u>, <u>Period Number</u>, Other Budget Amount)
MATERIAL ACTUAL ITEM (<u>Department No</u>, <u>Year</u>, <u>Period Number</u>, Material Actual Amount)
LABOR ACTUAL ITEM (<u>Department No</u>, <u>Year</u>, <u>Period Number</u>, Labor Actual Amount)
OTHER ACTUAL ITEM (<u>Department No</u>, <u>Year</u>, <u>Period Number</u>, Other Actual Amount)

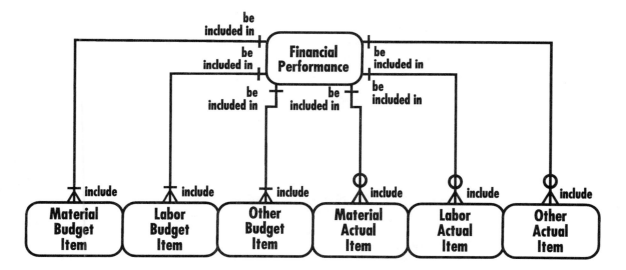

Figure 9-4. Budget and Actual Data Separated

Inconsistencies that become visible as a result of trying to generalize may suggest useful questions to be asked of the user. Why, for instance, are "other" budgets and expenditures recorded on an annual basis rather than quarterly? Do we want to bring them into line with labor and materials? Alternatively, do we need to provide for labor and materials also being reported at different intervals?

We can take generalization further, bringing together labor, material, and other budgets, and doing likewise for actuals. We gain the flexibility to introduce new types of financial reporting, but will need to add Budget Item Type and Actual Item Type attributes to replace the information lost from the data structure (Figure 9-5). Note that we can do this either by supertyping the entities in Figure 9-4, or generalizing the attributes in the original model of Figure 9-2.

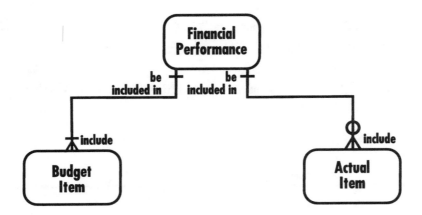

FINANCIAL PERFORMANCE (<u>Department No</u>, <u>Year</u>, Approved By, Discretionary Spending Limit)

BUDGET ITEM (<u>Department No</u>, <u>Year</u>, <u>Period Number</u>, <u>Budget Item Type</u>, Budget Amount)

ACTUAL ITEM (<u>Department No</u>, <u>Year</u>, <u>Period Number</u>, <u>Actual Item Type</u>, Actual Amount)

Figure 9-5. Generalization of Labor, Material, and Other Data

Finally, we could consider generalizing budget and actual data. After all, they are represented by identical structures. When I present this example on training courses, there is often strong support for doing this, perhaps because we have been doing so well with generalization to that point! But we need to ask: Does the business have processes that treat budget and actual items in much the same way? Is there the possibility of a new category (in addition to "budget" and "actual") arising that can take advantage of existing processes? Chances are that the answer to both is no, and we may achieve only unnecessary obscurity by generalizing any further. The data model may look elegant, but the program logic needed to unravel the different data will not. The best approach is to look always at how the business treats the data, using commonality of shape only as a prompt, not as a final arbiter.

9.4.4.   Limits to Attribute Generalization

In the preceding example, we reached the point of limited further gains from generalization while we still had a number of distinct attributes. But there are situations in which a higher level of attribute generalization is justified. Figure 9-6 shows an example of a very high level of attribute generalization, in which all attributes are generalized to a single "Parameter Value" attribute, and subsequently removed as a repeating group. I've called the new entity Parameter Value rather than Attribute – an entity named Attribute is not going to do much for communication with the uninitiated!

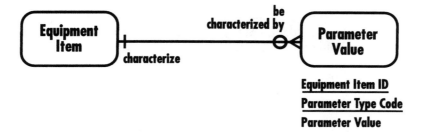

Figure 9-6. Highly Generalized Attributes

This is the attribute level equivalent of the Thing entity (Chapter 4). It has application when structures are genuinely unstable and unpredictable. In this example, every time we purchased a new type of equipment, we might want to record new attributes: perhaps bandwidth, range, tensile strength, or mean time between failures. Rather than add new attributes to Equipment Item, we simply record new values for Parameter Type Code.

Commercial software packages may employ high levels of generalization to support "user-defined attributes." I have seen the technique used very successfully in product databases, allowing new products with unanticipated attributes to be defined very quickly without altering the database structure. But I have also seen it used far too often as a substitute for rigorous analysis. You need to keep in mind the following:

1. Some of the entity's attributes may be stable and handled in a distinct way. Model them separately, and don't include them in the generic repeating group.

2. Consider subtyping Parameter Value based on data type, e.g., Numeric Parameter Value, Text Parameter Value.

3. You will need to add attributes to replace the information removed from the data structure. This includes anything you would normally specify for an attribute, including name, format, editing rules, and optionality. These become attributes initially of the Parameter entity, then, through normalization, of a Parameter Type entity (Figure 9-7). Parameter Types can be related to Equipment Types (not shown) to specify which parameter types are applicable to each type of equipment (see Chapter 11 for examples of this technique).

4. The technique is only useful if the different parameter types can utilize common program code. If not, you may as well make the change to the system in the conventional fashion by modifying the database and writing the necessary code. Good candidates for the parameter approach are attributes that are simply entered and displayed, rather than those which drive or are involved in more complex logic.

5. Programs will need to be suitably parameter-driven, to the extent that you may need to support run-time decisions on screen and report formatting. You will need to look hard at how well your tool set supports the approach. Many program generators cannot effectively handle challenges of this kind. Even human programmers will need guidance from someone very familiar with the data model if they are to exploit it properly.

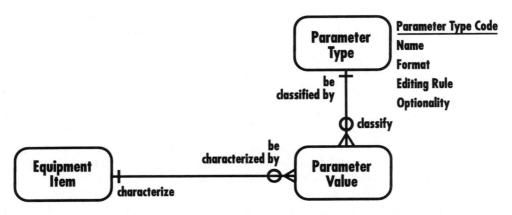

Figure 9-7. Highly Generalized Attributes with Look-Up Table

9.5.   DOMAINS, CONSTRAINTS, AND LOOK-UP TABLES

A domain is essentially the set of values that an attribute may legitimately take. For an attribute that represents a quantity or amount, the domain may be specified as a range of allowed values. System-generated keys may have as their domains a predetermined range of integers. Foreign keys will be subject to the same domain as their corresponding primary keys, or a subset of that domain . For nonnumeric descriptive attributes such as Gender, Status Code, and Country Code, the domain is likely to be a simple list of allowed values.

This broad classification of attributes into keys, quantities, and descriptions corresponds roughly to that advocated by Tasker.[1]

Simple range checks do not usually cause much difficulty. It's basically a matter of documenting the rules with their corresponding attributes, and using facilities provided by the database management system to enforce them. In the event that such facilities are not available, a single table "data dictionary" will usually suffice to record attribute names and ranges for checking at run-time. Alternatively, we can use the time-honored method of writing the checks into program logic.

Most of the issues that arise in practice concern domains for descriptive attributes.

---

[1] Tasker, D., *Fourth Generation Data – A Guide to Data Analysis for New and Old Systems*, Prentice Hall, Australia (1989).

9.5.1. Coding of Descriptive Attributes

Having decided that we require a descriptive attribute such as Account Status, we need to determine the set of possible values and how we will represent them. For example, allowed statuses might be "Active," "Closed," and "Suspended." Should we use these words as they stand, or introduce a coding scheme, such as "A", "C" and "S" or "1", "2", and "3" to represent "Active," "Closed," and "Suspended?"

Most practitioners would introduce a coding scheme automatically, in line with conventional practice since the early days of data processing. They would also need to provide somewhere in the system (using the word "system" in its broadest sense to include manual files, processes, and human knowledge) a translation mechanism to code and decode the fully descriptive terms.

Given the long tradition of coding, it's worth looking at what it actually achieves:

First, and most obviously, we save space. "A" is more concise than "Active." The analyst responsible for dialogue design may well make the coding scheme visible to the user, as one means of saving key strokes and reducing errors.

We also improve flexibility, in terms of our ability to add new codes in a consistent fashion. We don't have the problem of finding that a new value of Account Status is a longer word than we have allowed for.

The list of codes and their meanings can be incorporated into the system in a disciplined way. For example, we can refer to the list when vetting input data, and add new values and codes by adding to the list. This argument is less strong than it might appear at first glance, as there is nothing to stop us from simply maintaining a single-column table of allowed values. In practice, such tables are rarely seen, probably because normalization will not produce them, and they may not appear to hold any extra data.

Probably the most important benefit of using codes is the ability to change the text description of a code while retaining its meaning. Perhaps we wish to rename the "Suspended" status "Under Review." This sort of thing happens as organizational terminology changes, sometimes to conform to industry standards and practices. The coding approach provides us with a level of insulation, so that we distinguish a change in the meaning of a code (update translation table) from a change in actual status of an account (update Account table).

To achieve this distinction, we need to be sure that the code can remain stable if the full description changes. Use of initial letters, or indeed anything derived from the description itself, will interfere with this objective. How many times have you seen coding schemes that only partially follow some rule, because changes or later additions have been impossible to accommodate?

The issues of code definition are much the same as those of primary key definition, discussed in Chapter 8. This is hardly surprising, as a code is the primary key of a computerized or external look-up table.

9.5.2.   Simple Look-Up Tables

As soon as we introduce a coding scheme for data, we need to provide for a method of coding and decoding. In some cases, we may make this a human responsibility, relying on users of the computerized system to memorize or look up the codes themselves. Another option is to build the translation rules into programs. The third option is to include a table for this purpose as part of the database design. Such tables are commonly referred to as "look-up tables" by analogy with manual records in which we "look up" the meanings of codes.

In practice, I make a point of considering an entity for each code set in the initial data model. It's not as daunting a task as it may sound, and it forces me to think about how the translation mechanism will be handled in each case. However, in presenting a model, I frequently omit these domain entities in order to reduce the complexity of the diagram.

There are certain circumstances in which the look-up table approach should be strongly favored:

1.   If the number of different code values is large enough to make human memory, manual look-up, and programming approaches cumbersome. At 100 values, you are well into this territory.
2.   If the set of code values is subject to change. This tends to go hand in hand with large numbers of values. Changing a data value is simpler than updating code, or keeping people and manual documents up to date.
3.   If we want to hold further data about the code that is to be used by the system at run-time (as distinct from documentary data for the benefit of programmers, etc.) For example, we may need to hold a more complete description of the meaning of each code value for inclusion in reports, or maintain "Applicable From" and "Applicable To" dates.
4.   If the entity has relationships with other entities in the model, besides the obvious relationship to the entity in which the code is primarily used (see Section 9.5.4).

Conversely, the look-up table approach is less attractive if we need to "hard code" actual values into program logic. Adding new values will then necessitate changes to the logic, so the advantage of being able to add values without affecting programs is lost.

9.5.3.   Generalization of Look-Up Tables

The entities that specify look-up tables tend to follow a standard format: Code, Full Name, and possibly Description. This suggests the possibility of generalization, and I have frequently seen models that specify a single supertype look-up table (which, incidentally, should not be named "Look-Up Table," but something like "Code" in keeping with our rule of naming entities according to the meaning of a single instance).

Again, we need to go back to basics, and ask whether the various code types are subject to common processes. The answer is usually yes as far as their update is concerned, but the enquiry pattern is likely to be less consistent. A consolidated look-up table offers the possibility of a generic code update module, and easy addition of new code types, not inconsiderable benefits when you have seen the alternative of individual program modules for each code type. Views can provide the subtype level pictures required for enquiry.

Be ready for an argument with the physical database designer if you recommend implementation at the supertype level. The generalized table may well cause an access bottleneck. As always, you will want to see evidence that this is so, and will need to negotiate trade-offs accordingly. Programmers may also object to the less obvious programming required if full advantage is to be taken of the generalized design. On the other hand, I have seen generalization of all look-up tables proposed by database administrators as a general rule.

And, as usual, recognizing the generalization is valuable even if the supertype isn't implemented directly. You may still be able to write or clone generic programs to handle update more consistently and at reduced development cost.

9.5.4. Interdomain Constraints

We sometimes wish to enforce constraints on the *combinations* of values that two or more attributes can take. For example, the entity Job might have attributes Job Type and Risk Level, but only certain combinations of the two might be allowable. *One way* of handling this situation is to introduce a new code for each legitimate combination. This introduces an intermediate level of coding between the look-up tables and the entity, resulting in the structure of Figure 9-8.

Some DBMSs provide direct support for describing constraints across multiple attributes as part of the database structure definition. In my experience, however, such constraints are frequently volatile, and therefore better held as data values, which brings us back to tables again.

Chapter 11 is a fuller discussion of techniques for modeling rules in general. Much of the advice is relevant to enforcing constraints across attributes.

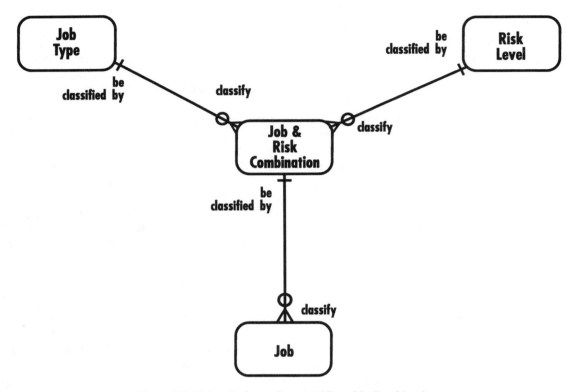

Figure 9-8. Using Codes to Restrict Allowable Combinations

9.6.   ATTRIBUTE NAMES

9.6.1.   Objectives of Standardizing Attribute Names

Much fuss is made about attribute names. Many organizations have put in place detailed standards for attribute naming, typically comprising lists of component words with definitions, standard abbreviations, and rules for stringing them together. Needless to say, there has been much "reinvention of the wheel." Names and abbreviations tend to be organization-specific, so most of the common effort has been in deciding sequence, connectors, and the minutiae of punctuation. IBM's "OF" language, originally proposed in the early 1970s, has been particularly influential. Attribute names constructed using the OF language consist of a single "class word" drawn from a short standard list (Date, Name, Flag, etc.) and one or more organization-defined "modifiers," separated by connectors (primarily "of" and "which is" – hence the name). Examples of names constructed using the OF language are "Date of Birth," "Name of Person," and "Amount which is Discount of Product which is Retail." Some of these names are more natural and familiar than others!

The objectives of an attribute-naming standard are usually to:

1. reduce ambiguity in interpreting the meaning of attributes (the name serving as a short form of documentation);
2. reduce the possibility of "synonyms" – two or more attributes with the same meaning but different names; and
3. reduce the possibility of "homonyms" – two or more attributes with the same name but different meanings.

The first objective makes reasonably good sense, although no naming convention completely eliminates the need for supporting definitions.

The second and third objectives are of less concern in practice than the proponents of naming standards might have us believe. Although we may deal with many hundreds or thousands of attributes, these should be grouped under entities, giving us a very significant start in identifying duplication. A further categorization by class word (as mentioned above) can usually reduce the problem to an easily managed level without any recourse to fully standardized names.

9.6.2. Some Guidelines for Attribute Naming

The naming standard you adopt may be influenced by the facilities provided by your CASE tool or data dictionary, and by earlier practices. Here are some basic guidelines and options:

1. Whether or not to include the name of the entity in the attribute name continues to be a matter of debate, probably because there is no overwhelming reason for choosing either option over the other. Workable variants (not mutually exclusive) include:
    Using the "home" entity name as the first word or words of the attribute name. The term "home" entity is introduced to cater to foreign keys, whose home entities are those in which they appear as primary keys, and for attributes inherited or rolled up from supertypes and subtypes. So attributes of Vehicle might include *Vehicle* Registration Number, *Asset* Purchase Date (inherited), *Truck* Capacity (rolled up), and *Organization Unit* Code Responsible (foreign key).
    Not using supertype or subtype entity names at all, or at least not in primary and foreign keys;
    Using entity names only in primary and foreign keys;
    Using entity names only in foreign keys.
2. Prefix foreign keys according to the name of the relationship they implement: e.g., *Issuing* Branch No, *Responsible* Branch No. This is not always easy, and it is reasonable to bend the rule if the relationship is obvious and the name clumsy, or an alternative role name is available (e.g., *Advanced* Customer No, meaning the key of the customer to whom a loan was advanced, could be better named Borrower (Customer) No).

3. Build a standard list of modifiers, and a separate short list of class words, as per the OF language, both with definitions. The objective is to avoid using different words for the same thing. The class word list can use the original IBM OF language as a guide, but examine the original list with a critical eye first. Your list needs to cover (at least):
    Unique and non-unique identifiers (ID, Name, Code)
    Numeric amounts (quantity, money amount, ratios)
    Description (text at least)
    Dates
    Try to select words that will result in minimum disruption to existing terminology.

4. Avoid abbreviations in attribute names, unless they are widely understood in your organization (by business people!) or you are truly constrained by your CASE tool or data dictionary. It's very likely that the DBMS will impose length and punctuation constraints. These apply to *columns*, not to attributes!

5. Don't feel obliged to include a Class Word in every name. In some cases, another word implies the class quite clearly: hence Communication Link Traffic Volume rather than Communication Link Traffic Volume Quantity. However, it is well worth supplementing the class word list with such implications: does "Rate" imply "Amount" or "Percentage"; does "Value" imply "Amount" or "Quantity?"

6. Sequence words using the "reverse" variation of the IBM OF language. The traditional way of achieving this is to string together the words using "which is" and "of" as connectors, to produce an OF language name, then to reverse the order and eliminate the connectors.
    For example an attribute to represent the average annual dividend amount for a stock could be (using OF language):
    Amount of Dividend which is Average which is Annual of Stock
    Reversing gives:
    Stock Average Annual Dividend Amount.
    This is pretty painful, but with a little practice you can move directly to the reverse OF language name, which usually sounds reasonable, at least to an information systems professional!

7. Don't throw away well-known names unless there are real ambiguity problems.

8. Look hard at any proposal to use "aliases" i.e., synonyms to assist access. This is really a data dictionary management issue rather than a modeling one, but take note that alias facilities are often established but relatively seldom used.

9. Establish a simple translation from attribute names to column names. Here is where abbreviations come in.

In the pursuit of consistency and purity, don't lose sight of one of the fundamental objectives of modeling: communication. Sometimes we must sacrifice rigid adherence to standards for familiarity and better-quality feedback from non-technical participants in the modeling process. Conversely, it is sometimes valuable to introduce a new term to replace a familiar, but ambiguous term.

A final word on attribute names. If establishing a data dictionary, do not use Attribute Name as the primary key for the table containing details of Attributes. Names and even naming standards will change from time to time, and we need to be able to distinguish a change in attribute name from the creation of a new attribute. A simple meaningless identifier will do the job – it need not be visible to anyone. Most CASE tools and data dictionaries support this; a few do not.

9.7. SUMMARY

Each attribute should represent one fact type only. The most common types of violations are simple aggregations, complex codes, meaningful ranges, and inappropriate generalization.

There is value in exploring different levels of generalization for attributes. Attributes can be allocated to different levels of the entity subtype hierarchy, and will influence the choice of level for implementation. Attributes belonging to the same entity may also be generalized, possibly resulting in repeating groups, which will be separated by normalization.

Attribute coding should follow the same basic principles as primary key definition: codes should be unique, stable, and singular. Look-up tables may be implemented to support interpretation and verification of code values.

Attribute naming should be guided, but not necessarily constrained, by a set of standards. The IBM OF language provides a useful starting point.

10

The Time Dimension

10.1. THE PROBLEM

Few areas of data modeling are the subject of as much confusion as the handling of time-related data.

Perhaps we're modeling data for an insurance company. It's certainly important for us to know the current status of a client's insurance policy – how much is insured and what items are covered. But in order to handle claims for events that happened some time ago, we need to be able to determine the status at any given date in the past.

Or, we may want to support planning of a railway network, and be able to represent how the network will look at various times in the future.

Underlying these questions is the concept of effective dates, past or future, and how we handle them in a data model.

A closely related issue is the maintenance of "audit trails": a history of changes to the databases, and of the transactions that caused them. What cash flows contributed to the current balance? Why was a customer's credit rating downgraded?

The difficulties that even experienced data modelers encounter in these areas are often the result of trying to find a simple recipe for "adding the time dimension" to a model. There are two problems with this approach: first, the initial model usually includes time-dependent data already, and second, we seldom need to maintain a full history and set of past positions for *everything* in the database.

In this chapter we look at some basic principles and structures for handling time-related data. You should be able to solve most problems you encounter in practice by selectively employing combinations of these. Once again, the choice of the best approach in a given situation is not always straightforward, and, as in all our modeling, we need to actively explore and compare alternatives.

10.2.   AUDIT TRAILS AND SNAPSHOTS

Let's start with a very simple example – a single entity. Our client is an investor, and the entity Share Holding represents their holdings of each share type (Figure 10-1).

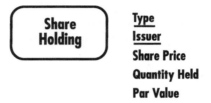

Figure 10-1. Model of Current Share Holdings

As it stands, the model enables us to record the *current* quantity and price of each type of share. But we may also need to hold data about past holdings and prices, to support queries such as "how many shares in company xyz did we hold on July 1, 1992?" or "by how much has the total value of our investments changed in the past month?"

There are essentially two ways of achieving this:

1.   Record details of each *change* to a share holding – the "audit trail" approach; or
2.   Include an "effective date" attribute in the Share Holding entity, and record new instances either periodically or each time there is a change – the "snapshot" approach.

If you are familiar with accounting, you can think of these as "profit and loss" and "balance sheet" approaches, respectively. Balance sheets are snapshots of a business's position at particular times, while profit and loss statements summarize changes to that position.

10.2.1   The Basic Audit Trail Approach

We'll start with the audit trail approach. Let's make the reasonable assumption that we want to keep track not only of changes, but of the events that cause them. This suggests the three-entity model of Figure 10-2. Note that Share Holding represents *current* share holdings.

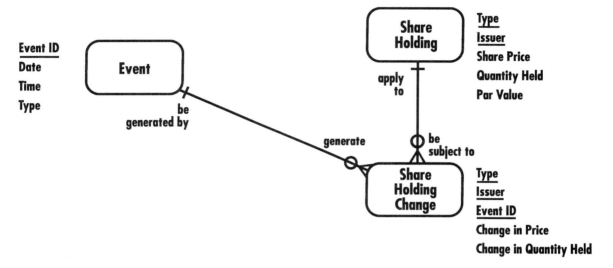

Figure 10-2. Basic Audit Trail Approach

This is the basic audit trail solution, and often quite workable as it stands. But there are a number of variations we can make to it.

Event is a very generic entity that may be usefully subtyped to reflect different sets of attributes and associated processes. In this example we might model separate entities for purchase, sale, rights issue, bonus issue, revaluation, etc.

There is often value in grouping events into higher level events, or, conversely, breaking them down into component events. For example, we might group a number of different share purchases into the aggregate event "company takeover," or break them down into individual parcels. We can model this with a variable or fixed-depth hierarchy – e.g., a recursive relationship on Event, or separate entities for Aggregate Event, Basic Event, and Component Event, suitably defined and/or subtyped.

In some circumstances, we may not require the Event entity at all. Attributes of the Share Holding Change entity (typically Date and Time, or External Reference Number) can sometimes provide all the data we need about the source of the change. One common situation in which this is likely to be so is when values are recorded at predetermined intervals. For example, we might record share prices on a daily basis, rather than each time there was a movement.

Another possibility is that each event affects only one share holding – i.e., generates only one share holding change. We can very often propose workable definitions of Event to make this so. For example, we could choose to regard a bundled purchase of shares of different types as several distinct "purchase events." This reduces the relationship between Event and Share Holding Change to a mandatory, non-transferable one-to-one, and suggests combining the two entities (see Section 6.4). Figure 10-3 shows the result.

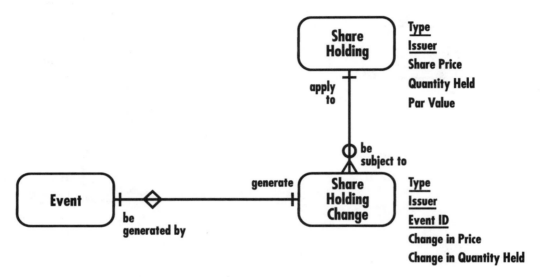

Figure 10-3. Event Defined as Generating Only One Change

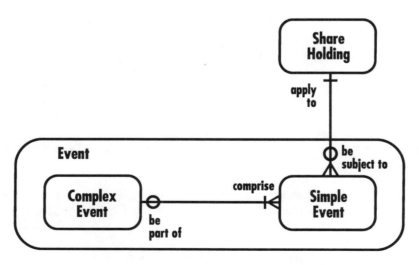

Figure 10-4. Separating Complex and Simple Events

Even if some types of event do cause more than one change, we can extend the model to accommodate them as in Figure 10-4.

Returning to the model in Figure 10-2, Share Holding Change can also be subtyped to distinguish price changes from quantity changes (Figure 10-5).

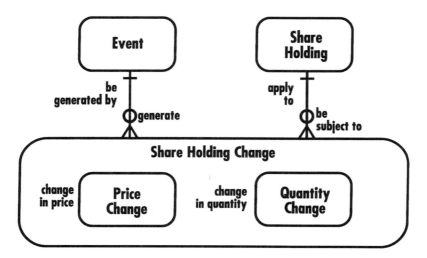

Figure 10-5. Subtyping to Reflect Different Types of Changes

With only two attributes, our choices are straightforward, but as the number of attributes increases, so does the variety of subtyping options. It can be helpful to look at the different types of events (whether formal subtypes or not) and the combination of attributes that each affects. This will often suggest subtypes based on groups of attributes which are affected by particular types of events. For example, "Share Acquisition" might be suggested by the Event Subtypes "Share Purchase," "Bonus Issue," "Rights Issue," and "Transfer In." But you do need to look closely at the stability of these groups of attributes. If they reflect well-established business events, there may be no problem, but if they are based around, for example, our current breakup of a dialogue, we may find ourselves changing the database structure simply because we want to update an attribute at a different point in the dialogue.

The Share Holding entity not only contains the current values of all attributes, but is the only place in which any static attributes (other than the primary key) need to be held. For example, the Par Value of the share never changes, and therefore should not appear in Share Holding Change.

Instead of defining Share Holding as representing current share holdings, we could have used it to represent *initial* share holdings (Figure 10-6).

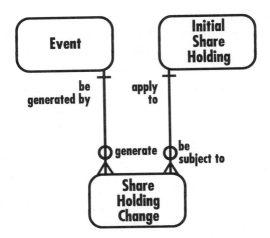

Figure 10-6. Model Based on Changes to Initial Share Holding

In one way this is more elegant, as updates will need only to create rows in the Event and Share Holding Change tables – they will not need to update the Initial Share Holding. On the other hand, inquiries on the current position require that it be built up by applying all changes to the initial holding. Note also that the collection of all the instances of Initial Share Holding will not represent our "opening position"; rather, they represent the opening position plus the initial quantities and values of each share acquired since.

One very important assumption in the model of Figure 10-6 is that Events and Share Holding Changes cannot themselves be updated (or, at least, that we are not interested in keeping any history of such changes). Imagine for a moment that we *could* update the attributes of Share Holding Change. Then we would need to extend the model to include "Share Holding Change Change" to keep track of these changes, and so on until we reached a "nonupdatable" entity – one in which each instance, once recorded, never changed. So an interesting feature of the audit trail approach to modeling time-dependent data is that it relies on defining some data that is invariant.

In our example, it's difficult to envision any business event that would cause the values of Share Holding Change attributes to change. But there is always the possibility that we record some data in error (perhaps we have miskeyed a price change). We then have essentially three options:

1. Correct the data without keeping a history of the change. This is a simple solution, but it will cause reconciliation problems if reports have been issued or decisions made based on the incorrect data.

2. Maintain a separate history of "changes to changes." This complicates the model, but does separate business changes from error corrections.

  3. Allow for a "reversal" or "correction" event, which will create another
  Share Holding Change row. This is the approach used in accounting. This
  is often the cleanest solution to the problems of 1, above, and to situations
  where the correction event can cause more complex changes to the
  database (e.g., reversal of commission and government tax).

All of these approaches may be used, depending on the circumstances. The
important thing is to plan explicitly for changes resulting from error corrections as
well as those caused by the more usual business events.

10.2.2. Handling Nonnumeric Data

You may have noticed that I conveniently chose numeric attributes (Number of
Shares and Share Price) as the time-dependent data in the example. It makes sense
to talk about the change (increase or decrease) to a numeric attribute. But how do
we handle changes to the value of nonnumeric attributes – for example "Share
Holding Custodian?" One approach is to hold the value prior to the change, rather
than the amount of change. The value *after* the change will then be held either in
the next instance of Share Holding Change or in the Current Share Holding.

Holding the prior value is also an option when dealing with numeric data. We
could just as well have held "Previous Price" as "Change in Price." One will be
derivable from the other, and selecting the best option usually comes down to which
is more commonly required by the business processes, and perhaps maintaining a
consistency of approach – elegance again!

10.2.3. The Basic Snapshot Approach

The idea of holding prior values rather than changes provides a nice lead-in to the
"snapshot" approach.

One of the options available to us is to consistently hold prior values rather than
changes, to the extent that "no change" is represented by the prior value being the
same as the new value. If we take this approach, then Share Holding Changes start
to look very like Current Share Holdings as they stood prior to updating. The only
difference in the attributes is the inclusion of the event identifier or effective date,
and the exclusion of data that is not time-dependent, such as Par Value.

Share Holding Change is now badly named, as we are representing past positions,
rather than changes. "Historical Share Holding" is more appropriate (Figure 10-7).
This change of name reflects a change in the flavor of the model. Queries of the form
"what was the position at a particular date" are now supported in a very simple way
(just find the relevant Historical Share Holding), while queries about changes are
still supported, but require some calculation to assemble the data. If typical updates
to share holdings involve changes to only a small number of attributes, this snapshot
approach will be less tidy than an audit trail with subtypes: we will end up carrying
a lot of data just to indicate "no change."

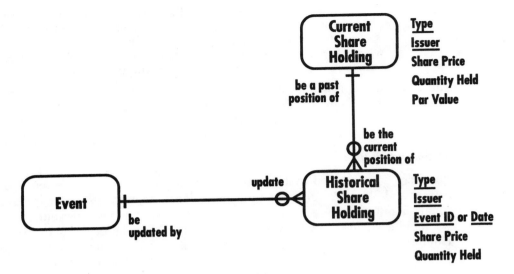

Figure 10-7. Basic Snapshot Approach

Note that the event associated with a particular historical share holding is the event that *ended* that set of attribute values – not the event that set them up. The relationship name "update" (in contrast to "create") reflects this. Another option is to link events to the historical share holding they *create*. In this case, we will also need to link Current Share Holding to Event (Figure 10-8).

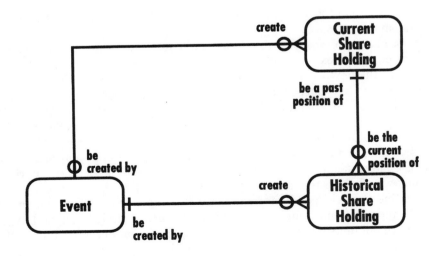

Figure 10-8. Linking Events to the Positions Which They Create

This gives us yet another option, with some advantages in elegance if the business is more interested (as it often is) in the event that *led* to a particular position.

Note that the two relationships to Event are now optional. This is because the initial share holding (which may be an instance of either Current Share Holding or Historical Share Holding) may represent an opening position, not created by any event we have recorded. Of course, we have the option of defining an "initialize" or "transfer in" event to set up the original holdings, in which case the two relationships would become mandatory.

The model as it now stands has at least two weaknesses. The first is the inelegance of having two separate relationships to Current Share Holding and Historical Share Holding. The second is more serious. Each time we create a new current share holding, we will need to create a historical share holding that is a copy of the previous current share holding. This is very close to breaking our rule of not transferring instances from one entity to another (Section 4.15.5).

We can overcome both problems by generalizing the two relationships, along with the two entities. We do this by first splitting out the time-dependent portion of Current Share Holding, using a one-to-one relationship, according to the technique described in Section 6.4.1. The result is shown in Figure 10-9.

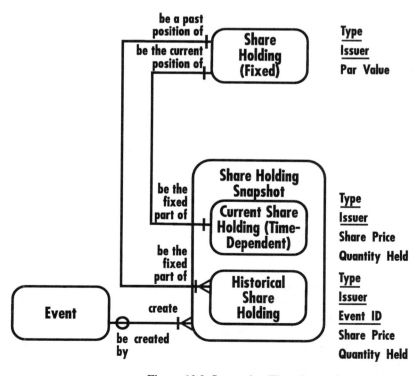

Figure 10-9. Separating Time-Dependent and Static Data

Historical Share Holding will have basically the same attributes as this extracted part of Current Share Holding, and there may well be important processes (e.g., portfolio valuation plotted over time) that treat the two in much the same way.

The Share Holding (Fixed) entity represents attributes that are not time-dependent, or for which we require only one value (perhaps the current value, perhaps the original value). If there are no such attributes besides the key, we will not require this entity at all. Nor will we require it if we take the "sledge hammer" approach of assuming at the outset that *all* data is time-dependent, and that we need to record all historical values.

We've now come quite some distance from our original audit trail approach. The path we took is a nice example of the use of creative modeling techniques. Along the way we've seen a number of ways of handling historical data, even for the simplest one-entity model. The one-entity example is quite general, and can easily be adapted to handle future positions (for example, the results of a planned share purchase) as well as (or instead of) past positions.

We often arrive at models like those discussed here without ever explicitly considering the time dimension. For example, a simple model of bank accounts and transactions is an example of the audit trail approach, and a "Staff Appraisal" entity, which represents multiple appraisals of the same person over time, is an example of the snapshot approach.

10.3.   DATES, VERSIONS, AND SEQUENCES

In our examples so far, we have used the term "time-dependent" in a very literal way, to mean that events, snapshots, and changes have an attribute of Date or Date and Time. We can equally apply these rules to sequences that are not explicitly or visibly tied to dates and times. For example, we may wish to keep track of software according to "Version No," or to record the effect of events that can be placed in sequence without specifying absolute times – perhaps the stages in a human-computer dialogue.

10.4.   HANDLING DELETIONS

Whether we take the audit trail approach, snapshot approach, or some hybrid of the two, we need to be able to accommodate to events that "delete" an entity instance, as well as those that merely change the values of its attributes. I've put "delete" in quotes, because we often don't want to simply delete the relevant row(s) from the database. This would effectively wipe out historical data which we may be interested in preserving, such as closed accounts or products no longer manufactured. Nor do we want to set all the attribute values to null, or use any other artifice that could be misinterpreted. The simplest solution is to add a "currency" or "deletion status" attribute. This attribute is then set to "noncurrent" or "deleted" to indicate that the data is no longer current.

Often these noncurrent entity instances will still have relevance in the context of relationships with other entities. For example, the country "East Germany" may no longer exist, and hence be flagged as non current; nevertheless it will still have meaning as a place of birth for a visa applicant.

It is possible for an entity instance to be deleted and then reinstated (see, for example, the Employee/Equipment Item example in Section 10.6.2). In these cases, we can simply keep a history of the currency attribute in the same way that we would for any other attribute.

10.5. ARCHIVING

In modeling time-dependent data, you need to take into account any archiving requirements, and the associated deletion of data from the database.

Snapshot approaches are generally amenable to having old data removed; it is even possible to retain selected "snapshots" from among the archived data. For example, we might remove daily snapshots from before a particular date, but retain the snapshots from the first day of each month, to provide a coarse history.

Audit trail approaches can be less easy to work with. If data is to be removed, it will need to be summarized into an aggregate "change" or "event," or a "starting point snapshot." Similarly, if a coarse history is required, it will be necessary to summarize intermediate events.

10.6. MODELING TIME-DEPENDENT RELATIONSHIPS

10.6.1. One-to-Many Relationships

We have now had a fairly good look at the simplest of models, the one-entity model. If we can extend this to a model of two entities linked by a relationship, we have covered the basic building blocks of a data model, and should be able to cope with any situation that arises. In fact, handling relationships requires no new techniques at all if we think of them as being represented by foreign keys: a change to a relationship is just a change to a (foreign key) data item.

So let's develop the share holding example further to include an entity representing the company that issued the shares (Figure 10-10).

We can use any of the preceding approaches to represent a history of changes to Company and Share Holding. Figure 10-11 shows the result of applying a version of the snapshot approach. The Event, Share Holding Snapshot, and Company Snapshot entities are a result of using the techniques for single-entity models. The new problem is what to do with the relationship between Company and Share Holding. In this case, we note that the "issued by" relationship is *nontransferable*, and hence is part of the *fixed* data about share holdings. (The foreign key – Issuer – will not change value for a given Share Holding).

We already hold the Company ID on Share Holding (Fixed), and the relationship is therefore between Share Holding (Fixed) and Company (Fixed), as shown.

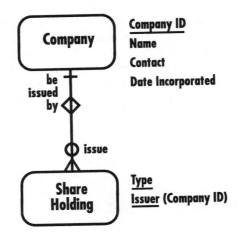

Figure 10-10. Companies and Shares - Current Position

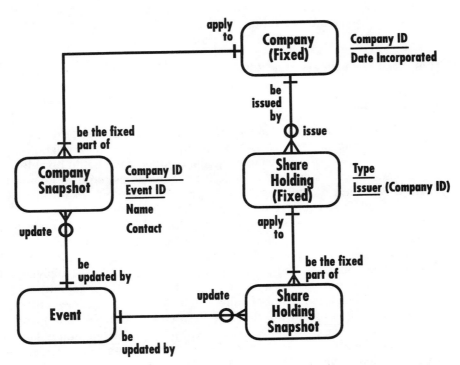

Figure 10-11. Basic Snapshot Approach Applied to Nontransferable Relationship

But what if the relationship were transferable? In Figure 10-12 we include the entity Location, and the rule that shareholdings can be transferred from one location to another. Each shareholding *snapshot* is now related to a single instance of Location. A new shareholding snapshot is created whenever a share holding is moved from one location to another. From a relational model perspective, the foreign key to Location is now time-dependent, and therefore needs to be an attribute of the Shareholding Snapshot (Figure 10-13).

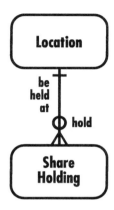

Figure 10-12. Location and Shareholding - Current Data

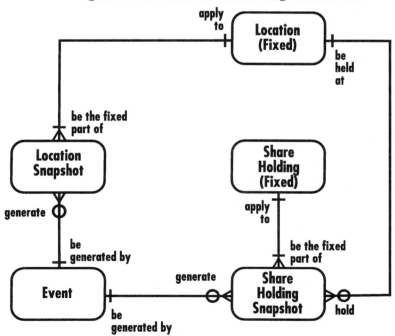

Figure 10-13. Basic Snapshot Approach Applied to Transferable Relationship

The effects on the original relationship under the two options (transferable and non-transferable) are summarized in Figure 10-14. Note the use of the nontransferability symbol introduced in Section 6-3.

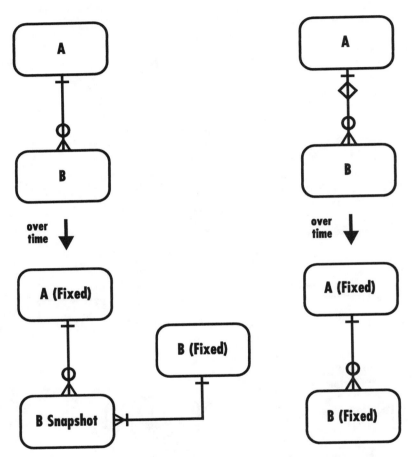

Figure 10-14. Adding History to Transferable and Nontransferable Relationships

You might find it interesting to compare this result with the often-quoted guideline that "when you include the time dimension, one-to-many relationships become many-to-many." If you think of the Shareholding Snapshot entity as a resolution entity, you will see that this guideline only applies to *transferable* relationships. This makes sense. If a relationship is nontransferable, it will not change over time; hence there is no need to record its history.

10.6.2. Many-to-Many Relationships

Many-to-many relationships present no special problems, as we can start by resolving them into two one-to-many nontransferable relationships, plus resolution entity.

Figure 10-15 shows a worked example using the snapshot approach (I've left out the individual histories of the Employee and Equipment Item entities).

In the simplest case, when the resolution entity does not contain any attributes other than the key, we need only keep track of the periods for which the entity applies (i.e., for which the relationship exists). We can use either of the structures in Figure 10-16. Option 1 is based on an audit trail of changes, option 2 on periods of currency.

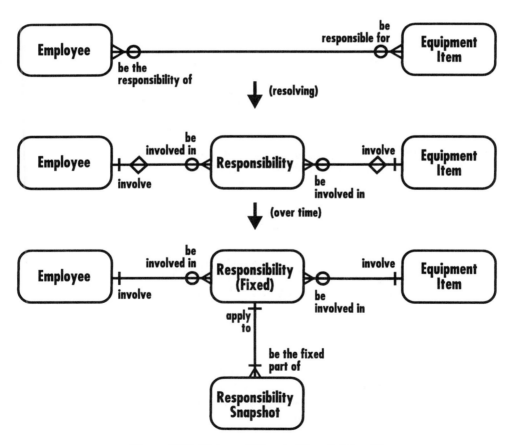

Figure 10-15. History of Many-to-Many Relationships

Option 1:

RESPONSIBILITY (<u>Employee ID</u>, <u>Equipment ID</u>, <u>Date Effective</u>, Currency Indicator)

Option 2:

RESPONSIBILITY (<u>Employee ID</u>, <u>Equipment ID</u>, <u>Date Effective From</u>, Date Effective To)

Figure 10-16. Alternatives for Handling History of Simple Resolution Entity

10.6.3. Self-Referencing Relationships

Handling self-referencing relationships is no different in principle from handling relationships between two entities, but it's easy to get confused. Figure 10-17 shows solutions to the most common situations.

10.7.   DATE ENTITIES

Occasionally, we need to set up an entity called Date or something similar, to record such data as whether a given date is a public holiday. (Incidentally, I've often seen this entity named "Calendar" – a violation of our "one instance" rule covered in Section 3.4.2.)

There is no problem with the entity as such; the difficulty arises when we note that the primary key is Date, and that this attribute appears in entities throughout the data model, where, technically, it is a foreign key to the Date entity. According to our diagramming rules we should draw relationships between the Date entity and all the entities in which the foreign key appears, a tedious and messy exercise.

My advice is to break the rules, and not to worry about drawing the relationships. The rules that the relationships enforce (i.e., ensuring that only valid dates appear) are normally handled by standard date-checking routines; our explicit relationships add virtually nothing except unnecessary complexity. The situation is different if the dates are a special subset – for example, public holidays. In this case, you should name the entity appropriately ("Public Holiday!") and show any relationships that are constrained to that subset (e.g., Public Holiday Bonus *paid for work on* Public Holiday).

10.7.1.   Changes to the Data Structure

Our discussion so far has related to keeping track of changes to data *content* over time. From time to time, we need to change a data model, and hence the database *structure*, to reflect a new requirement or changes to the business.

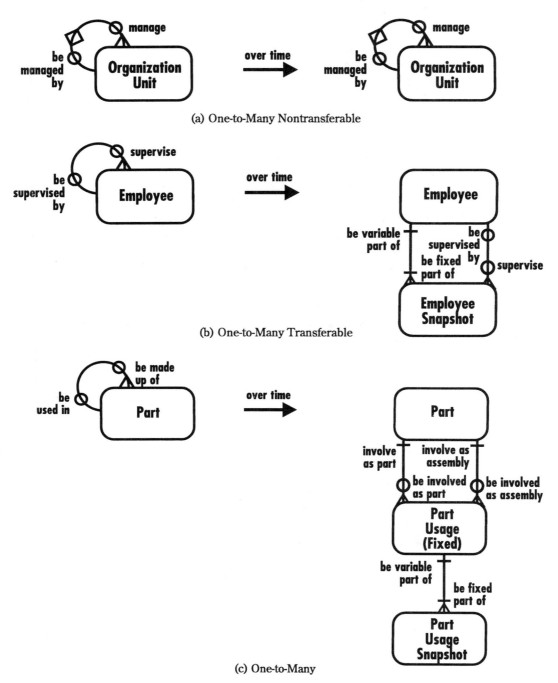

(a) One-to-Many Nontransferable

(b) One-to-Many Transferable

(c) One-to-Many

Figure 10-17. History of Self-Referencing Relationships

Handling this falls outside the realm of data modeling, and is a serious challenge for the database administrator. The problem is not only to implement the changes to the database, and the (often considerable) consequent changes to programs. The database administrator also needs to ensure the ongoing usefulness of archived data, which remains in the old format. Usually, this means archiving copies of the original programs, and of any data conversion programs.

10.8.   PUTTING IT INTO PRACTICE

In this chapter, we've worked through a number of options for incorporating time and history in data models. In practice, I suggest that you don't worry too much about these issues in your initial modeling. On the other hand, you should not consciously try to exclude the time dimension. You will find that you automatically include much time-related data, through the use of familiar structures such as account entries, transactions, and events.

You should then review the model to ensure that time-related needs are met. The best approach often does not become clear until attributes are well-defined, and functional analysis has identified the different event types and their effects on the data.

Keep in mind that every transaction that changes or deletes data without leaving a record of the previous position is destroying data the organization has paid to capture. It's important to satisfy yourself and the user that such data is no longer of potential value to the organization before deciding that it will be deleted without trace.

10.9.   SUMMARY

There are numerous options for modeling historical and future (planned or anticipated) data. The most appropriate technique will vary from case to case, even within the same model.

The two basic approaches are the "audit trail," which records a history of changes, and the "snapshot," which records a series of past or future positions. Other variations arise from different levels of generalization and aggregation for events and changes, and the choice of whether to treat current positions separately or as special cases of historical or future positions.

Transferable relationships that are one-to-many with the time factor excluded become many-to-many over time. Nontransferable relationships remain one-to-many.

11

Modeling Business Rules

11.1.   INTRODUCTION

Information systems contain and enforce *rules* about the businesses they support. (Some writers prefer the word *constraints* – I use the two interchangeably). For example, a human resource management system might incorporate the following rules (along with many others):

> "Each employee can belong to at most one union at any time."

> "A minimum of four percent of each employee's salary up to $80,000 must be credited to the company pension fund."

> "If salary deductions result in an employee's net pay being less than zero, include details in an exception report."

> "At most two employees can share a job position at any time."

> "Only employees of Grade four and above can receive entertainment allowances."

> "For each grade of employee, a standard set of base benefits applies."

> "Employee number 4787 has annual salary $82,000."

What distinguishes a rule from other facts? We shall adopt the guideline that a rule is a statement *about* data, which may exist in the absence of that data. In the above examples, the last "rule" may not seem to fit this guideline. However, if we think of it as being a rule about individual salary payments, insofar as they must reflect the annual salary, then it meets the criterion.

Deciding how and where each rule is to be held is the very essence of information system design. There are basically three different ways of representing a rule:

1. within program logic,
2. as data held in the database, and
3. within the structure of the database (as specified by the data model).

The best choice in each case will depend on two main factors.

First, some rules are most easily, or "naturally," supported by one particular option. In the preceding examples, most system designers would think immediately of implementing the union membership rule within data structure (a one-to-many relationship between Union and Employee entities), the pension deduction figures as data (or perhaps program constants), and the salary deduction exception handling within program logic.

Second, the processes and skills needed to change a rule differ significantly, depending on where the rule is held. Rewriting program logic or reorganizing the database structure are quite different tasks from updating a data value. It is important that volatile rules can be readily changed. On the other hand, stable rules form the framework on which we design the system, by defining the boundaries of what it must be able to handle. Without some stable rules, system design would be unmanageably complex – every system would need to be able to accommodate any conceivable possibility or change. We want to implement these stable rules in such a way that they cannot be easily bypassed or inadvertently changed.

In some cases, these two factors conflict. The most common situation involves rules that would most easily be enforced by program logic, but which need to be readily updatable by users. Increased pressure on businesses to respond quickly to market or regulatory changes has meant that rules which were once considered stable are no longer so. One solution is to hold the rules as data. If such rules are central to the system, we often refer to the resulting system as being "table driven."

A different sort of problem arises when we want to represent a rule within the data structure, but cannot find a simple way of achieving it. Rules that "almost" follow the pattern of those we are used to specifying in data models can be particularly frustrating. We can readily enforce the rule that only one person can hold a particular job position, but what if the limit is two? Or five? Or a minimum of two? How do we handle more subtle (but equally reasonable) constraints, such as "the customer who receives the invoice must be the same as the customer who placed the order?"

As data modelers, our primary interest is in rules that are to be enforced directly by data structure, or through data values (which, of course, the data structure must be able to hold). There is room for choice and creativity both in deciding where a rule will be held, and in specifying exactly how it will be represented. This chapter covers some basic principles and discusses the problems most commonly encountered in practice.

11.2.   GENERAL PRINCIPLES

I have seen even quite experienced data modelers get into real trouble, and waste considerable time, trying to model rules. Here are some guidelines that should help avoid the most common pitfalls.

11.2.1.   Describe the Rules in the Most Natural Form First

In Chapters 3 and 4, we looked at generating business sentences from the diagrams ("Each employee may submit one or more leave applications," "A maternity leave application is a type of leave application"). Don't use the data model as the *initial* medium for documenting rules that do not follow these simple forms.

Plain language, despite all its ambiguities, is still one of the most convenient and best understood ways to specify rules. Take advantage, too, of the range of techniques available to specify *process* logic: decision tables, decision trees, data flow diagrams, function decompositions, pseudo code, etc. These are particularly relevant for rules we would like to hold as data, in order to facilitate change, but which would more naturally be represented within program logic.

The resulting documentation serves as an intermediate representation. Incorporating the rules into the system may take some time and effort, and there is always the chance that something will "fall between the cracks." It is invaluable to be able to refer back to an agreed specification, rather than having to involve the user in developing each design option.

11.2.2.   Support the Rules with Examples

Examples serve not only to clarify and test the accuracy of our specified requirements, but provide "bullets" to fire at proposed solutions. They also serve to verify that the rules are real and important. On occasions, I have seen requirements dropped or significantly modified after the search for examples failed to turn up any, or confirmed that the few cases from which the rules had been inferred were in fact the only cases!

11.2.3.   Assess and Isolate Volatility

The volatility (or, conversely, stability) of a rule will be one of the major factors in deciding where to hold it. Given a choice of "flexible" or "inflexible," we can expect system users to opt for the former and, consequently, to err on the side of volatility when asked to assess the stability of a rule. But the net result can be a system that is far more sophisticated and complicated than it need be.

It is important, therefore, to gather reliable evidence as to how often and in what way we can expect rules to change. History is always a good starting point. We can prompt the user: "This rule hasn't changed in ten years; is there anything that would make it more likely to change in the future?" Volume is also an indication. If we have a large set of rules, of the same type or in the same domain, we can anticipate that the set will change.

When you find that a rule is volatile, at least to the extent that it is likely to change over the life of the system, it is important to identify the components that are the cause of its volatility. One useful technique is to look for a more general "higher level" rule that *will* be stable.

For example, the rule "Five percent of each contribution must be posted to the Statutory Reserve Account" may be volatile. But what about "A percentage of each contribution must be posted to the Statutory Reserve Account?" But perhaps even this is a volatile instance of a more general rule: "Each contribution is divided among a set of accounts, in accordance with a standard set of percentages." And will the division always be based on percentages? Perhaps we can envision in the future deducting, say, $10 from each contribution regardless of size to cover administration costs.

This sort of exploration and clarification is absolutely essential if we are to avoid going to great trouble to accommodate a change of one kind to a rule, only to be caught by a change of a different kind.

11.2.4.   Distinguish Rule Enforcement from Solution Finding

I have seen data modelers modeling highly complex, interrelated sets of rules, in the mistaken belief that by adequately constraining what can be held in the database, they will be well on the way to finding data that meets the constraints. Time-tabling and scheduling applications are good examples. It is usually possible, if difficult, to incorporate in a data model many of the constraints imposed by nature (a teacher can be in only one classroom at a time) and regulation (each flight must have at least two qualified pilots assigned). But coming up with sets of data that fit the constraints, or even establishing that the constraints can be met by any set of data, is another problem altogether. Data modelers presented with problems of this kind need to make their role very clear here, lest they be expected to find data that meets the constraints rather than merely model a database to hold it.

Often the best strategy is not to model all the constraints rigidly, but to allow data that breaks some of the rules to be held. This allows solutions to be approached progressively, with conformity to rules being checked rather than enforced, typically by batch programs with the rules built in. There is a good example of this in the automated support available for data modeling. Many data modelers prefer to work with CASE tools which do not enforce the rules of sound data modeling (such as relationships being properly named) at the time of data entry, but report on omissions and inconsistencies later.

11.2.5. Consider Different Techniques and Technologies

The time-tabling problems referred to in the previous section are at the edge of those that are best addressed by conventional database-centered systems, and hence of our data modeling techniques. Remember the old adage "to a child with a hammer, everything looks like a nail." All of us who have expertise in a particular technique are inclined to apply it to problems that come our way, even if they lie outside the domain for which the technique was originally developed. Occasionally this leads to effective new approaches, so we should certainly not be afraid to stretch the limits of data modeling from time to time. But we need to be aware of other techniques, and recognize when they may be better suited.

I have seen data modeling used for everything from business planning to optimizing message scheduling on a telecommunications network, without the more conventional alternatives being properly considered. *Don't try to solve every problem by developing a conventional data model.*

This book has focused on the widely used entity-relationship and relational approaches to modeling. But other approaches can offer greater power to represent rules. In particular, Nijssen's "fact based" approach provides a well-developed and much richer language for modeling constraints, and the resulting models can be converted to relational models fairly mechanically. Unfortunately, those constraints that cannot be implemented in relational models have to be identified and incorporated elsewhere in the system design. Nevertheless, it is a useful technique to have in reserve.[1]

When I get into trouble with modeling rules, I turn to colleagues with experience in two fields in particular: operations research (essentially the application of mathematics to business problems) and knowledge-based systems. In some cases, the problem has been solved or is well understood in one of these fields; in others they offer techniques better suited to expressing or solving the problem. In particular, you should consider the possibility of developing part of a system using knowledge-based systems technology, and the remainder using a conventional database. These hybrid approaches are becoming more practical, and offer a "best of both worlds" solution to some of the most awkward problems in systems design.

---

[1] Nijssen, G.M. and Halpin, T.A., *Conceptual Schema and Relational Database Design – A Fact Based Approach,* Prentice Hall (1989).

11.3.   WHERE TO HOLD RULES

As discussed earlier, we can hold rules in data structure, program logic, or data. In fact, the situation is a little more complex than this: Rules held primarily in one place may also affect the design of other parts of the system. For example, if we hold a rule in data structure, that rule will also be reflected in program structure; if we hold a rule in data, we will need to design the data structure to support the necessary data, and the programs to allow their processing logic to be driven by the data values.

This is an area in which it is crucial that data modelers and function modelers (analysts) work together. Many a data model has been rejected or inappropriately compromised because it placed demands upon function modelers that they didn't understand or were unprepared to tackle.

A simple example will illustrate the three major options. Figure 11-1 shows part of a model to support transaction processing for a medical benefits fund. Very similar structures occur in many systems that support a range of products against which specific sets of transactions are allowed. Note the use of the exclusivity arc introduced in Section 6.7.2 to represent, for example, that each dental services claim must be lodged by either a Class A member or a Class B member.

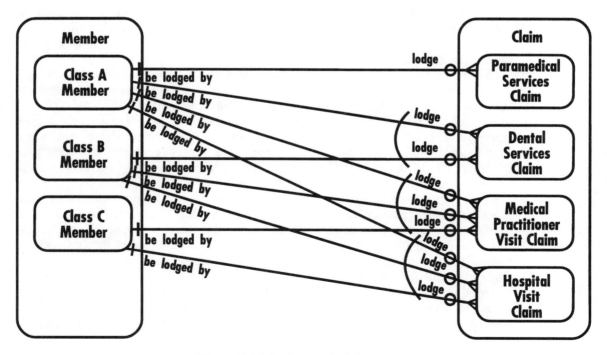

Figure 11-1. Members and Medical Insurance Claims

Let's consider just one rule that the model represents: "Only a Class A member can lodge a claim for paramedical services."

11.3.1. Rules in Data Structure

If we implement the model at the lowest level of subtyping, the rule restricting paramedical services claims to Class A members will be implemented in the data structure. The Paramedical Services Claim table will hold a foreign key supporting the relationship to the Class A Member table. Program logic will take account of this structure in, for example, the steps taken to process a paramedical claim, the layout of statements to be sent to Class B members (no provision for paramedical claims), and in ensuring that only Class A members are associated with paramedical claims, through input vetting and error messages. If we are confident that the rule will not change, then this is a sound design, and the program logic can hardly be criticized for inflexibility.

Suppose now that our assumption about the rule being stable is incorrect, and we need to change the rule to allow Class B members to claim for paramedical services. We now need to change the database design to include a foreign key for Class B members in Paramedical Claim. We will also need to change the corresponding program logic.

In general, changes to rules contained within the data structure require the participation of data modelers and database administrators, analysts, programmers, and, of course, the users. Facing this, we may well be tempted by "quick and dirty" approaches – perhaps we could transfer all Class B members to Class A, distinguishing them by a flag in a spare column. Many a system bears the scars of continued "programming around" the data structure rather than incurring the cost of changes.

11.3.2. Rules in Programs

From Chapter 4, we know broadly what to do with unstable rules in data structure: we generalize them out. If we implement the model at the level of Member, the rules about what sort of claims can be made by each type of member will no longer be held in data structure.

Instead, the model holds rules:

> "Each Paramedical Claim must be lodged by one Member";
> "Each Dental Claim must be lodged by one Member"; etc.

But we do need to hold the original rules somewhere. Probably the simplest option is to move them to program logic. The logic will look a little different from that associated with the more specific model, and we will essentially be checking the claims against the new attribute Member Type.

Enforcement of the rules now requires some discipline at the programming level. It is technically possible for a program that associates any sort of claim with any sort of member to be written. Good practice suggests a common module for checking, but good practice isn't always enforced!

Now, if we want to change a rule, only the programs that check the constraints will need to be modified. We will not need to involve the data modeler and database administrator at all. The amount of programming work will depend on how well the original programmers succeeded in localizing the checking logic. It may include developing a program to run periodic checks on the data to ensure that the rule has not been violated by a rogue program.

11.3.3. Rules in Data

Holding the rules in program logic may still not provide sufficient responsiveness to business change. In many organizations, the amount of time required to develop a new program version, fully test it, and migrate it into production may be several weeks or months.

The solution is to hold the rules in the data. In our example, this would mean holding a list of the valid member types for each type of claim. An Allowed Claim for Member Type table as in Figure 11-2 will provide the essential data.

Allowed Claim Type for Member Type (<u>Claim Type Code</u>, <u>Member Type Code</u>)

Figure 11-2. Table of Allowed Claim Types for Each Member Type

But our programs will now need to be a deal more sophisticated. If we implement the database at the generalized Member and Claim level (Figure 11-3), the program will need to refer to the Allowed Claim Type for Member Type table to decide which subsets of the main tables to work with in each situation.

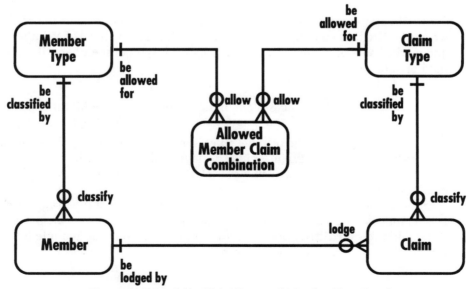

Figure 11-3. Model at Claim Type and Member Type Level

If we implement at the subtype level, the program will need to decide at run time which *tables* to access, by referring to the Allowed Claim Type for Member table. For example, we may want to print details of all claims made by a member. The program will need to determine what types of claim can be made by a member of that type, and then access the appropriate claim tables. This will involve translating Claim Type Codes and Member Type Codes into table names, which we can handle either with look-up tables or by translation in the program. The latter approach means that we will have to change the program if we add further tables; the former raises the possibility of a system in which we could add new tables without changing any program logic. Again, we would need to be satisfied that this sophisticated approach was better overall than simply implementing the model at the supertype level. Not all programming languages (in particular SQL) comfortably support run-time decisions about which table to access.

The payoff for the "rules in data" or "table-driven" approach comes when we want to change the rules. We can leave both database administrators and programmers out of the process, and handle the change with conventional transactions. Because such changes may have a significant business impact, they are typically restricted to a small subset of users, or a system administrator. Without proper control, there is a temptation for individual users to find "novel" ways of using the system, which may invalidate assumptions made by the system builders. The consequences may include unreliable or uninterpretable outputs, and unexpected system behavior.

For some systems and types of change, the administrator needs to be an information systems professional who is able to assess any systems changes that may be required beyond the changes to data values (not to mention taking due credit for the quick turnaround on the "systems maintenance" requests). In our example, the tables would allow a new type of claim to be added by changing data values, but this might need to be supplemented by changes to program logic to handle new processing specific to claims of that type.

11.4.   DOCUMENTING RULES IN DATA MODELS

Wherever the conventions of data modeling allow you to capture a business rule easily in the data model, I recommend that you do so, *even if you have little intention of actually implementing the rule in the final database design*. This advice is born of long experience reviewing models that were so generic as to be incomprehensible to users, and failed to document important rules and constraints the users had conscientiously provided, on the basis that they were potentially volatile. I'm often left with the suspicion that the data modelers have abdicated their responsibility for doing detailed and rigorous analysis, and that the assessment of volatility and subsequent move to a very generalized model have been made without adequate hard data.

One of the strengths of the two-stage modeling approach, wherein we model subtypes and supertypes initially, then level the model for implementation (Section 4.9), is that we can capture rules now and decide later where they will be held. Function modelers will thank us for saving them the embarrassment of asking the same questions again!

Our principal weapon in capturing detailed rules is the subtype, and a willingness to use it in situations where it is unlikely ever to be implemented directly as a table. This means using subtypes which may not be stable over the life of the system, allowing that entity instances may migrate from one subtype to another, and using multiple partitions (see Chapter 4).

We now look at some of the more common types of rules that can be modeled in this way.

11.4.1. Simple Inclusion and Exclusion

Figure 11-4 illustrates the simplest use of subtypes to represent a rule. The initial model relates workers and annual leave applications, but we are advised that only certain types of workers – employees – can submit annual leave applications. A straightforward subtyping captures the rule.

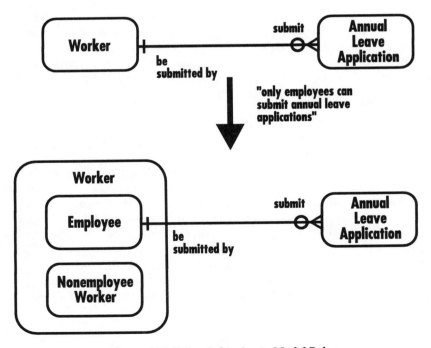

Figure 11-4. Using Subtyping to Model Rules

"Non Employee Worker" is not an elegant classification or name, and we should be prompted to ask what other sorts of workers the user was interested in. Perhaps we might be able to change the entity name to "Contractor." We may well decide to drop the subtypes at implementation time, perhaps because we can envision other worker types in the future, or a relaxation of the rule as to who can submit leave applications. We would then hold the rule either within program logic, or through a table listing the types of workers able to submit annual leave applications.

This simple example provides a template for solving more complex problems. For example, we might want to add the rule that "only noncitizens require work permits." This could be achieved by using the partitioning convention introduced in Chapter 4 to show alternative subtypings (Figure 11-5).

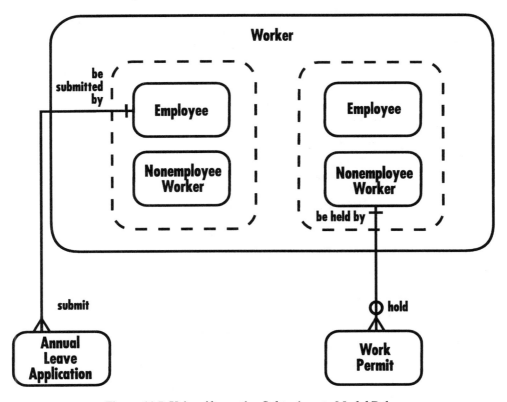

Figure 11-5. Using Alternative Subtypings to Model Rules

Note that the relationship from Noncitizen to Work Permit is *optional*, even though the original rule could have been interpreted as requiring it to be mandatory. We would have checked this by asking the user: "Could we ever want to record details of a noncitizen who did not have a work permit – perhaps prior to their obtaining one?" With more than one subtyping, the term "Worker Type" becomes ambiguous. It is always best to use more descriptive terms if available – perhaps Employment Status and Citizenship Status. A useful convention is to reserve the term "type" for stable (*intrinsic*) types, in the sense that an instance is not allowed to change types.

11.4.2. Participation in Relationships

Suppose we wanted to model the organizational structure of a company so as to enforce the rule that an employee could be assigned only to a lowest level organizational unit. This kind of structure also occurs in hierarchical charts of accounts, in which transactions can be posted only to the lowest level.

Figure 11-6 shows the use of subtypes to capture the rule. Note that the structure effectively *defines* a Lowest Level Organization Unit as an Organizational Unit which cannot control other Organizational Units (since it lacks the "controls" relationship). Once again, we might not implement the subtypes, perhaps because a given lowest level organizational unit could later control other organization units, thus changing its entity classification. (Section 4.15.15 discusses why we want to avoid instances changing from one entity to another.)

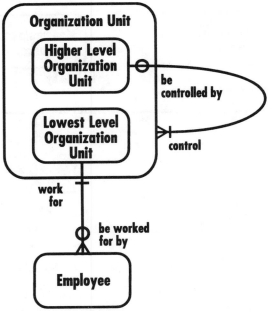

Figure 11-6. Using Unstable Subtypes to Capture Rules

POST OFFICE CLOSURE (<u>Branch No</u>, <u>Date</u>, Reason)

Post Office Closure Table

Branch No	Date	Reason
18	*12/21/93*	*Maintenance*
63	*12/23/93*	*Local Holiday*
1	*12/25/93*	*Christmas Day*
2	*12/25/93*	*Christmas Day*
3	*12/25/93*	*Christmas Day*
4	*12/25/93*	*Christmas Day*
5	*12/25/93*	*Christmas Day*
6	*12/25/93*	*Christmas Day*

Figure 11-7. Post Office Closures Model

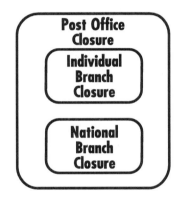

INDIVIDUAL BRANCH CLOSURE (<u>Branch No</u>, <u>Date</u>, Reason)

NATIONAL BRANCH CLOSURE (<u>Branch No</u>, <u>Date</u>, Reason)

Individual Branch Closure		
Branch No	**Date**	**Reason**
18	*12/21/93*	*Maintenance*
63	*12/23/93*	*Local Holiday*

National Branch Closure		
Branch No	**Date**	**Reason**
1	*25/12/93*	*Christmas*
2	*25/12/93*	*Christmas*
3	*25/12/93*	*Christmas*
4	*25/12/93*	*Christmas*
5	*25/12/93*	*Christmas*
6	*25/12/93*	*Christmas*

Figure 11-8. Subtyping Post Office Closure

11.4.3.   Rules With Exceptions

Subtypes are also valuable in handling "rule with exceptions" situations. Figure 11-7 is a table recording the dates on which post office branches are closed. (A bit of creativity may already have been applied here – the user is just as likely to have specified a requirement to record when the post offices were *open*.)

Look at the table closely. There is a definite impression of repetition for national holidays, such as Christmas Day, but the table is in fact fully normalized. We might see what appears to be a dependency of Reason on Date, but this only applies to some rows of the table.

The restriction "only some rows" provides the clue to tackling the problem. We use subtypes to separate the two types of row, as in Figure 11-8.

The National Closure table is not fully normalized, as Reason depends only on Date; normalizing gives us the three tables of Figure 11-9.

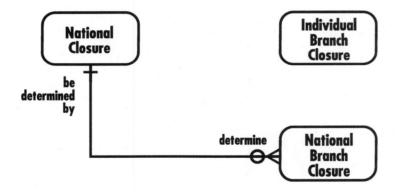

INDIVIDUAL BRANCH CLOSURE (<u>Branch No</u>, <u>Date</u>, Reason)

NATIONAL BRANCH CLOSURE (<u>Branch No</u>, <u>Date</u>)

NATIONAL CLOSURE (<u>Date</u>, Reason)

Individual Branch Closure		
Branch No	Date	Reason
18	12/21/93	Maintenance
63	12/23/93	Local Holiday

National Branch Closure	
Branch No	Date
1	12/25/93
2	12/25/93
3	12/25/93
4	12/25/93
5	12/25/93
6	12/25/93

National Closure	
Date	Reason
12/25/93	Christmas

Figure 11-9. Post Office Closures – Normalized After Subtyping

We now need to ask whether the National Branch Closure table holds any information of value to us. It is fully derivable from a table of branches (which we probably have elsewhere), and the National Closure data. Accordingly, we can delete it. We now have the two table solution of Figure 11-10.

INDIVIDUAL BRANCH CLOSURE
(Branch, Date, Reason)

NATIONAL CLOSURE
(Date, Reason)

Individual Branch Closure		
Branch	**Date**	**Reason**
18	12/21/93	Maintenance
63	12/23/93	Local Holiday

National Closure	
Date	**Reason**
12/25/93	Christmas

Figure 11-10. Final Post Office Closure Model

In solving the problem of capturing an underlying rule, we have produced a far more elegant data structure. Recording a new national holiday, for example, now requires only the addition of one row. In effect we found an unnormalized structure hidden within a more general structure, but with all the redundancy and update anomalies that we expect from unnormalized data.

11.5. CONSTRAINTS ON ATTRIBUTES

The most common rules associated with attributes are simple domain specifications (e.g., Gender must take the value "M" or "F"), discussed in Section 9.5, and those implied by the rules of primary and foreign keys (e.g., referential integrity requirements, as discussed in Section 2.7.6).

Occasionally, we encounter a rule that involves two or even more attributes, usually but not always from the same entity. If the rule simply states that only certain combinations of attribute values are permissible, we can set up a table of the allowed combinations. If we introduce a surrogate key for the table of allowed combinations, we can replace the two or more original attributes with this. The second approach might seem to enforce the rule more strongly, but both capture the rule in data structure, and rely on checking that only values appearing in the relevant look-up tables are used. Referential integrity features of the database management system, if provided, can be used to support this. The principles are much the same as those discussed in the earlier section on modeling rules in data.

Other interdomain constraints, such as range checks (if Product Type is "Vehicle," Price must be greater than $10,000) and cross-entity constraints (only a customer with a credit rating of "A" can have an account with an overdraft limit of over $1,000) can be readily implemented by simple tables specifying the allowed combinations of domains, or in process logic. The ability to enforce them in data structure is largely determined by the database management system; some will allow domain constraints to be specified in the logical database design.

As always, the best approach is to document the constraints as you model, in this case as attribute or domain descriptions, and defer the decision as to exactly how they are to be enforced until you finalize the logical database design.

11.6.   ENFORCEMENT OF RULES THROUGH PRIMARY KEY SELECTION.

The structures available to us in data modeling were not designed as a comprehensive "tool kit" for representing rules. To some extent, the types of rules we are able to model are a byproduct of database management system design, in which other objectives were at the fore. Most of these are well-understood (cardinality, optionality, etc.), but others arise from quite subtle issues of key selection.

In Section 6.2.3, we looked at an apparently simple customer orders model, reproduced with different primary keys in Figure 11-11.

By using a combination of Customer No and Order No as the key for Order, and Customer and Branch No as the key for Branch, as shown, we are able to enforce the important constraint that the customer who placed the order also received the order (because the Customer No in the Ordered Item table is part of the foreign key to both Order and Branch). But this is hardly obvious from the diagram, or even from fairly close perusal of the attribute lists, unless you are a fairly experienced and observant modeler. Don't expect the database administrator, user, or even your successor to see it.

I counsel you not to rely on these subtleties of key construction to enforce constraints. Clever they may be, but they can easily be overridden by other issues of key selection, or forgotten as time passes. It is better to handle such constraints with a check within a common program module, and strongly enforce use of that module.

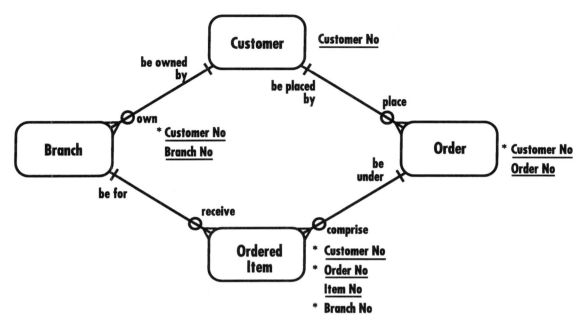

Figure 11-11. Constraint Enforced by Choice of Keys

11.7.   SUMMARY

A conventional information system may hold rules as data, data structure, or program logic. Rules held in data structure are difficult to circumvent or change. Rules held in data values are more readily changed, but may demand more sophisticated programming.

Some unstable rules are not readily held as data. In such cases, alternative techniques and technologies should be considered.

Subtypes provide a powerful mechanism for capturing rules, and can be used even when there is no intention of implementing them directly.

Subtleties of key construction should not generally be used to enforce rules.

12

Corporate Data Modeling

Always design a thing by considering it in its next larger context – a chair in a room, a room in a house, a house in an environment, an environment in a city plan.
– Eliel Saarinen

12.1. INTRODUCTION

So far, we have discussed data modeling in the context of database design: We have assumed that our data models will ultimately be implemented more or less directly using some database management system. Our focus has been on the data requirements of individual application systems.

But data models also have a role to play in data planning and management for an enterprise as a whole. A *corporate data model* (sometimes called an *enterprise-wide data model*) is a model that covers the whole of, or a very significant part of, an organization. We can use such a model to:

1. Classify or index existing data
2. Provide a target for database and systems planners
3. Provide a context for specifying new databases
4. Guide data modelers in the development of individual databases
5. Provide input to business planning
6. Specify an organization-wide database

These activities are part of the wider discipline of *data management* – the management of data as a corporate resource – that warrants a book in itself. In this chapter, we look briefly at data management in general, then discuss the uses of corporate data models. Finally, we examine how development of a corporate data model differs from development of a conventional project-level data model.

But first, a word of warning. Far too many corporate data models have ended up "on the shelf" after considerable expenditure on their development. The most common reason appears to be a lack of a clear idea of how the model is to be used. It is vital that any corporate data model be developed in the context of a data management strategy, within which its role is clearly understood, rather than as an end in itself.

12.2. Data Management

12.2.1. Problems of Data Mismanagement

The rationale for data management is that data is a valuable corporate resource, and therefore needs to be properly managed. Parallels are often drawn with physical assets, people, and money, all of which need to be managed explicitly if the enterprise is to derive the best value from them. But as with management of other assets, we can best understand the need for data management by looking at the results of *not* doing it.

Databases have traditionally been developed on an application-by-application basis – one database per application system. Indeed, databases are often seen as being "owned" by their parent applications. The problem is that some data may be required by more than one application. For example, a bank may build separate applications to handle personal loans and savings accounts, but both will need to hold data about customers. Without some form of planning and control, we will end up holding the same data in both databases. This is where the element of choice in data modeling works against us – we have no guarantee that the modelers working on the two systems will have represented the common data in the same way. Not only will the data be duplicated, it will be very difficult to document, reconcile, and control the duplication.

The effects of duplication and inconsistency across multiple systems are similar to those that arise from poor data modeling at the individual system level.

There are the costs of keeping multiple copies of data in step (and repercussions from data users, including customers, managers, and regulators, if we don't). It is not uncommon to have had the experience of notifying an organization of a change of address, and later discovering that only some of their records have been updated.

Pulling data together to meet management information needs is far more difficult if definitions, coding, and formats vary. An airline wants to know the total cost of running each of its terminals, but the terminals are identified in different ways in different systems – sometimes only by a series of account numbers. An insurance company wants a breakdown of profitability by product, but different divisions have defined "product" in different ways. Problems of this kind have been a serious impediment to implementing effective management and executive information systems, which typically need to consolidate data from diverse operational systems.

Finally, poor overall data organization can make it difficult to use the data in new ways as business functions change in response to market and regulatory pressures and internal initiatives. Often, it seems easier to build yet another single-purpose database than to attempt to use inconsistent existing databases. A lack of central documentation also makes reuse of data difficult – we may not even know that the data we require is held in an existing database. The net result, of course, is still more databases, and an exacerbation of the basic problem. Alternatively, we may decide that the new initiative is "too hard" or economically untenable. Advocates of Business Process Re-engineering point out that good data management is a prerequisite for organizations that want to be responsive and "nimble" in changing their processes.

I have seen banks with fifty or more "Branch" files, retailers with more than thirty "Stock Item" files, and organizations that are supposedly customer-focused with dozens of "Customer" files. Often, just finding out the scope of the problem has been a major exercise. Not surprisingly, it is the data that is most central to an organization (and hence used by the greatest number of applications) that is most frequently mismanaged.

12.2.2. Managing Data as a Shared Resource

Data management aims to address these issues by taking an organization-wide view of data. Instead of regarding databases as the sole property of their parent applications, we treat them as a shared resource. This may entail documenting existing databases; encouraging development of new, sharable databases in critical areas; establishing standards for data representation; and setting an overall target for data organization. These tasks are usually assigned to a data management (or "data administration") team, which may also serve as a center of expertise in data modeling.

The ideal solution to data management problems would be to build a single shared database covering all of the enterprise's data requirements. Unfortunately, the approach seldom makes sense logistically or economically, as some organizations found to their cost in the 1970s. (Some who failed to learn from others' experiences discovered the same thing for themselves in the 1980s!)

In practice, data managers are akin to town planners. They cannot tear down existing databases and start again, but need to coordinate an orderly migration to a better overall position. Data managers seldom initiate projects, but are responsible for ensuring that individual initiatives contribute to an harmonious whole. And like town planners, they can expect to fight a few political battles along the way, as builders assert their preference for operating without outside interference!

A corporate data model can play a number of roles in supporting data management. In the following sections, we examine the most important of these.

12.3.   CLASSIFICATION OF EXISTING DATA

Most organizations have a major investment in existing databases and files. Often, the documentation of these is of variable quality and held locally with the parent applications.

The lack of a central, properly indexed register of data is one of the greatest impediments to data sharing. If we don't know what data we have (and where it is), how can we hope to identify opportunities for its reuse? The problem is particularly apparent to builders of management information systems and executive information systems. Much of the data needed to provide summarized information for management must be drawn from existing operational systems. The data required by senior executives frequently crosses organizational and application boundaries. Sourcing this data, often at short notice, has proved a major challenge. Correctly interpreting it in the absence of adequate documentation has proved an even greater one, and serious business mistakes have been made as a result of incorrect assumptions.

Commercial data dictionaries have been around for many years to address this need, and they are now being supplanted by more sophisticated "repositories." Some organizations have built their own, with mixed success. But data inventories are of limited value without an index of some kind: We need to be able to ask, "What files or databases hold data about flight schedules" or "Where is 'Country Code' held?," remembering that "Country Code" may be called "CTRY-ID" in one system, and "E12345" in another. Or an attribute named "Country Code" may mean something entirely different to what we expect. I recall encountering a "Vehicle ID," which in fact identified salespersons; the salesperson was the "vehicle" by which the sale was made.

A standard set of "keywords" that are then associated with each existing data item provides a partial solution to the indexing problem. But by the time we provide a tight definition for each keyword, and handle the problems of completeness and overlap, we have performed a task not too dissimilar to defining entities and attributes for a corporate data model. Given the value of a corporate data model for other purposes, it makes sense to use it, rather than keywords, as our indexing technique.

In developing a corporate data model specifically to index existing data, remember that the mapping between entities and existing files will be simpler if the two are based on similar concepts. Avoid radically new, innovative corporate data models unless there is an adequate payoff! Of course, if the business has changed substantially since the databases were built, the corporate data model may well, by necessity, differ significantly from what is currently in place. It then becomes an important tool for assessing the completeness and quality of information systems support for the business.

One of the most effective approaches to building an indexed inventory of data is to develop a fairly generalized corporate data model, and to devote the major effort to improving documentation of individual databases. The corporate model is mapped against existing data at the entity level, and serves as a coarse index to identify databases in which any required data may be held; the final assessment is made by close examination of the local documentation.

12.4.   A TARGET FOR PLANNING

Just as a town plan describes where we aim to be at some future date, a corporate data model can describe how we intend to organize our total set of computerized data at some point in the future.

It is here that corporate data modelers have frequently encountered trouble. It is one thing to start with a blank sheet of paper and develop an ideal model that may be conceptually quite different from the models on which existing systems are based. It is quite another to migrate from existing databases and files to new ones based on the model.

In the first place, there is a natural (and often economically sound) reluctance to replace current databases that are doing an adequate job. We may need to accept, therefore, that large parts of the corporate model will remain unimplemented, at least in the medium term.

This leads to a second problem: Should developers of new systems aim to share data from existing databases, or duplicate the data, following the specification of the corporate data model? The former approach perpetuates the older structures; the latter increases the problems of data duplication. I have even seen developers refusing to use databases that were designed in accordance with a corporate data model because the corporate model has since changed.

Third, in many business areas, the most economical approach is to purchase a packaged system. In these cases, we have little choice about the underlying data models (except insofar as we may be able to choose among packages that are better or worse matches with the corporate data model). With one purchase decision, we may render a large part of the corporate data model irrelevant.

Corporate data modelers frequently find themselves fighting both systems developers and users, who want economical solutions to their specific problems, and who feel constrained by the requirement to fit in with a larger plan. There are arguments for both sides. Without an overall target, it will certainly be difficult to achieve better sharing of data. But too often data modelers forget the basic tenet of creative data modeling: There may be more than one good answer. I have seen data modelers arguing against purchase of a package because it does not fit "their" corporate model, when in fact the underlying database is built on a sound model and could readily be incorporated into the existing set of databases.

The most practical solution lies in the "town planning" paradigm mentioned earlier. The target needs to be a combination of existing databases that are to be retained, databases to be implemented as components of packages, and databases to be developed in-house. It is, in fact, a corporate data model produced within the constraints of other commitments, the most important being the existing systems and the applications development strategy. Some of it will be less than ideal: the structures that fit in best will often differ from those we would use if we had started with a "clean slate."

In developing this sort of model, you should set a specific date – typically, three to five years hence, and aim to model how the organization's data will look at that time. Some areas of the model can be very precise indeed, as they merely document current databases; others may be very broad because we intend to purchase a package whose data structure is as yet unknown.

Such a model represents a realistic target that can be discussed in concrete terms with systems planners, developers, and users, and used as a basis for assessing individual proposals.

12.5.   A CONTEXT FOR SPECIFYING NEW DATABASES

12.5.1.   Determining Scope and Interfaces

In specifying a new database, three of the most fundamental questions we need to ask are:

> What is included?
>
> What is excluded?
>
> What do we have to fit in with?

These questions need to be answered early in a systems development project, as an important part of agreeing expectations and budgets, and of managing overlaps and interfaces among databases. Once a project team has planned and budgeted to design their own database in isolation (and all the associated processing to maintain it), it can be virtually impossible to persuade them to use existing files and databases. Similarly, once it has been decided (even if only implicitly) not to include certain data, it is very difficult to change the decision.

A "big picture" of an organization's overall data requirements – a corporate data model – is an invaluable aid to answeing questions of scope and overlap, and highlighting data issues before it is too late to address them.

12.5.2. Incorporating the Corporate Data Model in the Development Lifecycle

Here is how a typical large organization ensures that databases are specified in the context of an overall data plan.

The organization requires that every information systems development project beyond a certain size receive funding approval from a committee of senior managers, which looks at proposals in terms of overall costs and benefits to the business. The committee's brief is far broader than data management; its prime concern is that the organization's total investment in information systems is well directed, and that local needs do not override the best interests of the organization as a whole. (For example, they may enforce a preferred supplier policy for hardware.)

The committee requires that each proposal include a one-page "data management" statement, prepared in consultation with the data management group. This involves project and data management representatives looking at the corporate data model and identifying the entities that will be required by the proposed system. The resulting "first-cut" data model for the system is a subset of the corporate data model produced by "slicing" in two dimensions: horizontally, to select which entities are to be included and vertically to select which subtypes of those entities are applicable to the project. For example, the project might decide that it requires the entity "Physical Asset" (horizontal selection), but only in order to keep data about vehicles (vertical selection). This exercise may lead to reconsideration of system scope, often to include other subtypes that are handled similarly. For example, it might turn out that with some minor enhancements the vehicle management system could handle all movable assets.

The data management group then advises on whether and in what form the required data is currently held, by reference to the data inventory. This in turn provides a basis for deciding where data will be sourced, and what new data structures the project will build. Where data is to be duplicated, and the need for common representation and/or interfaces can be established. The results of the discussions form the data management statement.

From time to time, disagreements as to data sourcing arise, typically because the project prefers to "roll its own" and the data management group favors data reuse. Ultimately, the committee decides, but most situations are resolved when the implications of each option are laid out and discussed.

In practice, this is a very simple process, with the data management statement typically taking less than a day to prepare. But it can make a real difference to the scope and cost of projects, and to the integration of systems. It does, however, depend upon having a corporate data model, and someone in authority (perhaps the "Chief Information Officer") who is interested in *overall* costs and benefits to the organization rather than the cost justification of each project in isolation.

The first-cut project data model can also be a valuable tool for estimating and budgeting. It is possible to make an estimate of system size in terms of function points using only a data model and some rules of thumb, such as average number of functions per entity. The accuracy of the estimate depends very much on how well data boundaries are defined; the corporate model approach does much to assist this.

Another benefit of an early look at project data requirements in the context of a corporate data model is that the terminology, definitions, and data structures of the corporate data model are communicated to the project team before they embark on a different course. The value of this in improving the quality and compatibility of databases is discussed in the next section.

12.6.   GUIDANCE FOR DATABASE DESIGN

A corporate data model can provide an excellent starting point for the development of project-level data models (and hence database designs).

It contains information about business data requirements that might not otherwise be available to data modelers working on a specific project. A corporate data model takes a broad view of the business, and is likely to incorporate contributions from senior management and strategic planners. In particular, it may highlight areas in which change can be expected, vital input to decisions as to the most appropriate level of generalization.

Because a corporate data model is usually developed by very experienced data modelers, it should specify technically sound data structures, and may include good and perhaps innovative ideas.

The corporate data model can also provide standard names and definitions for common entities (and attributes as well, though corporate modeling to this level of detail is less common). Pulling together data from multiple databases, or transferring data from one to another, is much easier if definitions, formats, and coding are the same. More and more, we need to be able to exchange data with external bodies, as well as among our own databases. The corporate data model can be the central point for specifying the necessary standard definitions and formats.

Achieving genuine consistency demands a high level of rigor in data definition. I recall an organization that needed to store details of languages spoken. One database treated Afghani as a single language, while another treated it as two – Pushtu and Pashto. What might seem to be an academic difference caused real problems when transferring data from one system to another, or attempting to answer simple questions requiring data from both databases. In cases of code sets like this, reference to an external standard can sometimes assist in resolving the problem. Often decisions at this level of detail are not taken in the initial corporate modeling exercise, but are "fed back" to the model by project teams tackling the issue, for the benefit of future project data modelers.

12.7. INPUT TO BUSINESS PLANNING

A corporate data model provides a view of an important business resource (data) from what is usually a novel perspective for business specialists. As such, it may stimulate original thinking about the objectives and organization of the business.

In business, new ideas frequently arise through generalization: a classic example is redefining a business as "transportation" rather than "trucking." We as modelers make heavy use of generalization, and are able to support it in a formal way through the use of supertypes.

So we find that even if the more specialized entities in a corporate data model represent familiar business concepts, their supertypes may not. Or, commonly, the supertypes represent critical high-level concepts that cut across organizational boundaries, and are not managed well as a whole. In a bank, we may have "Loan" (whereas individual organization units manage only certain types of loan), in a telecommunications company "Customer Equipment Item" (whereas different organization units manage different products).

I have seen some real breakthroughs in thinking stimulated by well-explained corporate data models. Some of these have been attributable to a multi disciplinary, highly skilled corporate modeling team looking closely at a business's aims and objectives as input to the modeling exercise. Others have appeared as a result of the actual modeling.

Nevertheless, I would not encourage corporate data modeling for this reason alone. Better results can usually be achieved by the use of specific business-planning techniques. We need to remember that data modeling was developed as a stage in database design, and its conventions and principles reflect this. Normalization is unlikely to help you set your business direction!

Unfortunately, there is a tendency among data modelers to see a business only from the perspective of data, and to promote the data model as representing a kind of "business truth." Given the element of choice in modeling, the argument is hard to sustain. In fact, corporate data models usually encourage a view of the business based on *processes*, as distinct from products, customers, or projects. For example, the high-level supertype "Policy" in an insurance model might suggest common handling of all policies, rather than distinct handling according to product or customer type. Sometimes the new view leads to useful improvements; sometimes it is counterproductive. The business strategy that allows for the most elegant handling of data certainly has advantages, but these may be outweighed by other considerations.

12.8. SPECIFICATION OF A CORPORATE DATABASE

The last use of a corporate data model was historically the first. The dream in the early days of database management systems was to develop a database embracing all of an organization's computer data, fully normalized, nonredundant, and serving the needs of all areas of the organization.

A number of organizations actually attempted this, almost invariably without success. The logistics of developing a database of the necessary size and complexity and providing the associated processing were well beyond the project management capabilities (and budgets) of most organizations. Eventually, more urgent business priorities overrode these grand plans.

A variant is the "subject database" approach, in which the corporate data model is carved up into smaller, more manageable components, which are to be built one at a time. The difficulty lies in deciding how to partition the data. If we partition the data on an application-by-application basis we end up with duplication, resulting from data being required by more than one application (the same as if we had developed application databases without any plan!).

An alternative approach is to divide the data by supertypes: thus a bank might plan subject databases for Loans, Customers, Transactions, Branches, and so on. The problem here is that most practical systems require data from many of these subject databases. To implement a new loan product, the bank would probably require all of the databases mentioned above. The subject database approach is viable, but requires very careful management of the migration from existing databases. The subject databases are developed tactically, to complement application-specific databases. Organizations that have attempted to use subject databases to meet all of their data requirements have run into conflict between this long-term ideal and immediate business needs.

The choice of subject databases is important. Successful strategies have focused on widely used but centrally updated data, typically of low to medium volume. These databases are usually implementations of entities near the top of the one-to-many relationship hierarchy. Examples include data about products, organizational structure, regulations, and staff, as well as common codes and their meanings. Customer data does not quite fit the criteria, but is of sufficient importance to most organizations that support can frequently be gained for a customer database project.

Finally, it is almost always a mistake to develop databases in isolation. Successful projects deliver a *system*, even if this only provides for update and basic inquiries on the data. For example, rather than deliver a product database, we should aim to deliver a product management system for the marketing division. By doing this, we bring the subject database initiative into the mainstream of systems development and can manage it using well-understood procedures and roles. Most importantly, organizations have proved more reluctant to abandon the development of a conventional system with specific user sponsorship than an infrastructure project whose benefits may be less obvious and less clearly "owned."

12.9.   CHARACTERISTICS OF CORPORATE DATA MODELS

Although corporate data models use the same building blocks – entities, relationships, and attributes – as individual database models, they differ in several ways. Most of the differences arise from the need to cover a wide area, but without the detail needed to specify a database.

Ultimately, the level of detail in a corporate data model depends upon its role in the data management strategy – in other words, what it is going to be used for. An extreme example is the organization that produced, after considerable effort and investment, a corporate data model with only six entities. But suppose the organization was a bank, and the entities were Customer, Product, Service, Contract, Account, and Branch. If the model was successfully used to win agreement throughout the organization on the meaning of these six terms, drove the construction of six shared databases, and encouraged a review of the way each was managed, then the six-entity model would have justified its cost many times over.

More typical corporate data models contain between 50 and 200 entities. This relatively low number (in comparison with the model that would result from consolidating all possible project-level models) is achieved by employing a high level of generalization – often higher than we would select for implementation. Corporate models, as initially developed, seldom specify the full set of attributes for each entity. In some cases no attributes at all are recorded; in others, sample and key attributes may be included to clarify entity definitions.

Corporate models may also omit some of the "less important" entities, or incorporate them into other entities through denormalization. For example, a model might include the entity Contract, but exclude Contract Change, Contract Type, and Client Involvement in Contract. The last is a resolution entity that could be implied through a many-to-many relationship (Client may be involved in Contract) rather than shown explicitly.

Even after this amount of trimming, a corporate data model may still be too complicated to be readily understood. Many business specialists have been permanently discouraged from further participation in the modeling process by a forbiddingly complex "circuit diagram" of boxes and lines. In these cases, it is worth producing a very high-level diagram showing less than ten very generalized entities. Ruthless elimination of entities that are not critical to communicating the key concepts is essential. Such a diagram is intended solely as a starting point for understanding, and you should therefore make decisions as to what to generalize or eliminate on this basis alone.

12.10.   DEVELOPING A CORPORATE DATA MODEL

In developing a corporate data model, we use the same basic techniques and principles as for a project-level model. The advice in Chapter 5 about using patterns and exploring alternatives remains valid, but there are some important differences in emphasis and skills.

12.10.1. The Development Cycle

Project-level models are developed reasonably quickly to the level of detail necessary for implementation. Later changes tend to be relatively minor (because of the impact on system structure), and driven by changes to business requirements.

In contrast, corporate models are often developed progressively over a long period. The initial modeling exercise may produce a highly generalized model with few attributes. But project teams using the corporate model as a starting point will need to "flesh it out" by adding subtypes, attributes, and new entities resulting from detailed analysis and normalization. To do so, they will spend more time analyzing the relevant business area, and will be able to cross check their results against detailed function models. They may also receive better quality input from users, who have a more personal stake in specifying a system than in contributing to the planning exercise that produced the corporate data model.

The results of project-level modeling can affect the corporate model in two ways. First, more detailed analysis provides a check on the concepts and rules included in the corporate model. Perhaps a one-to-many relationship is really many-to-many, or an important subtype of an entity has been overlooked. The corporate model will need to be corrected to reflect the new information.

Second, the additional subtypes, entities, and attributes that do not conflict with the corporate model, but add further detail, may be incorporated into the corporate model. Whether this is done or not depends on the data management strategy, and often on the resources and tools available to maintain a more complex model. Many organizations choose to record only data of "corporate significance" in the corporate data model, leaving "local" data in project models.

In planning a corporate modeling exercise, then, you need to recognize that development will extend beyond the initial study, and put in place procedures to ensure that later "field work" by project teams is appropriately incorporated.

12.10.2. Partitioning the Task

Project-level data models are usually small enough that one person or team can undertake all of the modeling. While a model may be notionally divided into sections that are examined one at a time, this is usually done by the team as a whole rather than by allocating each section to a different modeler.

With corporate models, this is not always possible. For many reasons, including time constraints, skill sets, and organizational politics, we may need to divide up the task, and have separate teams develop parts of the model in parallel.

If doing this, the rule is to *partition by supertype, not by functional area,* as data is often used by more than one functional area. For example, assign a team to examine Physical Assets (supertype) rather than Purchasing (functional area). Although this approach may be less convenient from an organizational perspective, it means that different teams will not be modeling the same data. The element of choice in modeling inevitably leads to different models of the same data and long arguments in their reconciliation. I have seen teams spend far longer on reconciliation than on modeling, and corporate modeling projects abandoned for this reason.

If you *must* partition by functional area ("Purchasing is my responsibility and I insist on doing the modeling"), ensure that you have an agreed framework of supertypes in place before starting, and meet very regularly to fit results into the framework and identify any problems.

The initial high-level model is essential whichever approach is taken. Its development provides a great opportunity for creative exploration of options – so great that corporate data modeling projects frequently spend months arguing or become seriously stuck at this point looking for the "perfect" solution. Beware of this. Document the major options and move quickly to collect more detailed information to allow them to be better evaluated.

12.10.3. Inputs to the Task

Few things are more helpful to corporate data modelers than a clearly documented business strategy that is well supported by management. In developing a corporate model, overall business objectives need to take the place of system requirements in guiding and verifying the model. The best answer to "why did you choose this particular organization of data?" is "because it supports the following business objectives in the following way."

Business objectives prompt at least three important questions for the data modeler:

1. What data do we need to *support* the achievement of each objective? A welfare organization might need a consolidated register of welfare recipients to achieve the objective "reduce the incidence of persons illegally claiming more than one benefit."

2. What data do we need to *measure* the achievement of each objective? A police force may have the objective of responding to urgent calls as quickly as possible, and could specify the key performance indicator (KPI) "Mean time to respond to calls classified as urgent." Base data needed to derive the KPI would include time taken to respond to each call, and classification of call.

3. How will pursuit of the objectives change our data requirements over time? An investment bank may have the objective of providing a full range of investment products for retail and commercial clients. Meeting the objective could involve introduction of new products and supporting data.

Ideally, the corporate data model will be developed within the context of a full information systems planning project, following establishment of a comprehensive business plan. In many cases, however, data modeling studies are undertaken in relative isolation, and we need to make the best of what we have, or attempt to put together a working set of business objectives as part of the project. Interviews with senior staff can help, but it is unrealistic to expect a corporate modeling project to produce a business strategy as an interim deliverable!

The best approach in these cases is to make maximum use of whatever is available: company mission statement, job descriptions, business unit objectives, annual plans. Interviews and workshops can then be used to verify and supplement these.

One of the most difficult decisions facing the corporate modeling team is what use to make of existing project-level models, whether implemented or not, and any earlier attempts at corporate or business unit models. I find the best approach is to commit only to taking them into account, without undertaking to include any structures uncritically. These existing models are then used as an important source of requirements, and for verification, but are not allowed to stand in the way of taking a fresh look at the business.

The situation is different if our aim is to produce a realistic target for planning that incorporates databases to which we are committed. In this case, we will obviously need to copy structures from those databases directly into the corporate model.

12.10.4. Expertise Requirements

Data modelers working at the project level can reasonably be forgiven any initial lack of familiarity with the area being modeled. The amount of knowledge required is limited by the scope of the project, and expertise can be gained as the model is developed, typically over several weeks or months.

In the case of a corporate data model, the situation is quite different. A wide range of business areas need to be modeled, with limited time available for each. And we are dealing with senior members of the organization whose time is too precious to waste on explaining basic business concepts.

Conducting an interview with the finance manager without any prior knowledge of finance will achieve two things: a slightly improved knowledge of finance on the part of the interviewer, and a realization on the part of the finance manager that he/she has contributed little of value to the model. On the other hand, going into the interview with a good working knowledge of finance in general, and of the company's approach in particular, will enable the interview to focus on rules specific to the business, and will help build credibility for the model and data management.

In corporate data modeling, then, modeling skills need to be complemented by business knowledge. The modeling team will usually include at least one person with a good overall knowledge of the business. In complex businesses, it can be worthwhile seconding business specialists to the team on a temporary basis to assist in examining their area of expertise. I find that there is also great value in having someone whose knowledge of the business area was acquired outside the organization: experienced recruits, consultants, and MBAs are often better placed to take an alternative or more general view of the organization and its data.

12.10.5. External Standards

External data standards are an important, but often overlooked input to a corporate data model. There is little point in inventing a coding scheme if a perfectly good (and hopefully well-thought-out) one is accepted as an industry, national, or international standard, nor in rewriting definitions and inventing data names for entities and attributes.

A major payoff in using an external standard is in facilitating Electronic Data Interchange (EDI) with other organizations. Indeed, the corporate model can be the means by which the necessary standards are made available to development teams.

12.11.   CHOICE, CREATIVITY, AND CORPORATE DATA MODELS

Corporate data models can be a powerful means of promulgating innovative concepts and data structures. Equally, they can inhibit original thought by presenting each new project with a *fait accompli* as far as the overall structure of its model is concerned. In my experience, both situations are common, and frequently occur together in the one organization.

With their access to the "big picture" and strong data modeling skills, a corporate data modeling team is in a good position to propose and evaluate creative approaches. They are more likely than a conventional application project team to have the necessary access to senior management to win support for new ideas. Through the data management process, they have the means to at least encourage development teams to adopt them. Some of the most significant examples of business benefits arising from creative modeling have been achieved in this way.

On the other hand, a corporate data model may enshrine poor or outdated design, and inhibit innovation at the project level. There needs to be a means by which the corporate model can be improved by ideas generated by systems developers, and at least some scope for breaking out of the corporate data modeling framework at the project level. Too often, a lack of provision for changing the corporate data model in response to ideas from project teams has led to the demise of data management as the model ages.

It is vital that both systems developers and corporate modelers clearly understand the choice factor in modeling and recognize that:

1. If the project model meets the user requirements but differs from the corporate model, the corporate model is not necessarily wrong; and

2. If the corporate model meets business requirements but the project model differs, it too is not necessarily wrong.

Indeed, both models may be "right," but in the interests of data management we may need to agree on a common model, ideally one that incorporates the best of both.

A genuine understanding of these very basic ideas will overcome many of the problems that occur between corporate modelers and project teams, and provide a basis for workable data management standards and procedures.

12.12.   SUMMARY

Corporate data models cover the data requirements of complete enterprises or major business units. They are generally used for data planning and coordination rather than as specifications for database design.

A corporate data model should be developed within the context of a data management strategy. Data management is the management of data as a corporate resource, typically involving central control over its organization and documentation, and encouragement of data sharing across applications.

A corporate data model can be mapped against existing data, and thereafter used as an index to access it. It may also serve as a starting point for detailed project-level data modeling, incorporating ideas from senior business people and experienced data modelers.

Development of a corporate data model requires good business skills as well as modeling expertise. If the task is partitioned, it should be divided by data supertype rather than functional area.

While corporate data models can be powerful vehicles for promulgating new ideas, they may also stifle original thinking by requiring conformity.

APPENDICES

A

Check List for Data Model Review

I use the following check list as a framework for reviewing data models developed by others. It is equally relevant to checking your own work. Refer also to the list of deliverables at the end of Chapter 5.

THE CONTEXT OF THE MODEL

Is there a formal data model? (Chapter 1)

Some projects still do not include a formal data modeling phase at all, leaving all data organization decisions to the technical database designer.

Is there a commitment to using the model as a specification for database design? (Chapter 1)

Modern methodologies generally require delivery of a data model. Sometimes, there is no real commitment to actually using it as a specification for the database. Always review the logical database design as well as the model.

Who has been involved in developing the model? (Chapters 1 and 5)

Look for evidence that users and business specialists participated in developing and reviewing the model.

Have other candidate models been proposed? (Chapter 5)

Look for evidence that the modeler has not merely adopted the first workable solution.

How will performance problems be managed? (Chapter 1)

There should be a formal procedure in place for dealing with performance problems. Resolution should involve data modelers and users as well as physical database designers.

Is there a data management strategy in place? Does the model conform to this? (Chapter 12)

Check with the Data Administrator as well as the project data modeler.

Are there any constraints imposed by existing systems and data? Does the model take these into account? (Chapter 12)

Frequently, the data requirements of an application can be met at least partially from existing databases, either through direct data sharing or data transfer. The data model should identify any areas that are constrained to match existing structures.

Does the model conform to corporate standards for presentation, naming, and supporting documentation? (Chapters 5 and 9)

Check with the Data Administrator and standards group.

THE MODEL AS A WHOLE

How well-presented and understandable is the model? (Chapter 4)

Consider the intended audience(s). There may be a need to present the model at different levels, or to provide "subject area" models for particular audiences. Ask other stakeholders whether they understand the model.

Does the model cover the full scope required?

Check with the initial project proposal; verify against a high-level function model.

Have history requirements been taken into account? (Chapter 10)

> Identify any situations in which no mechanism exists for recording changes or past positions. Ensure that the user is willing to lose such data.

Has the data model been checked against a detailed function model? (Chapter 5)

> Look for documented interaction analysis.

Is there any redundancy? (Chapter 4)

> Look particularly for entities that overlap. The most common situations involve external people and organizations.

Have subtypes and supertypes been removed? (Chapter 4)

> The final model for implementation should be supported by a fully subtyped model, and documentation justifying the chosen level of subtyping in each case.

ENTITIES

Do all of the entities have meaningful, reasonably unambiguous names? (Chapter 3)

> Some ambiguity is unavoidable, but watch out for genuinely misleading names and names that have multiple distinct meanings in the business. Names should be in the singular.

Are all the entity names supported by good definitions? (Chapter 3)

> The definition should clearly state what is included and what is excluded and give examples of both. Poor entity definitions are one of the most common faults in data models.

Is the level of generalization appropriate? (Chapters 4 and 11)

> Check that the rules implied by entities are expected to be stable for the life of the system. Ensure that higher levels of generalization are not an excuse for incomplete analysis (look for subtypes as evidence of more detailed investigation).

RELATIONSHIPS

Are relationships correctly documented? (Chapter 3)

Relationships should be named, preferably in both directions. Cardinality, optionality, and ideally transferability should be shown.

Have all many-to-many relationships been resolved? (Chapter 3)

Resolution is not totally mechanical – ensure that the key of the resolution entity is defined.

Is the level of generalization appropriate? (Chapter 6)

Look particularly at self-referencing many-to-many relationships – check that they do not hide simple hierarchies.

Are any relationships derivable? (Chapter 6)

Look particularly for "relationships" derivable from inequalities.

ATTRIBUTES

Is there a full attribute list for each entity? (Chapters 2 and 6)

The documentation should include a full list of attributes for each entity including foreign keys.

Do the attribute names conform to (internal) standards? (Chapter 9)

If no naming standard is in place, look for inconsistencies, synonyms, and homonyms.

Do all attributes have definitions? (Chapters 2 and 9)

Look also for definitions of derivable attributes that do not appear in the entity lists.

KEYS AND NORMALIZATION

Are primary keys defined for all entities? (Chapter 2)

It is not sufficient to identify all candidate keys – one key must be nominated as primary.

Do all primary keys meet the basic criteria of applicability, uniqueness, minimality, and stability? (Chapter 8)

Give special attention to stability, particularly for meaningful keys.

Have surrogate keys been used indiscriminately? (Chapter 8)

If all entities use surrogate keys, check that this is not expected to cause performance problems.

Are all candidate keys identified? (Chapters 6 and 7)

Multiple candidate keys may be associated with BCNF problems or indicate that an entity should be disaggregated into two or more entities linked by one-to-one relationships.

Are all foreign keys identified? (Chapter 6)

Ensure that the notation allows the related entity to be identified in each case. Check for overlapping and split foreign keys.

Are all tables fully normalized? (Chapters 2 and 7)

Check particularly for 4NF and 5NF problems with all-key tables.

INDEX

INDEX